Fonti tradotte per la storia dell'Alto Medioevo

Italian Carolingian Historical and Poetic Texts

Edited and translated by

Luigi Andrea Berto

PISA
UNIVERSITY
PRESS

Italian Carolingian historical and poetic texts / edited and translated by Luigi Andrea Berto - Pisa : Pisa University Press, 2016. - (Fonti tradotte per la storia dell'Alto Medioevo)

945.02 (22.)
I. Berto, Luigi Andrea 1. Italia - Storia - Sec. IX - Fonti

CIP a cura del Sistema bibliotecario dell'Università di Pisa

GERDA HENKEL STIFTUNG   The preparation of this book has been funded by the
Gerda Henkel Foundation

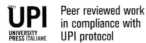 Peer reviewed work
in compliance with
UPI protocol

Redazione e impaginazione
Ellissi

ISBN 978-88-6741-664-6

TABLE OF CONTENTS

PREFACE

by François Bougard

The Kingdom of Italy during the Carolingian period does not stand out certainly as an area of prolific historical text production. For instance, the writing of annals, which was so diffuse north of the Alps, failed to gain any popularity in Italy, and the entire period passed as if not only the court of Pavia, but all areas of Carolingian Italy simply lacked any identity in terms of the writing of history. Between Paul the Deacon (ca. 720s-ca. 799) and the works of the late ninth century (the chronicle of Andreas of Bergamo and the so-called *Small book on the imperial power in the city of Rome*, probably composed in Spoleto), the absence of historical production is unmistakable. We know that a people without problems is often a people without a history, and one of the reasons for this rarity may simply be attributed to the relative state of domestic peace within the Kingdom of Italy, at least until the «great distress» that followed the death of Emperor Louis II (875). Another explanation might be the demand for historical writing of the Church on the borders of the Kingdom of Italy. In Ravenna and in Naples the deeds of local bishops were narrated. Rome, in particular, experienced its own cultural "renaissance" in the ninth century and attracted the brilliant scholar Anastasius Bibliothecarius, who proved capable of composing letters for the Frankish emperor and who placed his talent as a historian at the service of the *Book of the Pontiffs*.

Given this state of affairs, we must make use of everything that we can lay our hands on. We should, of course, utilize the "major" works, but we should also employ anonymous texts and the less extensive works, both those in prose and those in verse, which are often mentioned only in passing, as if no more than a cursory glance were sufficient to extract from them the scanty information that they contain.

The texts edited and translated by Luigi Andrea Berto constitute a welcome invitation to re-explore this literature and place it in an appropriate context. They cast a light on two distinct periods. First comes the happy reign of Pippin (781-810), who governed Italy at the orders of his father Charlemagne. The *History of the Lombards of Gotha's codex* (hereafter HLCG), which is in no way derived from Paul the Deacon's *History of the Lombards*, but has been completely out-shown by it in terms of popularity, first emphasizes that the Lombard conquest of Italy was the will of God, and then goes on to clearly state how decisive the transition to Carolingian rule proved to be: «The rule of the Lombards ended and the Kingdom of Italy began.» But continuity from one regime to the next was assured by the production of laws whose corollary is justice (let us keep in mind the fact that this chronicle occupies three folios of a manuscript, and the rest of that manuscript is juridical in nature). Laws were issued by the Lombard King, Rothari, by Charlemagne, and then by Pippin, under whose rule "law" was synonymous with «abundance and quietness.» The poem *King Pippin's Victory over the Avars*, on the other hand, describes an episode that occurred outside Italy. It sings Pippin's praises and points out that his reign was also notable for the victorious campaign of 796 against the Avars, hailed as the submission of the pagan world to the armies of the Catholic king, who was buttressed by Saint Peter. Both the HLCG and the poem were produced at Pippin's court, which was the sole court until the rule of King Berengar († 924) to boast a full-fledged literary existence, both in terms of original creations and of the transcription of existing works.

The other two texts offered here, written three-quarters of a century later, do not possess the same degree of unity. Certainly, the chronicle by the priest Andreas of Bergamo and the *Rythmus on Emperor Louis's Captivity* both feature Louis II as their main character. But the first work has a largely local focus, extending, at most, to include the interests of the Church of Milan, and its links to the court are only represented by the accounts of those who took part in the campaigns in southern Italy in the 860s and 870s. The *Rythmus*, on the other hand, seems to have been a product of the milieu of Benevento, which was much more productive in literary terms than its northern Italian counterparts. Its aim is far narrower and more specific. A careful and accurate translation provides a new interpretation of this text. Rather than seeing it as a parody of the misadventures of Louis II, who was imprisoned for a month in Benevento immediately after he conquered Bari in 871 and freed it from Muslim control, why not view it as a text composed on the occasion of the embassy of the southern Italian Lombards, who went to Louis II's court in 872 asking for aid against the Saracen threat, entreating a sovereign who had recently been betrayed, but who had been able to reacquire full political legitimacy through a new imperial coronation?

The assembling of texts in verse with works that are more traditionally examined by historians, who are often all too willing to overlook the existence of poetry, is one of the many merits of this volume. Among those merits, the most notable is how light is cast on the many ways in which the events of Carolingian Italy were narrated. Another considerable merit is found in the substantial challenge involved in translation. Translations are frequently considered with a degree of condescension by purists. Those purists are wrong on this point, because it is not merely a matter of rescuing the entire humanist education as well as popularizing texts that are increasingly beyond the understanding of readers who have been failed by questionable education at the primary, the secondary, and the university levels. Translation is also key to a better understanding and, therefore, a better utilization of sources by historians. Luigi Andrea Berto has been carrying this task forward for some time and with success with some Venetian and Cassinese texts. We all owe him a considerable debt of gratitude for his gift of these works.

PART I

INTRODUCTION

1. Carolingian Italy[1]

Taking advantage of the problems created in Byzantine Italy by the iconoclastic policy of Emperor Leo III (717-741) and his son, Constantine V (741-775), the King of the Lombards, Aistulf (749-756), attempted to conquer the parts of Italy that were not under his rule. After occupying Ravenna in 750/751, he began to threaten Rome.[2] In the wake of these events Pope Stephen II traveled to France in order to request assistance from the King of the Franks, Pippin III. In 754, the pontiff bestowed royal unction on the Frankish sovereign and his sons, thereby legitimizing Pippin III, who had deposed the previous king. With this gesture, Stephen II secured the intervention of the Franks against the Lombards. On two occasions Pippin III defeated Aistulf (754 and 756) and forced the return of all the territories the Lombards had conquered.[3] Yet the Frankish ruler could not intervene against Desiderius (757-774), the new Lombard king, who had once again invaded some of the former Byzantine territories. Desiderius's position was strengthened by the disagreements between Pippin III's heirs, Carloman and Charlemagne. The situation appeared to turn further in favor of the Lombard sovereign when Charlemagne, in need of an ally against his brother, married one of Desiderius's daughters.[4] However, the death of Carloman at the end of 771 rendered this alliance unnecessary and Charlemagne repudiated his Lombard wife. The Lombard ruler welcomed Carloman's wife and children who had been ousted from their paternal inheritance by Charlemagne. Meanwhile, at Rome, Hadrian, a supporter of an anti-Lombard policy, was elected pope.[5]

In 773, Desiderius took action, reaching the vicinity of Rome. Charlemagne then decided to answer the pontiff's pressing request for aid, and, having easily bypassed the Lombard defenses in the Alps, effortlessly penetrated the Po valley, laying siege to Pavia where Desiderius had taken shelter. In June 774, the Lombard king surrendered and Charlemagne assumed his crown.[6] Since he was heavily engaged in a war against the

---

[1] The goal of this section is to provide the non-specialist with an overview of the main events mentioned in the texts.

[2] Delogu, *Lombard and Carolingian Italy*, pp. 294-299; Noble, *The Republic of St. Peter*, pp. 29-60; Wickham, *Early Medieval Italy*, pp. 45-46.

[3] Delogu, *Lombard and Carolingian Italy*, pp. 298-300; Noble, *The Republic of St. Peter*, pp. 74-94; Barbero, *Charlemagne*, pp. 18-20 and 24-25; Gasparri, *Il passaggio dai Longobardi ai Carolingi*, pp. 28-29.

[4] Delogu, *Lombard and Carolingian Italy*, pp. 300-301; Gasparri, *Il passaggio dai Longobardi ai Carolingi*, pp. 29-30.

[5] Delogu, *Lombard and Carolingian Italy*, pp. 300-301; Gasparri, *Il passaggio dai Longobardi ai Carolingi*, p. 30.

[6] Delogu, *Lombard and Carolingian Italy*, pp. 301-303; Wickham, *Early Medieval Italy*, p. 47; Barbero, *Charlemagne*, pp. 26-32; Gasparri, *Il passaggio dai Longobardi ai Carolingi*, p. 30.

Saxons, the new sovereign initially chose not to replace all the members of the Lombard ruling class (above all those who, upon Charlemagne's arrival, had immediately abandoned Desiderius), but to pursue a policy of continuity. Yet, in 775-776, when several Lombard dukes fomented a rebellion in north-eastern Italy, Charlemagne seized the opportunity to eliminate those Lombards who still opposed the Franks. In replacing such men with lords from beyond the Alps, the Frankish ruler increased the number of non-Lombards holding office in Italy.[7] Charlemagne kept the title of king of the Lombards, but he granted the Kingdom of Italy to his son Pippin who was obliged to cooperate with several tutors because of his young age.[8]

Like his father, Pippin exhibited notable military activity and sought to expand his domains. Nevertheless, Pippin's only relevant victory came during the campaign against the Avars who resided in an area corresponding approximately to present-day Hungary.[9] His attempts to seize the Italian territories left unconquered by his father[10] ended in failure.[11]

Pippin died in 810, and his son, Bernard, became king.[12] The new sovereign was not able to keep the title for long because Charlemagne's death in 814 changed the political scenario. In 817, the new emperor, Louis the Pious, decreed that, on his own death, the Empire should be divided among his three sons: Lothar, Pippin, and Louis.[13] The Kingdom of Italy should have passed to Lothar who was appointed co-emperor as well; Bernard's fate was not mentioned. It was probably a work in progress which aimed at excluding him, since he was not a direct heir of the new sovereign. Bernard, feeling himself excluded, rebelled. Louis the Pious immediately sent an army to Italy and Bernard was easily captured and taken to Francia, where he was blinded and died as a result of the wounds inflicted.[14]

Because Lothar was entangled in the struggles between his father and brothers over the division of the Empire,[15] he was frequently gone from Italy. With recourse to central power being unavailable, a rise in local aristocratic autonomy soon developed.[16] The Italian Kingdom had a "full time" ruler again only from 844 onwards, when Lothar, busy defending his transalpine inheritance, sent his son Louis II to rule over Italy. Louis II, co-emperor in 850 and emperor on his father's death in 855, did not embroil himself in conflicts over the division of the Carolingian

[7] Krahwinkler, *Friaul im Frühmittelalter Geschichte einer Region*, pp. 125-129; Wickham, *Early Medieval Italy*, pp. 47-48; Cammarosano, *Nobili e re*, pp. 102-103.

[8] Manacorda, *Ricerche sugli inizii della dominazione*; Wickham, *Early Medieval Italy*, p. 49; Barbero, *Charlemagne*, p. 37.

[9] Pohl, *Die Awaren*, pp. 312-323; Barbero, *Charlemagne*, pp. 67-73.

[10] These areas were the former Lombard Duchy of Benevento, which had become an independent principality after the fall of the Lombard Kingdom, and the Venetian Duchy, that was theoretically a part of the Byzantine Empire, but it was, in practice, autonomous.

[11] Bertolini, *Carlomagno e Benevento*, pp. 609-611; Gasparri, *Il ducato e il principato di Benevento*, pp. 110-112; Ortalli, *Il ducato e la «civitas Rivoalti»*, pp. 725-731.

[12] Wickham, *Early Medieval Italy*, p. 49; Albertoni, *L'Italia carolingia*, p. 33; Barbero, *Charlemagne*, p. 140.

[13] Riché, *The Carolingians*, pp. 147-148.

[14] Depreux, *Das Königtum Bernhards von Italien*, pp. 1-25; Cammarosano, *Nobili e re*, pp. 144-146.

[15] Nelson, *Charles the Bald*, pp. 76-129; Boshof, *Ludwig der Fromme*, pp. 178-195.

[16] Wickham, *Early Medieval Italy*, pp. 50-51; Delogu, *Lombard and Carolingian Italy*, p. 309.

Empire. Instead, he dwelt permanently in Italy with the exception of a brief period when he went to Provence in order to inherit territory from his brother Charles who had died without an heir. Louis II managed, albeit with difficulty, to restore internal order. Following the example of his great-grandfather Charlemagne, who had held an itinerant court, he traveled his kingdom, seeking to remedy problems personally. His provisions, which aimed at ensuring that wrongdoers did not go unpunished, bear testimony to his strength and, at the same time, highlight the gravity of the previous state of affairs.[17]

Louis II made a concerted effort to defeat the Muslims in southern Italy as well. Not only did the Saracens undertake to seize Sicily from the Byzantines, but they also ventured throughout southern Italy with frequent incursions, reaching as far as Rome in 846 and sacking St. Peter's. They took advantage of the continual struggles between the various magnates of southern Italy, fighting as mercenaries and establishing some dominions, such as the emirates of Bari and Taranto.[18] Because Louis II lacked southern Lombard support, his campaigns were ultimately unsuccessful. Moreover, he was believed to harbor hegemonic aims over southern Italy.[19] In 866, Louis II organized a large expedition against the Saracens and in 871, with the aide of a Byzantine fleet, succeeded in conquering the Emirate of Bari. This victory seemed to have paved the way for the complete expulsion of the Muslims from southern Italy.

The sovereign had not, however, considered the political situation of the area nor the Lombards' overwhelming desire for independence. With the disappearance of the Emirate of Bari, the greatest enemy of the Lombards was, in fact, Louis II himself. The Prince of Benevento, Adelchis, imprisoned the emperor, releasing him only after having extracted the promise that he would no longer go to southern Italy on his own initiative. This episode proved to be a harsh blow to the prestige of the emperor, who, with the exception of an expedition to aid Salerno during a Saracens' siege, was never able to interfere in the South again.[20] Louis II died in 875 without an heir which led to conflict amongst his relatives who wanted to take possession of the Kingdom of Italy and the prestige of the imperial title. The King of the western Franks, Charles the Bald, was eventually crowned emperor at the end of 875, but he died in 877 and the struggles for the control of the Italian crown consequently continued.[21]

---

[17] Delogu, *Strutture politiche*, pp. 137-189; Wickham, *Early Medieval Italy*, pp. 60-62; Albertoni, *L'Italia carolingia*, pp. 42-51.

[18] Musca, *L'emirato di Bari*; Gabrieli, *Storia, cultura e civiltà*, pp. 109-112; Kreutz, *Before the Normans*, pp. 19-20, 25-27, 38-40.

[19] Gasparri, *Il ducato e il principato di Benevento*, pp. 123-124; Musca, *L'emirato di Bari*, pp. 64 ff.

[20] Musca, *L'emirato di Bari*, pp. 117-120; Gasparri, *Il ducato e il principato di Benevento*, pp. 125-126; Kreutz, *Before the Normans*, pp. 46-47, 55-57.

[21] Nelson, *Charles the Bald*, pp. 230-235; Delogu, *Lombard and Carolingian Italy*, pp. 313-315; Cammarosano, *Nobili e re*, pp. 198-200.

2. The *History of the Lombards of Gotha's codex*

This anonymous work has no dedication, prologue or title.[22] It reports events from the Lombard people's origins to the beginning of the ninth century and ends with the expedition of Charlemagne's son, Pippin, against the Muslims in Corsica,[23] which took place in 806, according to the Frankish Annals,[24] and with a praise for Pippin's campaigns in Italy. The chronicle therefore must have been completed[25] between 806 and Pippin's death († 810).[26]

The author's celebration of the victories of Charlemagne and Pippin[27] might suggest that he was a Frank who had moved to Italy after Charlemagne's conquest of the Lombard kingdom.[28] However, the chronicler refers to what «our ancient forefathers» said when describing the Lombards' settlement in Saxony,[29] a statement suggesting that he was probably of Lombard origin.[30] Another biographical detail can be observed in the chronicler's description of how, in his days, one could still see the remains of the residence of Wacho,[31] king of the Lombards in the early sixth century when his people had settled in an area between Bohemia and Hungary.[32] This could mean that the author participated in one of Pippin's expeditions against the Avars. Nevertheless, the chronicler does not state that he saw the ruins in person, so it is also possible that he learned of them from someone who had traveled to that region.

The text's rough Latin indicates that the author had a fairly low level of education, perhaps acquired as a young man. This theory becomes more likely when one considers his erroneous attribution of an observation by Isidore of Seville to Saint Jerome;[33] such a mistake could easily have been made by someone reciting from memory facts he had learned many years before. On the other hand, the chronicler shows a good grasp of Holy Scripture.[34] Moreover, it is noteworthy that, when narrating the period under King Rothari, the anonymous author uses the Lombard term *cadarfada* to describe the customary regulations used to solve disputes.[35] In King Liutprand's legislation, the same

---

[22] The title *Historia Langobardorum codicis Gothani* stems from the fact that the only manuscript containing this chronicle is in the Forschungsbibliothek of Gotha (Germany).

[23] HLCG, ch. 11.

[24] *Annales regni Francorum*, year 806.

[25] The work is not unfinished as it ends with the word *Amen*. HLCG, ch. 11.

[26] Pohl, *Memory, Identity and Power*, p. 21; Coumert, *Origines des Peuples*, p. 251.

[27] HLCG, chs. 10-11.

[28] *Le leggi dei Longobardi*, p. lviii.

[29] HLCG, ch. 2.

[30] Stefano Cingolani, Bruno Luiselli, and Magali Coumert agree with this opinion. Cingolani, *Le storie dei Longobardi*, p. 35; Luiselli, *Storia culturale dei rapporti*, p. 723; Coumert, *Origines des Peuples*, p. 251. Walter Pohl hypothesizes that the HLCG was composed in Milan while Magali Coumert believes that it might have been written in Montecassino. Pohl, *La costituzione di una memoria storica*, p. 574; Coumert, *Origines des Peuples*, pp. 563-580, 252. I think that it is more likely that the HLCG was composed in Northern Italy.

[31] HLCG, ch. 2.

[32] Christie, *The Lombards*, pp. 18-30.

[33] HLCG, ch. 2.

[34] HLCG, ch. 1.

[35] HLCG, ch. 8.

regulations were defined using the similar terms *cawerfeda* and *cawerfida*,[36] a detail suggesting that the author was familiar with Lombard law. It is nonetheless possible that he copied such terms from a source unknown to us. There is a further point linking this work with Lombard legislation: the HLCG survives in a manuscript that also contains the *corpus* of Lombard laws, thus suggesting that this chronicle could have been intended as an introduction to the latter.[37] However, as the codex dates to the eleventh/twelfth century, it is impossible to be certain that this brief chronicle was intended for such a purpose. For example, the HLCG could have been inserted in front of the laws some time after it had been written.

Unlike the other early medieval Italian chroniclers narrating the history of the Lombards,[38] the HLCG's author did not know Paul the Deacon's *History of the Lombards*.[39] His main source (along with some unknown texts) is the *Origin of the Lombard People*, a text written down around the mid-seventh century.[40]

The Lombards' various movements towards Italy are described as a sort of journey inspired by God which ended with their arrival in Italy (depicted as the Promised Land). There, through baptism, the redemption of this people was realized.[41] The chronicler emphasizes the ferocity of the first Lombards, comparing them to rapacious wolves and stating that they originated from serpents.[42] It is noteworthy that the author includes a quotation from Holy Scripture: «Do not accuse them of sin as they have no law.»[43] This observation underlines the chronicler's recognition of the fundamental importance of the Lombards' conversion to Catholicism and that he did not want to portray their early history in a purely negative light. Indeed, they could not be blamed for their past, because they did not know the true faith. This is an implicit sentiment, yet it draws attention to the author's desire not to undermine the origins of his own people entirely.

This first part of the HLCG differs from Paul the Deacon's *History of the Lombards* in its reference to the leaders of the Lombards during their migration. The HLCG relates that they were guided by Gambara alone, without the aid of her two sons, Ibor and Aio.[44]

---

[36] *Livtprandi leges*, chs. 77, 133.

[37] Cingolani, *Le storie dei Longobardi*, p. 35.

[38] For example, the chronicles of Andreas of Bergamo and Erchempert and the *Chronicon Salernitanum*.

[39] As it has been also emphasized by Coumert, *Origines des Peuples*, p. 219, this detail represents a strong argument against the hypothesis of Rosamond McKitterick, who maintains that Paul the Deacon wrote the *Historia Langobardorum* as an informative text on the Lombards for Pippin and his court. If this were the case, it would be very difficult to explain why the author of the only chronicle produced by a member of Pippin's entourage did not know the *Historia Langobardorum*. McKitterick, *History and Memory in the Carolingian World*, pp. 77-83.

[40] Luiselli, *Storia culturale*, p. 760, note 1272; Coumert, *Origines des Peuples*, p. 253. The chronicler used chs. 3-6 of the *Origo gentis Langobardorum*. According to Cingolani, the HLCG and the *Origo* copied from the same source. Cingolani, *Le storie dei Longobardi*, p. 94. Walter Goffart and Nicholas Everett instead believe that the author of the HLCG took his information from Paul the Deacon's *Historia Langobardorum*. More nuanced is Eduardo Fabbro, who maintains that the anonymous author likely knew this work. Goffart, *The Narrators of Barbarian History*, p. 382, note 163; Everett, *Literacy in Lombard Italy*, p. 94; Fabbro, *Charlemagne and the Lombard Kingdom That Was*, p. 14.

[41] HLCG, ch. 1. Cf. Cingolani, *Le storie dei Longobardi*, pp. 50-54, and Pohl, *Memory, Identity and Power*, p. 27.

[42] HLCG, ch. 1.

[43] HLCG, ch. 1.

[44] Paul the Deacon, *Historia Langobardorum*, I, 7.

Another striking difference is that, when the chronicler explains the origins of the change of name from Winili to Lombards, he maintains only that it was due to their long beards.[45] In contrast, the *Origin of the Lombard People* and Paul the Deacon both state that Gambara turned to Wotan's wife, Frea, to ask how the Winili could achieve a victory over the Vandals who consulted Wotan about the same matter. Wotan told the Vandals that the victors would be the ones who appeared first at dawn. Frea suggested to Gambara that the Winili women use their hair to cover their faces like beards and go along with their men at first light to the place where Wotan was usually found. The next day Wotan saw the disguised women and asked: «Who are those longbeards (*longibarbi*)?» Frea then asked him to bestow the victory on those whom he had named. He agreed to this and, from that time on, the Winili bore the name Lombards.[46]

These differences and the fact that the anonymous chronicler emphasizes that Gambara's talent for foresight was due to divine inspiration[47] have led to the hypothesis that the author wished to censor the pagan aspects of this story and gloss over the warlike characteristics of the migration.[48] It is, perhaps, more likely that he did not include the above story purely because it was unhelpful for his purposes; indeed he wanted to describe the pagan origins of the Lombards but at the same time to highlight the path to salvation represented by their migration to Italy.

Having narrated how the Lombards acquired their name, the author gives a very succinct account of their movements to Pannonia and then to Italy. For his account of the invasion of the peninsula and the first years of Lombard dominion, the chronicler used the *Origin of the Lombard People* which does not mention these events in a particularly tragic way.[49] By contrast, the author of the HLCG, in recounting the submission of the Italian cities to the Lombard King Alboin, states that this had been the will of God.[50] This detail is not mentioned by Paul the Deacon, who tells instead of how, after the fall of Pavia, Alboin's horse collapsed at the city's entrance and got up again only when the king swore not to carry out his former promise to exterminate all the inhabitants of Pavia, a clear sign of the divine protection they enjoyed.[51] Once again there seems to be evidence of a desire not to paint too dark a picture of the Lombards' past.

The anonymous author dwells on the death of Alboin,[52] but, in contrast to Paul the Deacon, he does not report the most scandalous parts of the episode, i.e. what made Rosemund turn against her husband and how she managed to persuade Peredeus to participate in the sovereign's murder.[53] Like Paul the Deacon, the anonymous chronicler narrates that

---

[45] HLCG, ch. 2.

[46] *Origo gentis Langobardorum*, ch. 1. Paul the Deacon, *Historia Langobardorum*, I, 8. For the meaning of this account, see the different interpretations of Gasparri, *La cultura tradizionale dei Longobardi*, pp. 12-33, Cingolani, *Le storie dei Longobardi*, pp. 69-79, and Coumert, *Origines des Peuples*, pp. 153-214.

[47] HLCG, ch. 1. Paul the Deacon does not mention this.

[48] Cingolani, *Le storie dei Longobardi*, pp. 86-87.

[49] HLCG, ch. 5. Cf. *Origo gentis Langobardorum*, ch. 5.

[50] HLCG, ch. 6.

[51] Alboin was reminded that the Pavians were good Christians and that he would be allowed to enter Pavia only if he broke his vow. Paul the Deacon, *Historia Langobardorum*, II, 27.

[52] HLCG, ch. 6.

[53] According to Paul the Deacon, Rosemund decided to kill Alboin as he forced her drink from a cup

Rosemund wanted to eliminate her accomplice Helmechis in order to marry Longinus, the prefect of Ravenna.[54] In addition, he uses a typical medieval ecclesiastical *topos* with regard to women, saying that Rosemund's behavior was due to a natural female propensity to sin, which is explained by the fact that a woman instigated the first sin.[55] Strikingly, unlike the other early medieval Italian chroniclers,[56] this author very explicitly expresses his misogyny.

The chronicler gives little information concerning the other Lombard sovereigns, and most of it is limited to listing the years of their rule. The sole king to whom he seems to dedicate more of his attention is Rothari, depicting him in a flattering light. Indeed, the author states that it was thanks to this ruler that the Lombards had laws and a justice system and that under Rothari the Lombards «devoted themselves to the canonical disputes and became helpers of the priests.»[57]

In the final section of the *Historia* the anonymous author describes Charlemagne's conquest of the Lombard kingdom. He recounts how the Frankish sovereign went to Italy to defend the pope,[58] but he does not say from whom. There is no mention of the threat the Lombards posed to Rome or of the confrontations between the Franks and the Lombards. The chronicler continues by praising Charlemagne's behavior, emphasizing that he was not pushed into action because of a thirst for conquest and that, even though he had the power to destroy everything in his path, he showed himself to be merciful. Charlemagne even allowed the Lombards to keep their own laws with minimal, but necessary, additions on his part.[59] Furthermore, the Frankish king pardoned a great number of men even though they had acted against him. God rewarded Charlemagne by increasing his riches a hundredfold.[60] Having mentioned Charlemagne's other victories and his coronation as emperor, the author sings Pippin's praises, saying that he enjoyed the same kind of divine favor as had his father,[61] and reporting his military victories.[62] Finally, the author characterizes the reign of Pippin as an era of splendor comparable to that of ancient times.[63]

To conclude, the HLCG was likely the work of a Lombard from North Italy, probably a member of Pippin's court, who accepted the new dominion and wanted to emphasize the well-being it had created and, at the same time, the bloodless nature of the change.[64]

---

made from the skull of her father. She convinced Peredeus to murder the king, by taking the place of the girl who was Peredeus's lover one night and, after Peredeus made love to her, Rosemund threatened to reveal all to Alboin if he refused to do as she asked. Paul the Deacon, *Historia Langobardorum*, II, 28.

[54] Paul the Deacon, *Historia Langobardorum*, II, 29.

[55] HLCG, ch. 6. This detail is not actually found in the *Origo gentis Langobardorum*, which the anonymous author used as a reference for these events.

[56] For example, see Skinner, *Women in Medieval Italian Society*, pp. 54-59, and Colonna, *Figure femminili*, pp. 29-60.

[57] HLCG, ch. 8.

[58] HLCG, ch. 10.

[59] HLCG, ch. 10.

[60] HLCG, ch. 10.

[61] HLCG, ch. 11.

[62] HLCG, ch. 11.

[63] HLCG, ch. 11.

[64] Magali Coumert has maintained that the fact that both the first King of the Lombards, Agelmund, and Pippin fought against the Beovinides (HLCG, chs. 2, 11) indicates that the HLCG established a sense of continuity between the first Lombard sovereign and Charlemagne's son and that it «présentait une identité lombarde fondée sur leur propre histoire, mais compatible avec une domination carolingienne. Malgré le changement de dynastie,

He was thus trying to make the Lombards forget the suffering, shame, and anger the Frankish conquest had caused.[65] Yet, his *Historia* is not merely a call to forget the past and look to the future. Indeed, it is very significant that, from the very beginning of his work, the author insists that the migration of the Lombards was divinely inspired and that, once they arrived in Italy, the Lombards became good Christians. As such, they should not be reproached for their pagan background. If the chronicler had not thought it important to highlight such features, he could simply have referred to them in passing. Hence his aim was not simply to record the purging of paganism from the Lombard population. It is likely that, despite his willing acceptance of the new rulers, the anonymous author still felt a proud attachment to his Lombard ancestry. Precisely because of this sentiment, he would have been determined to emphasize that his compatriots adhered with sincerity and devotion to Christianity as soon as they settled in Italy. In this way, he may have been trying to confute various papal sources, which, even in the eighth century, seemed to cast doubt on the faith of the Lombards.[66]

3. The *Historia* of Andreas of Bergamo

The little information known about this author comes from his work. The chronicler states that his name is Andreas, that he is a priest[67] and that he went from the Oglio river to the Adda river in the funeral procession carrying the coffin of Emperor Louis II from Brescia to Milan.[68]

The chronicle ends abruptly with an incomplete sentence mentioning an event that happened shortly after the year 877,[69] which leads one to suppose that Andreas died soon afterwards. There is no other evidence to support this hypothesis, yet it can be

---

les Lombards combattaient toujours les mêmes ennemis et en étaient de nouveau vainquers.» Moreover, she believes that «le point commun d'une ville de Pannonie comme étape importante du trajet des Francs depuis Troie et des Lombards depuis les confins de la Gaule soulignait leur communauté de destin» and that the mention in the *Historia* of a 200-year pact between the Avars and the Lombards when the latter left Pannonia to invade Italy (HLCG, chs. 5, 10) underscores in particular that «l'alliance avec les Avars eut lieu avec les Lombards païens, avant qu'ils n'aient reçu la grâce du baptême. La durée précise de l'alliance permettait de sous-entendre qu'il s'agit d'une époque révolue et que les Francs peuvent désormais unir leur force contre les païens qui occupent la Pannonie.» Coumert, *Origines des Peuples*, pp. 258-260. These hypotheses are interesting, yet these feelings are not explicit at all, and therefore they certainly did not represent one of the main goals of the author. Furthermore, the chronicler never says that Franks and Lombards fought together against the Beovinides and the Avars. Indeed, the successes against those peoples were obtained by Pippin alone. HLCG, ch. 11.

[65]   On the way in which the Lombards remembered the conquest of their kingdom, see Capo, *La polemica longobarda sulla caduta del regno*, pp. 5-35, Gasparri, *Prima delle nazioni*, pp. 206-207, and the part of this book dedicated to Andreas of Bergamo.

[66]   For a few examples, see Capo, *Il «Liber Pontificalis»*, pp. 217-224, and Pohl, *Invasions and ethnic identity*, pp. 29-30.

[67]   Andreas of Bergamo, *Historia*, ch. 2.

[68]   The author highlights that he helped to carry the sovereign's coffin. Andreas of Bergamo, *Historia*, ch. 22.

[69]   Andreas of Bergamo, *Historia*, ch. 24: «While he (Charles the Bald) was gathering his army to fight him, some of his men, whose fidelity he trusted greatly, abandoned him and joined Carloman. Having seen that, Charles fled and went to Gaul, but died suddenly during the journey. Having established order in the kingdom of Italy, Carloman returned to his father in Bavaria shortly thereafter. Meanwhile, King Louis.» The reference is to the death of Charles the Bald, which occurred in 877.

assumed that the work was compiled not long after 877, since the oldest manuscript of this text, which does not seem to be an autograph, dates to the end of the ninth century.

The lack of any other biographical details in the work makes it impossible to be sure which episodes were contemporary with Andreas's life. The eclipse and the aurora borealis he describes took place not long before Emperor Louis the Pious's death (840). His account of the widespread fear following these two unusual phenomena[70] could imply that he witnessed them. If this is the case, then it would be possible to deduce that he was already an adult by that time and so was born between 810 and 820. Nonetheless, this is just a hypothesis; the possibility that he was a young man in his twenties in 875 and heard about the strange natural events of 840 from an elder should not be ruled out.

The latter case would explain a factual error in the chronicle: Andreas's description of Pope Leo III traveling to Francia to ask for Charlemagne's help to combat the Lombards.[71] In reality, it was Pope Hadrian who asked the Frankish sovereign to intervene in the conflict, but the pontiff never actually crossed the Alps. A voyage into the land of the Franks was made, however, by one of his predecessors, Stephen II, who made the trip at the end of 753 when the ruler of the Franks was Pippin III, Charlemagne's father. Leo III crossed the mountains in 799, but with the aim of obtaining Charlemagne's help against the Romans who had made an attempt on the pope's life.[72] This type of error is understandable if one assumes that the chronicler learned of these events from people who were not actually contemporaries of that period.

G. La Placa, on the other hand, speculates that Andreas was born between 830 and 840. To support this claim, she argues that, in 875, the chronicler was a *presbyter*, a position rarely bestowed on young men. She also contends that, as he was one of Louis II's coffin bearers, a task that would have required a certain amount of physical strength, he must not have been too old at that time.[73]

Andreas says nothing about his birthplace or residence. He is normally referred to as Andreas of Bergamo,[74] but there is no clear evidence in his writings to suggest that he came from that city. There are three details in his work that do, however, support the assumption that the chronicler lived in Bergamo or its vicinity.

The first is that he records having participated in the procession taking Louis II's mortal remains from the Oglio river to the Adda river,[75] in other words the district of Bergamo.[76] The second detail is that the sole area the chronicler mentions when he describes the devastation caused by the raids taking place after Louis II's death is the territory around Bergamo.[77] The final point can be found in the section describing Louis II's campaigns

---

[70] Andreas of Bergamo, *Historia*, ch. 12.
[71] Andreas of Bergamo, *Historia*, ch. 4.
[72] Noble, *The Republic of St Peter*, pp. 292-293.
[73] La Placa, *Andrea di Bergamo*, p. 61.
[74] Bertolini, *Andrea da Bergamo*, p. 79.
[75] Andreas of Bergamo, *Historia*, ch. 22.
[76] Bertolini, *Andrea da Bergamo*, p. 79, and La Placa, *Andrea di Bergamo*, p. 62.
[77] The chronicler reports that Berengar of Friuli stayed in the monastery of Fara for a week. During that time, he carried out various raids in the surrounding countryside causing many inhabitants of the Bergamo area to seek refuge in the mountains or the city. Andreas of Bergamo, *Historia*, ch. 23. Cf. La Placa, *Andrea di Bergamo*, p. 62.

against the Muslims in southern Italy. In this part, Andreas mostly expanded upon an expedition the Count of Bergamo, Otto, had undertaken in Calabria.[78] Andreas's detailed account of the Calabrian expedition, which was relatively unimportant to Louis II's overall campaign in southern Italy,[79] was probably included because the chronicler would have heard about the victory from Count Otto or other men from Bergamo who were in his service.[80] These men would have possibly emphasized the campaigns in which they took part as principal protagonists rather than those in which they were of secondary importance.

Although Andreas never says anything about his ethnicity, it has been argued that «he saw himself as a man of Bergamo, a Lombard and a Frank.» This would be suggested by «his inconsistent use of ethnic labels,»[81] but this evaluation is based on a misunderstanding of the text.[82]

Some scholars have attempted to identify the chronicler as more specific individuals living in the 870s and 880s. It has been supposed that he was the *presbyter Andrea* mentioned in a document from 870, who was the representative of the Bishop of Bergamo, Garibald,[83] and who would, therefore, have been a member of the Bergamo clergy.[84] M. Lupo has also speculated that the *Andrea presbyter*, whose signature is one of those on a document from 881,[85] was the chronicler in question.[86] He has further maintained that the work was left unfinished not because the author died unexpectedly in 877, but rather because he abandoned it voluntarily.

G. La Placa has studied the parchments on which these documents of 870 and 881 are found, and concluded that the signatures are too dissimilar to belong to the same person, even if the possibility of a change in handwriting style over the eleven-year gap is considered. La Placa is cautious, but maintains that the author of the *Historia* is more likely to be the cleric of the 881 document.[87] Her theory is based on the fact that the historian signs his name *Andreas*, as does the *presbyter* of 881, whereas the individual in

---

[78] Andreas of Bergamo, *Historia*, chs. 17-18. Andreas does not write that Otto was the count of Bergamo, but that he was from the territory of Bergamo. Andreas of Bergamo, *Historia*, ch. 17. Other documents dating back to this period name the count of Bergamo as Otto, thus demonstrating that the character mentioned by Andreas of Bergamo was indeed the count of Bergamo. Jarnut, *Bergamo 568-1098*, pp. 21, 22, 68, 256.

[79] On this campaign of Louis II, see Gasparri, *Il ducato e il principato di Benevento*, pp. 124-125; Kreutz, *Before the Normans*, pp. 40-45.

[80] La Placa, *Andrea di Bergamo*, p. 62, note 7.

[81] MacLean, *Kingship and Politics*, p. 63. This scholar has also maintained that «these categories were not mutually exclusive.» This opinion has been reported in Wikipedia. https://en.wikipedia.org/wiki/Andreas_of_Bergamo (accessed on Februay 25, 2016).

[82] MacLean emphasizes that «this is especially clear in encounters with the Arabs and Beneventans.» MacLean, *Kingship and Politics*, p. 63, note 83. In reality, in the passage he refers to – the above-mentioned expedition of Count Otto in Calabria and the Muslim reaction to it –, the Lombards are never mentioned, only Otto is said to be «from the territory of Bergamo,» and Louis II's troops are defined as Franks and christians. Andreas of Bergamo, *Historia*, chs. 17-18. There is no «inconsistent use of ethnic labels» when Andreas narrates that Louis II besieged Bari with the Franks, the Lombards, and soldiers of «other nations» and that the same peoples fought the Muslims near Capua. Andreas of Bergamo, *Historia*, chs. 15, 19.

[83] *Le pergamene degli archivi di Bergamo*, pp. 35-36.

[84] Bertolini, *Andrea da Bergamo*, p. 79; Balzaretti, *Spoken Narratives*, pp. 35-36.

[85] *Le pergamene degli archivi di Bergamo*, pp. 42-44.

[86] *Codex diplomaticus civitatis et ecclesiae Bergomatis*, I, col. 914.

[87] La Placa, *Andrea di Bergamo*, p. 64.

the 870 source calls himself *Andrea*. As she also observes, Andreas was a fairly common name at the time and for this reason it is perfectly possible that the chronicler and the *presbyteri* of 870 and 881 were actually three different people.

N. Gray's theory is to be excluded entirely. She has speculated that the chronicler was *Andreas laevita*, author of the epitaph of the Archbishop of Milan, Anspertus, who died in 882.[88] The writing on the inscription actually demonstrates a high level of education,[89] contrasting completely with the ungrammatical Latin of the chronicler.[90]

The author's interest in the rural world is apparent in the *Historia*. This would suggest that he was familiar with such an environment, though it cannot be determined whether he lived in it. In fact, he states that it snowed so much in one year that the snow settled on the plains for one hundred days and the cold was so intense that many seeds and most of the vineyards were destroyed and wine froze in its barrels.[91] In the early 870s, the wine went bad not long after the wine harvest,[92] in May of the following year, a late frost destroyed the vineyards and the leaves on the trees, while in August locusts severely damaged the crops. In the latter case, Andreas even specifies that the damaged grain types were millet and foxtail millet.[93] When he recounts how the Bergamasques living in the countryside abandoned their homes to escape Berengar of Friuli's raid, the chronicler states that they had to flee in such a hurry that they took with them only their wives and a few essential items, thus leaving the wine and the crop harvest behind.[94] These are doubtless extraordinary events that do not reflect the reality of daily life, yet that Andreas is the only early medieval Italian chronicler to report specific information of this kind makes his interest in the countryside significant.[95]

Andreas does not explain why he wrote his work nor does he dedicate it to anyone. This and the fact that the chronicler states that he enjoyed writing his work[96] seem to imply that he composed the *Historia* for his own satisfaction. Along with many other medieval authors, Andreas affirms that he has written this chronicle despite being unworthy of the task,[97] a statement indicating that he did have a readership in mind.

The chronicler does not label his work in any way; the title *Historia* was assigned by the modern editors of his chronicle.[98] It can be said that he used the terms *cronica*

[88] Gray, *The Paleography of Latin Inscriptions*, pp. 93-94.

[89] Ferrari, *Manoscritti e cultura*, pp. 259-260.

[90] La Placa, *Andrea di Bergamo*, p. 66. For Andreas's Latin, see Pitkäranta, *Zur Sprache des Andreas von Bergamo*, pp. 129-149, and Molinelli, *Riflessi di un mondo plurilingue*, pp. 255-272.

[91] Andreas of Bergamo, *Historia*, ch. 14.

[92] Andreas of Bergamo, *Historia*, ch. 21.

[93] Andreas of Bergamo, *Historia*, ch. 21. At this time, these types of cereals were chosen for their resistance to bad weather. Montanari, *L'alimentazione contadina*, pp. 114, 133-144.

[94] Andreas of Bergamo, *Historia*, ch. 23.

[95] A similar attitude can be found in Paul the Deacon's *Historia Langobardorum*, where the chronicler relates that the plague that broke out in Narses's time killed off such a large number of men that neither the crops nor the grapes were harvested. Paul the Deacon, *Historia Langobardorum*, II, 4.

[96] Andreas of Bergamo, *Historia*, ch. 2.

[97] Andreas of Bergamo, *Historia*, ch. 2. For this *topos*, see Curtius, *European Literature*, pp. 83-85.

[98] The first editor, J. B. Mencke, entitled it *Chronicon. Andreae presbyteri, Itali, scriptoris seculi IX, Chronicon breve*.

(chronicle) and *historia* (history) as synonyms, because he defines the *History of the Lombards* by Paul the Deacon equally as a *historia*[99] and a *cronica*.[100]

It has been maintained that his poor Latin grammar indicates that Andreas was not very well educated.[101] Yet, the fact that the first section of his *Historia* is a summary of the *History of the Lombards* by Paul the Deacon[102] and that the chronicler quotes Holy Scripture on several occasions suggest that he was at least moderately educated.[103]

As for the sources on which the part following the summary of the *History of the Lombards* is based, the chronicler states that he utilized several letters and collected accounts from a number of old men.[104]

Except for the description of the motives inducing the Byzantine general Narses to invite the Lombards to invade Italy and the account of the conquests made by Alboin, Andreas's synthesis of Paul the Deacon's text is very succinct. For the most part, it is simply a list of Lombard kings, how long they were in power and their most important deeds.[105] Because of certain phrases he uses, such as *Quid multu?* and *Quid plura?*, (which can be translated as «why saying many things?») and the fact that, concerning King Rothari, he affirms «are not the other things concerning his rule, his strength, and the wars he had made written in the chronicle of the Lombards, like the things mentioned above?,»[106] it seems that the summary functioned purely as an introduction and that Andreas presupposed that his target audience had a good knowledge of the *History of the Lombards*.

An important aspect in the section dedicated to the history of the Lombard kingdom is that, along with all the sovereigns' actions, the chronicler also relates how many new laws they added to the *corpus* of Lombard legislation (something not reported by Paul the Deacon). This might suggest that Andreas was able to consult a manuscript containing

[99]   Andreas of Bergamo, *Historia*, ch. 2.
[100]   Andreas of Bergamo, *Historia*, ch. 1. Many medieval chroniclers did not distinguish between *chronica* and *historia*. Cf. Guenée, *Histoire et Culture historique*, pp. 200-207, and Arnaldi, *Annali, cronache, storie*, pp. 463-466.
[101]   Andreas's style and language have been called barbarous and rough. Balzani, *Le cronache italiane nel Medio Evo*, p. 112; Bertolini, *Andrea da Bergamo*, p. 80. Less severe was the evaluation of Viscardi, *Le Origini*, p. 77.
[102]   Andreas of Bergamo, *Historia*, ch. 1.
[103]   M. G. Bertolini claims that Andreas received some education, but only during his youth. Bertolini, *Andrea da Bergamo*, p. 80.
[104]   Andreas of Bergamo, *Historia*, ch. 2. M. G. Bertolini maintains that Andreas could have consulted some papal letters. Bertolini, *Andrea da Bergamo*, p. 80. However, there is no evidence in the work to support this hypothesis. Chris Wickham states that *series litterarum* could be king-lists appended to some legal texts. Wickham, *Lawyers' Time*, p. 279. As for the inclusion of testimonies of old men, this is a characteristic of many medieval chronicles. See, for example, the cases related by Skinner, *Gender and Memory*, pp. 39-40.
[105]   For example, about Authari, Andreas reports: «After ten years, they elected Authari, Cleph's son. Authari married a woman named Theodelinda, the saintly and most noble daughter of the Bavarians' King Garibald [...] King Authari, as they narrate, died in Ticinum from taking poison after reigning for six years.» Andreas of Bergamo, *Historia*, ch. 1, p. 71. About Liutprand, he reports: «Liutprand was very learned, merciful, virtuous, eloquent, tireless worshipper, and generous in alms. He augmented the laws of the Lombards and ordered them to be written in the collection of the Edict. He reigned for thirty-one years and seven months and died.» Andreas of Bergamo, *Historia*, ch. 1, p. 75.
[106]   Andreas of Bergamo, *Historia*, ch. 1, p. 71.

the Lombard laws.[107] However, one must point out that he makes a few mistakes.[108] Therefore, he was either reciting from memory or he learned this information from another person's account.

After the summary of the *History of the Lombards*, which ends at the reign of Liutprand (712-744), Andreas gives an account of the Lombard kingdom's final years and its conquest by Charlemagne. Without knowing exactly what sources Andreas used, it is impossible to discern whether the information he provides is his own conscious selection or merely what was said by those «old men» from whom he gathered testimonies.[109] What is certain is that the events are narrated from a Lombard point of view.

The accounts of the rules of Ratchis (744-749) and Aistulf (749-756) are obscurely worded. Indeed, they seem to have been designed to eliminate from memory the conflicts that occurred between the faction which wanted peaceful coexistence with the Papacy and the one which aimed at completing the conquest of Italy and provoked the deposition of Ratchis.[110] The defeats suffered by Aistulf at the hands of the Franks who came to the defense of Rome[111] are overlooked as well. With regard to these two kings, Andreas only writes the following sentence: «We cannot say what they did; we have only heard that they were both courageous and during their era the Lombards did not fear any other people.»[112]

Regarding Charlemagne's conquest of the Lombard kingdom, on the other hand, the author goes into much greater detail. Even though he makes a mistake about the pope's name, there are no relevant omissions in his account like those present in the passage about Ratchis and Aistulf.

There is a lot of evidence to show that Andreas narrates events from a Lombard standpoint and demonstrates rancor towards the Franks, but this is not always the case. In actual fact, the chronicler does not cover up the Lombards' responsibility for their own downfall and he expresses a certain amount of admiration for their conquerors. A list of the episodes clearly emphasizes an oscillation between the two viewpoints.[113]

Blame for the dissolution of the marriage between Charlemagne and the daughter of the Lombard King Desiderius is placed not on Charlemagne, but on his brother, the «terrible and evil» Carloman who paid for his behavior with a painful death.[114] Next, Andreas recounts that the pontiff traveled to *Francia* because of the Lombard «oppressions.» Here, the pope discovered how «astute and noble» the Franks were and he asked them to conquer

---

[107] I believe that this kind of information is not enough for maintaining that Andreas of Bergamo had an «exact knowledge of Lombard legal texts» and that his chronicle demonstrates the existence of a strong connection between history and legislation. For these opinions, see Balzaretti, *Spoken Narratives*, p. 36, and Gasparri, *Italia longobarda*, p. 175. More cautious is Wickham who has correctly noted that the chronicler reports how many laws the Lombard kings issued. Wickham, *Lawyers' Time*, p. 279.

[108] Andreas of Bergamo states that Ratchis and Aistulf added eight and fourteen new laws respectively whereas Ratchis actually added fourteen and Aistulf twenty-two. Andreas of Bergamo, *Historia*, ch. 3.

[109] According to Chris Wickham, Andreas wrote more or less all he knew. Wickham, *Lawyers' Time*, p. 279.

[110] Andreolli, *Una pagina di storia longobarda*, pp. 281-327; Jarnut, *Geschichte der Langobarden*, pp. 106-109.

[111] Wickham, *Early Medieval Italy*, p. 46.

[112] Andreas of Bergamo, *Historia*, ch. 3. Cf. Capo, *La polemica longobarda*, p. 25.

[113] By contrast, C. G. Mor believes that Andreas's work only expresses a grudge towards the Franks. Mor, *La storiografia italiana del sec. IX*, p. 243. Of the same opinion is Fasoli, *Carlo Magno*, p. 350.

[114] Andreas of Bergamo, *Historia*, ch. 3.

Italy.[115] Like the Frankish and papal sources,[116] Andreas does not neglect to mention that the pope's actions were legitimate because the Lombards were oppressing him. In addition, he highlights the good qualities of the Lombards' enemies. The observation that they were «astute» could indicate that Andreas wanted to stress that the Franks had astutely taken advantage of the situation in order to take over the Lombard kingdom. Yet, such an interpretation contrasts with Andreas's description of the Franks as «noble.»

Andreas takes a more "pro-Lombard" stance, when he recounts that Charlemagne prepared to attack the Lombards, by underlining that thus the Frankish king forgot all the good things Desiderius had done for him.[117] This stance disappears as quickly as it emerged, however. Andreas follows this statement by explaining that the oaths between the Frankish and Lombard sovereigns had been rendered null and void by the pope,[118] so Charlemagne could not be accused of betrayal. He then points out that the Franks took possession of Italy without any arduous battles, because God had spread terror among the Lombards,[119] thus implying that God was on the Franks' side.[120]

The chronicler continues to oscillate between praising and criticizing the Franks.[121] In reporting the pernicious effects of their victory, he tells of how «in Italy there were, therefore, many misfortunes; some were killed by the sword, others struck by famine, others were killed by beasts so that few remained in the villages and towns.»[122]

In his account of the Lombard revolt of 775-776, the author shows a tendency to exalt the Lombards and belittle Charlemagne's actions. Firstly, Andreas does not say that the Lombards staged a rebellion. He narrates instead that the dukes of Cividale and Vicenza heard of the devastation caused by the Franks and of how they were heading for Cividale. The Lombards confronted and beat the Franks at the river Livenza.[123] The chronicler adds that Charlemagne eventually managed to win only by corrupting a Lombard who convinced his companions to lay down their arms.[124] The Frankish annalist, who was writing at the same time, perhaps went to the other extreme by not mentioning the earlier defeat suffered by the Franks, and reporting only that Charlemagne put an end to the uprising by killing the duke of Cividale and conquering the rebellious cities.[125]

---

[115] Andreas of Bergamo, *Historia*, ch. 4. As has already been stated, the chronicler makes an error in reporting that it was Pope Leo III who went to Charlemagne for help against the Lombards. It was Pope Stephen II who crossed the Alps to get help from Pippin III, Charlemagne's father.

[116] For example, *Annales qui dicuntur Einhardi*, year 773.

[117] Andreas of Bergamo, *Historia*, ch. 5.

[118] Andreas of Bergamo, *Historia*, ch. 5.

[119] Andreas of Bergamo, *Historia*, ch. 5.

[120] The claim that God supported Charlemagne is also found in the Chronicle of Novalesa, a text written around the middle of the eleventh century. It narrates that God appeared to the Frankish king in a vision prompting him to go to Italy. *Cronaca di Novalesa*, III, 6.

[121] These features of Andreas's work are not taken into consideration by Gasparri, who only provides a brief summary of the chronicler's account. Gasparri, *Italia longobarda*, p. 175.

[122] Andreas of Bergamo, *Historia*, ch. 5. Here, the chronicler is probably exaggerating, but the hard times of this period are testified in other contemporary sources as well. Capo, *La polemica longobarda*, p. 7, note 7; Cammarosano, *Nobili e re*, p. 102; Barbero, *Charlemagne*, pp. 35-36.

[123] Andreas of Bergamo, *Historia*, ch. 6.

[124] Andreas of Bergamo, *Historia*, ch. 6. This detail is overlooked by Gasparri, *The Fall of the Lombard Kingdom*, p. 64, and Gasparri, *Italia longobarda*, p. 125.

[125] *Annales regni Francorum*, years 775-776. According to Barbero, «Andreas's account could be interpreted

That Andreas does not report the coronation of Charlemagne as emperor and never refers to him as *imperator* or *augustus* could mean that he wished to omit the event in order to diminish the success of the Lombards' adversary. This is clearly a very strange omission, especially if one considers that the chronicler makes a point of referring to Charlemagne's son, Louis the Pious, who took the throne after his father's death, as emperor.[126] Even if it is obvious that this omission was intentional, it is still important to bear in mind that the chronicler, during the account of Charlemagne's death, attributes the great fame of the Franks to this sovereign.[127] This last point again highlights the author's complex stance towards Charlemagne and the Franks.

A similar position can be also found later in the work. Andreas of Bergamo says nothing about Charlemagne's son, Pippin, who took over the kingdom of Italy, but the fact that he mentions the great famine afflicting the kingdom during his rule[128] is further proof that he wanted to provide a negative image of the Frankish domination of Italy as well.

From a narrative point of view, the reference to the problems during Pippin's reign allows Andreas to exalt the rule of Bernard, Pippin's son. Andreas states that, as soon as Bernard's reign began, appeared «prestige and abundance» which were to last throughout his rule.[129] It has been argued that these praises reveal the existence of a nationalistic Lombard spirit aimed at extolling the actions of Bernard, who rebelled against Louis the Pious probably because of his exclusion from the Empire's subdivision in 817.[130] This is a suggestive interpretation, but there is no evidence to prove it. Unlike the Frankish sources,[131] Andreas makes no mention of Bernard's rebellion and he places the responsibility for the death of the king of Italy entirely on Louis the Pious's wife. According to the chronicler, when she entered into a conflict with Bernard for unspecified reasons, the empress had him blinded and he died from the injuries. It is noteworthy that Andreas is keen to emphasize Louis's lack of involvement in the affair, explaining that everything took place without the emperor's knowledge.[132] Moreover, immediately after recounting Bernard's death, the chronicler describes Louis the Pious in a positive way, calling attention to his wisdom and love of peace.[133]

---

as the wishful ramblings of a Lombard who, even after so much time, found it difficult to accept the defeat of his people at the hands of the Franks.» Barbero, *Charlemagne*, p. 35. On the other hand, Pierandrea Moro believes that Andreas of Bergamo is a more reliable source than the Frankish Annals. Moro, «*Quam horrida pugna*», p. 35.

[126] Andreas of Bergamo, *Historia*, ch. 7.

[127] Andreas of Bergamo, *Historia*, ch. 7.

[128] Andreas of Bergamo, *Historia*, ch. 7.

[129] Andreas of Bergamo, *Historia*, ch. 7.

[130] For example, C. G. Mor maintains that Andreas's benevolence towards Bernard was because the sovereign wanted independence from the Empire and to reunite Italy. Mor, *La storiografia italiana del sec. IX*, p. 242. In general on the revolt of Bernard, see Noble, *The Revolt of King Bernard*, pp. 315-326; Jarnut, *Kaiser Ludwig der Fromme*, pp. 637-648; Depreux, *Das Königtum Bernhards*.

[131] *Annales regni Francorum*, years 817-818; Thegan, *Gesta Hludowici imperatoris*, chs. 22-23; Astronomer, *Vita Hludowici imperatoris*, chs. 29-30. Regino of Prüm, who wrote at the beginning of the tenth century, also reports a similar version of events. Regino of Prüm, *Chronicon cum continuatione Treverensi*, year 818.

[132] Andreas of Bergamo, *Historia*, ch. 8.

[133] Andreas of Bergamo, *Historia*, ch. 9.

In line with this positive portrayal of Louis the Pious is the account the author gives of the Archbishop of Milan, Angilbert, who was accused of having induced Lothar, Louis the Pious's son, to abduct his stepmother Judith. According to the chronicler, the prelate managed to persuade Louis the Pious to pardon the crime by reminding him of the love one ought to show even to one's enemies.[134]

Andreas probably had limited information concerning the conflicts over the subdivisions of the Empire that broke out between Louis the Pious and his sons. He states correctly that Lothar had Charles the Bald's mother, Judith, imprisoned in Tortona,[135] but he does not explain why. Nor does Andreas report the revolts that Lothar and his brothers instigated against Louis the Pious. Most significantly, he does not express any judgment concerning the aforementioned affair.

Andreas briefly tells of the quarrels that broke out among Louis the Pious's sons after his death and underscores that these conflicts caused the battle of Fontenoy (841).[136] Unlike the contemporary Frankish records, Andreas never accuses Lothar of being responsible for the situation. Instead, the Italian chronicler states that Lothar joined in the conflict because Louis the Pious's heirs could not agree over the division of the Empire. The commentary Andreas gives about the battle of Fontenoy is noteworthy both in its originality and in the sentiments it brings to light. He is actually indifferent to the outcome of the conflict and dwells upon the recklessness of the battle itself, in which many men, who could have made a valuable contribution to the fight against the pagans, died. Andreas adds that most of those killed at Fontenoy were from Aquitania, with the result that there were no noblemen left in the area to fight the Northmen who were attacking that region.[137]

The final account Andreas gives of the Carolingians concerns Lothar II, Lothar I's son. It concerns an episode that took place in 869.[138] He narrates that Lothar II traveled to Italy to meet his brother, Louis II, who was in southern Italy, and explains that, during the journey, Lothar II committed many blasphemous acts and destroyed the homes of many poor people.[139] Since the author was a contemporary of this event, it is surprising that he does not mention that Lothar II went to Italy in order to obtain the annulment of his marriage to Theutberga from the pope, an affair that provoked a scandal of large proportions in the 860s.[140] Andreas may not have known anything about this, but his silence could be also due out of a desire to draw the reader's attention to the damage caused in Italy by a Frank on this occasion. The reference to the suffering inflicted on the poor is noteworthy precisely because their protection was one of the main and widely acknowledged tasks of any sovereign.

---

[134] Andreas of Bergamo, *Historia*, ch. 11.
[135] Andreas of Bergamo, *Historia*, ch. 10. Cf. Thegan, *Gesta Hludowici imperatoris*, ch. 42, and Astronomer, *Vita Hludowici imperatoris*, ch. 48.
[136] Andreas of Bergamo, *Historia*, ch. 13.
[137] Andreas of Bergamo, *Historia*, ch. 13.
[138] Andreas does not give the date, but the fact that he states that Lothar II died in Piacenza means that the episode took place in 869, the year Lothar II passed away. *Annales Bertiniani*, year 869.
[139] Andreas of Bergamo, *Historia*, ch. 13.
[140] For further information about this case, see Heidecker, *The Divorce of Lothar II*.

The passages concerning Italy and Louis II indicate that Andreas concentrated almost entirely on the final phase of Louis II's campaigns against the Muslims in southern Italy. The sole exceptions are brief mentions of the problems the Slavs caused to the subjects of the Italian kingdom before Everard became the leader of Friuli,[141] of Louis II's repression of a revolt led by the Burgundian Hupert,[142] and of the baptism at Rome of the king of the Bulgarians.[143]

The first important feature that comes to light is that Andreas never writes about the difficulties the emperor had with the Lombards of southern Italy before 871, but only reports the sovereign's victories. These are not all described in the same way, however. The most important success, the conquest of Bari in 871, which came after a long siege and represented the end of the emirate of Bari, the main Muslim dominion in the southern part of Italian peninsula at that time,[144] is concisely narrated,[145] whereas the earlier victories in Calabria and Apulia are described in far greater detail.[146] This is probably because, as we have already stated, Andreas was able to gather information from the Bergamasques who had taken part in those battles.

The numerous details provided by the chronicler show that he was aware of the image of "holy war" which the Frankish sovereigns wanted to attribute to their campaigns against the Saracens.[147] The chronicler blames the Muslims not only for making raids, but also for the destruction of churches.[148] They are referred to as pagans, while Louis II's soldiers are called Christians.[149] Moreover, Andreas recounts that, before a battle, the emperor's troops attended mass, taking Holy Communion and receiving the blessing of priests.[150] Then, before beginning the fighting, Louis II's soldiers – called «faithful of Christ» – prayed: «O Lord Jesus Christ, you said: "He who eats my flesh and drinks my blood will remain in me and I with him." So, if you are with us who is against us?»[151] On this occasion Andreas also explains that, in virtue of the commitment to battle, that the Christians demonstrated, «heavenly weapons» helped them to win.[152]

A reference to divine aid is also present in the account of a later confrontation in which the Muslims are depicted as braggarts. When they learned of the fall of Bari, the Saracens arrived in droves to assist their compatriots. Once they had landed, the

---

[141] Andreas of Bergamo, *Historia*, ch. 14.
[142] Andreas of Bergamo, *Historia*, ch. 14.
[143] Andreas of Bergamo, *Historia*, ch. 16.
[144] Musca, *L'emirato di Bari*.
[145] Andreas of Bergamo, *Historia*, ch. 19.
[146] Andreas of Bergamo, *Historia*, chs.17-18.
[147] The lack of available sources on Louis II makes it difficult to study this aspect in much detail. Suffice to say that Andreas's description of the anti-Muslim campaigns has some similarities with the capitulary issued by Lothar in 847, in which there is an account of the preparation for the expedition against the Saracens, following the sack of Rome that they perpetrated in 846. *Capitularia regum Francorum*, II, number 203, chs. 2, 3, 7, 13.
[148] Andreas of Bergamo, *Historia*, ch. 17.
[149] Andreas of Bergamo, *Historia*, ch. 18.
[150] Andreas of Bergamo, *Historia*, ch. 18.
[151] Andreas of Bergamo, *Historia*, ch. 18 (John 6: 56, and Rom. 8: 31).
[152] Andreas of Bergamo, *Historia*, ch. 18.

Muslims destroyed their own boats, saying that they were no longer necessary because the Franks were powerless against them.[153] The Saracens, however, paid dearly for their presumption as they suffered a terrible defeat. Andreas narrates the whole event effectively, remarking that «those who had come exalted were humbled.»[154]

In his perspective, these conflicts were waged only in order to defeat the enemy of God, not out of a desire for conquest or booty. In full agreement with this particular interpretation is the passage in which the chronicler points out that Louis II sent troops to save the Calabrians who were being oppressed by the Muslims. The emperor did not take this decision because their ambassadors had promised him loyalty and tribute, but because he was moved by the dire situation they were experiencing.[155]

Once the threat posed by the Muslims had been dealt with, the Prince of Benevento, Adelchis, immediately imprisoned Louis II because he feared that the emperor would conquer all of southern Italy.[156] The subsequent scandal was huge, since the abrupt *volte-face* of the Beneventans showed not only their ingratitude, but their true feelings towards the Franks as well. The affair, moreover, was embarrassing for the Franks. The ease with which Louis II's capture took place exposed the sovereign's lack of foresight as the Lombards had already in the past shown themselves to be untrustworthy allies.

Andreas appears to have perceived the complexity of the situation. Indeed, he does not limit his narrative to the ingratitude of the Beneventans, who gave «evil for good» to Louis II, who had in contrast shown the deepest loyalty to them. To justify what happened, he also brings supernatural intervention into play. The account of Louis II's capture begins with a description of the devil, charged with inciting the Beneventans to act against the Franks.[157] If the devil were really to blame for the betrayal, any fault on the Beneventans' and on Louis II's part would be diminished. This is the sole time Andreas assigns the devil responsibility for a wrongdoing, a peculiarity that makes this narrative decision even more significant. In effect, the implication is that this is not just the simple utilization of a *topos*; rather the author perceived the need for a special explanation for the incident. Noteworthy too is the detail that the chronicler emphasizes that God ensured that Louis II was released after a brief period of imprisonment by spreading a «heavenly fear» among the Beneventans.[158] Furthermore, Andreas shows that the sovereign constantly enjoyed God's favor, thus implicitly freeing the emperor from any responsibility for what had happened. Despite this happy conclusion, Louis II's imprisonment was a pernicious event and the prelude to a period of adversities.

The chronicler's tone changes immediately after the liberation of the emperor, and takes on dramatic nuances. Andreas was likely influenced by the conviction, spread by

---

[153] Andreas of Bergamo, *Historia*, ch. 19.
[154] Andreas of Bergamo, *Historia*, ch. 19 (Math. 23: 10, and Luke 14: 10). Andreas indicates the location of the battles, but never mentions any details about the fightings, focusing instead on the major losses suffered by the Muslims.
[155] Andreas of Bergamo, *Historia*, ch. 17.
[156] Russo Mailler, *La politica meridionale di Ludovico II*, pp. 12-15; Gasparri, *Il ducato e il principato di Benevento*, pp. 125-126, and Kreutz, *Before the Normans*, pp. 45-47.
[157] Andreas of Bergamo, *Historia*, ch. 20.
[158] Andreas of Bergamo, *Historia*, ch. 20.

apocalyptic literature, that the end of the world would be anticipated by terrible events, as he goes on to list a series of progressively negative occurrences: the wine went bad as soon as it was made;[159] at Easter, earth fell from the sky;[160] in May, frost caused serious damage to the vines and trees;[161] in August, locusts destroyed harvests;[162] in June of the following year, a comet appeared,[163] and in July, the Saracens sacked Comacchio.[164] This series of disastrous events ended with the death of Louis II in August 875.[165]

In effect, the sovereign's passing represented the end of an era. The quarrels that broke out among his relations over the succession to the throne marked the end of nearly a century of peace in the Italian kingdom.[166] Andreas was probably aware of this, as he affirms that after the death of Louis II a great *tribulatio* (distress) fell over Italy.[167] He also explains that the people responsible for this situation were the aristocracy and Louis II's wife, Angelberga, who asked both Charles the Bald and Louis the German to come to Italy.[168] As has already been pointed out, the reports Andreas gives of the destruction and raids that characterized this period only concern the area around Bergamo.[169]

The rest of Andreas's chronicle contains no other points of interest since the events between the arrival of Charles the Bald in Italy and his death are referred to only briefly. There is, nevertheless, a surprising error in it, given that the chronicler was living at that time. According to Andreas, Charles the Bald, having reached an agreement with his nephew Carloman, went to Rome, where the pope crowned him emperor, after which he returned to Pavia.[170] When he heard that Carloman was going to attack him, Charles the Bald rounded up his troops to confront him. However, a number of his men went over to the enemy and, therefore, Charles the Bald went back to France; he never arrived as he died along the way.[171] In reality, once Charles the Bald had been elected emperor on Christmas day in 875, he did not reside in Pavia for long, but returned to France. At the pope's invitation, in 877 he went back to Italy with a few of his men, leaving the rest

---

[159] Andreas of Bergamo, *Historia*, ch. 21.

[160] Andreas of Bergamo, *Historia*, ch. 21.

[161] Andreas of Bergamo, *Historia*, ch. 21.

[162] Andreas of Bergamo, *Historia*, ch. 21.

[163] Andreas of Bergamo, *Historia*, ch. 22.

[164] Andreas of Bergamo, *Historia*, ch. 22.

[165] Andreas of Bergamo, *Historia*, ch. 22.

[166] However, it is an exaggeration to maintain that Andreas of Bergamo was a «supporter of Louis II.» Moreover, there is no evidence that the chronicler perceived Louis II as an «Italian sovereign.» For these opinions, see Gasparri, *Italia longobarda*, p. 176.

[167] Andreas of Bergamo, *Historia*, ch. 23. The fact that Andreas also uses the word *tribulatio* (distress) to describe the situation in which Italy found itself after Charlemagne's defeat of the Lombards could serve as evidence to suggest that the author wanted to show that intervention from across the Alpine border always produced the same results. Andreas of Bergamo, *Historia*, ch. 5. Still, it cannot be excluded that the repetition is purely due to limited linguistic ability or knowledge of synonyms on Andreas's part. Having reported that, not long before Louis the Pious had died, an eclipse had occurred, Andreas writes *facta est tribulatio magna* (there was a great distress). Andreas of Bergamo, *Historia*, ch. 12.

[168] Andreas of Bergamo, *Historia*, ch. 23.

[169] He also adds that they were carried out by Berengar of Friuli who sided with the Eastern Franks. Andreas of Bergamo, *Historia*, ch. 23.

[170] Andreas of Bergamo, *Historia*, ch. 23.

[171] Andreas of Bergamo, *Historia*, ch. 24.

to follow later. When he heard that Carloman was about to cross the Alps and that his own army was not going to arrive, because many noblemen had defected, he turned back hastily, but passed away in October 877 in Nantua, a few miles from Geneva.[172] In the *Historia*, then, any narration of Charles the Bald, who went back to France in 876 before returning to Italy the following year, is lacking. This error likely signifies either that Andreas wrote this last passage several years after the events had transpired or that another non-contemporaneous author completed Andreas's work.

To conclude, the fact that the public officials are never mentioned with their title in the chronicle and that important events regarding Louis II – for example, when he assumed leadership of the kingdom of Italy or his coronation as emperor – are not recorded lead to the assumption that Andreas did not belong to Louis II's entourage. He likely spent most of his life in Bergamo or in the surrounding territory and perhaps collected the testimonies of his fellow citizens, who had fought in the ranks of the emperor's army, and of travelers passing through Bergamo.

The episode concerning the Archbishop of Milan, Angilbert, which underscores the pride of the Ambrosian Church, suggests that Andreas had been in contact with Milanese ecclesiastics. The modest size of Andreas's work is, therefore, due more to the sources that he had at his disposal than to his meager descriptive ability. In the cases, in which Andreas was sufficiently well-informed, he demonstrates, despite his incorrect use of Latin, that he did not want to write a simple account of the events and that he possessed a reasonable narrative talent. One of the most relevant aspects of this text is the preservation of a Lombard version of the Lombard kingdom's fall – probably due to the fact the author did not belong to official circles. In spite of the existence of a certain acrimony for the Franks, however, it must be noted that the chronicler's attitude towards them is not uniformly negative. In fact, Andreas demonstrates admiration for the new rulers as well. He appears, therefore, to be a spokesman for those who accepted the Frankish domination, while remarking with a certain pride that the defeat of the Lombards was not a complete debacle and highlighting the negative aspects that followed the Frankish conquest.[173]

4. The Poem *King Pippin's Victory over the Avars*

The author of this poem, narrating the 796 expedition led by Charlemagne's son, Pippin, against the Avars, is anonymous.[174] Yet, unlike other coeval Frankish sources, he mentions the name of the Avar sovereign's wife[175] and provides the title by which the Avar dignitaries

---

[172] Nelson, *Charles the Bald*, pp. 243-253.
[173] A version of the sections on the HLCG and the *Historia* of Andreas of Bergamo has been published in Berto, *Remembering Old and New Rulers*, pp. 23-53.
[174] Manacorda believes that the poet was a Frank living at Pippin's court. Manacorda, *Ricerche sugli inizii della dominazione*, p. 16.
[175] The author relates that the khagan's wife was called *Catuna*. In reality, this was not a name, but the title held by Avar rulers' consorts. *De Pippini regis victoria*, lines 17-18. Cf. Pohl, *Die Awaren*, pp. 305-306.

were known,[176] which leads to the supposition that the poet himself participated in the campaign or that he may have interviewed someone who had taken part in it.

In the first part of the work the poet highlights that the Avars had not been converted to Christianity and mentions numerous misdeeds they carried out to the detriment of churches. Emphasized in particular is that, at the devil's suggestion, the Avars carried out the blasphemous gesture of handing the ecclesiastics' clothing to their women.[177] The author then recounts that the Lord sent Saint Peter to assist Pippin, who, with God's help, encamped with his own troops alongside the Danube.[178] The most original part of the work comes at this point. The poet describes the Avars' reaction to the news of Charlemagne's son's arrival, and reports the words addressed by the Avar Unguimeri to the khagan[179] and to his wife. Unguimeri told them that the Avars' reign was over and that, if they wanted to live, they would have to go immediately to Pippin, pay homage, and bring him gifts.[180] The khagan, terrified by this threat, submitted to Charlemagne's son and begged him to withdraw his army.[181] The author concludes his piece by thanking God for the victory over the pagans, praising Pippin for having created a kingdom that not even Caesar or the pagans had managed to establish, and wishing the sovereign a long life and numerous children.[182]

No other work was written to celebrate the campaigns against the Avars. For this reason, it is possible to make a comparison only with the Frankish Annals, which are generally less descriptive than Carolingian poems. It is noteworthy that the anonymous poet highlights above all the edifying aspects of Pippin's feat, i. e. that he was supported by God and aimed at punishing the pagans who had destroyed numerous churches and monasteries and carried out blasphemous acts. No aspect of war is mentioned.[183] The author says only that the Avars surrendered immediately, implicitly emphasizing Pippin's power. The Frankish Annals, however, report that Charlemagne's son drove the Avars further back than the river Theiss and that he razed their camp, the Ring, where the khagan resided, to the ground taking possession of the numerous riches stored there. He then went to his father's court in Aachen to show him the plunder.[184]

Unless the poet composed his work before the destruction of the Ring, it seems that he wished to make Pippin's campaign appear as a feat driven by noble ideals and not by material interests. The lack of any information about the author unfortunately does not enable us to determine whether this attitude was his choice or whether it represented the will of Pippin who probably commissioned these verses.[185]

---

[176] *De Pippini regis victoria*, line 29. Cf. Pohl, *Die Awaren*, pp. 301-302.

[177] *De Pippini regis victoria*, lines 3-9.

[178] *De Pippini regis victoria*, lines 10-15.

[179] The rulers of the Avars held the title of khagan. Pohl, *Die Awaren*, pp. 293-300.

[180] *De Pippini regis victoria*, lines 16-27.

[181] *De Pippini regis victoria*, lines 28-36.

[182] *De Pippini regis victoria*, lines 37-46.

[183] R. Bezzola is therefore wrong when he states that this poem has «un accent guerrier.» Bezzola, *Les origines et la formation de la littérature courtoise*, p. 130.

[184] *Annales regni Francorum*, year 796.

[185] Rosamond McKitterick has hypothesized that this poem was sent to the court of Charlemagne «as a form of report and homage for his son.» McKitterick, *Charlemagne*, p. 367.

5. The *Rythmus on Emperor Louis's Captivity*

The author of this *Rythmus* is unknown, but the fact that the sole extant manuscript of this text dates to the ninth century and that this work mentions numerous details concerning Emperor Louis II's imprisonment by the Beneventans in 871 imply that he was contemporary with this event, and either witnessed it or had the opportunity to question someone who had been present. According to the anonymous poet, Adelferius and Saductus played an important role in the conspiracy. The former, who persuaded the Beneventans to capture the sovereign,[186] probably held a high position in the court of the Prince of Benevento, Adelchis.[187] The latter, on the other hand, mentioned alongside the Emir of Bari, Sawdān,[188] was likely a member of the Saducti, a family from Capua, who had fled to Benevento some years previously because of a clash with the gastald of Capua.[189] The author, moreover, reports that Louis II was liberated because Christ had arranged for a large number of Muslims to arrive at Salerno,[190] a detail recorded by Erchempert, one of the most well-informed chroniclers on this episode.[191]

The *Rythmus* is structured as a sort of trial of Louis II in which the wide use of direct discourse contributes notable dynamism and drama to the account.[192] Adelferius has the role of the accuser; he incites Prince Adelchis and the Beneventans to arrest and kill the emperor, who was accused of trying to seize Benevento and of not taking the Beneventans into any consideration.[193] Louis II, depicted as a martyr, is brought before the Beneventan prince. After being mocked by the Emir of Bari, Sawdān,[194] and by Saductus, the emperor, described as holy and pious, turns to the Beneventans, telling them that they arrested him like a thief, even though he had come to their land induced by love for the Church and to liberate them from the Muslims.[195] Sawdān responds with a parody, putting the imperial crown on his head and declaring himself emperor.[196] Yet he does not succeed in continuing this farce because he is immediately possessed by the devil and falls to the ground, a miraculous event large numbers of people rush to observe.[197] The author declares that in this way Christ expressed his verdict and goes on to narrate how many Muslims went to besiege Salerno and that Louis II promised to defend those lands without trying to conquer them.[198]

---

[186] *Rythmus de captivitate Lhuduici imperatoris*, lines 4-9.

[187] Russo Mailler, *La politica meridionale*, p. 23.

[188] *Rythmus de captivitate Lhuduici imperatoris*, line 13.

[189] The Saducti's escape is described by the ninth-century southern Lombard chronicler Erchempert, *Ystoriola Longobardorum Beneventum degentium*, ch. 15. The significant role that this family then assumed in Benevento seems to be suggested by the fact that a Saductus is among the signatories of the division of the principality of Benevento in 849. *Chronicon Salernitanum*, ch. 84ᵇ. Cf. Russo Mailler, *La politica meridionale*, p. 24.

[190] *Rythmus de captivitate Lhuduici imperatoris*, lines 28-30.

[191] Erchempert, *Ystoriola Longobardorum Beneventum degentium*, ch. 35.

[192] Dronke, *Generi letterari della poesia ritmica altomedievale*, p. 176.

[193] *Rythmus de captivitate Lhuduici imperatoris*, lines 4-9.

[194] After the fall of Bari, Sawdān was taken to Benevento, where it seems that he enjoyed a certain freedom. Musca, *L'emirato di Bari*, pp. 124-126.

[195] *Rythmus de captivitate Lhuduici imperatoris*, lines 10-21.

[196] *Rythmus de captivitate Lhuduici imperatoris*, lines 22-24.

[197] *Rythmus de captivitate Lhuduici imperatoris*, lines 25-27.

[198] *Rythmus de captivitate Lhuduici imperatoris*, lines 28-32.

It has been supposed that the author was a cleric in Louis II's entourage, who later became a «jongleur,» and that this *Rythmus* parodies Louis II. Such a hypothesis would be supported by the fact that this text is characterized by dialogues and that the manuscript in which the *Rythmus* is reported is written in Carolingian minuscule and is in a library in Verona, details that might indicate that this work was composed in Carolingian Italy.[199]

In my opinion, the *Rythmus* is not satire. Firstly, one must observe that the *Audite* (Hear) with which this text opens does not necessarily mean that it is the work of a storyteller. In fact, numerous early medieval rythms start with this *incipit*, above all the *abecedarii*.[200] Moreover, that Louis II defends himself by pointing out the ingratitude of the Beneventans, and that the emir of Bari places the imperial crown on his own head do not represent the ridiculing of the sovereign. In fact, Louis II says the very words used by Christ when he was captured at Gethsemane,[201] Sawdān is punished immediately for what he did, while the emperor is liberated and asked to protect the principality of Benevento from the Muslims.[202]

The hypothesis that the anonymous poet was someone in Louis II's entourage is not to be ruled out. The sovereign appears to be the innocent victim of a conspiracy and it is clearly understood from the text that Christ had made sure that the emperor was saved. It is not absurd, however, to suppose that the author came from southern Italy. The *Rythmus*, in fact, gives voice to the fears of the Beneventans, who were worried that they would be subjugated by Louis II; yet, at the same time, it highlights the innocence of the holy and pious emperor and emphasizes the wish of the Lombards to be defended by him. The imprisonment of Louis II had embarrassing implications: the emperor was jailed without clear provocation and immediately after his conquest of Bari, the most dangerous Saracen base in southern Italy. Besides, the Muslim threat did not cease and the Lombards demonstrated their inability to resist it. Consequently they were forced, through the mediation of the Bishop of Capua, Landulf, to ask for the intervention of the emperor, who agreed to the request for help and defeated the Saracens.[203] The *Rythmus* could, therefore, be the expression of the embarrassment of the Beneventans, who asked for the help of the very person they had betrayed. It is noteworthy that in the text the Prince of Benevento, Adelchis, is never mentioned. It is only reported that Adelferius spoke to the prince, telling him of Louis II's faults.[204] Only Adelferius, Saductus, and Sawdān acted against the emperor. The *Rythmus* could represent the version of the events presented by the Lombards who went to solicit the sovereign's help against the Muslims. The Beneventan prince had not actually wanted Louis II to be imprisoned and

---

[199] Russo Mailler, *La politica meridionale*, pp. 17 and 24-25.

[200] The *abecedarii* are poems in which the lines begin with the letters of the alphabet in sequence.

[201] *Rythmus de captivitate Lhuduici imperatoris*, line 15. Cf. Luke 22:52.

[202] One of the reasons for C. Russo Mailler's flawed interpretation is poor comprehension of the text. She translates lines 31 and 32 «Iuratum est ad sancte Dei reliquie / ipse regnum defendendum et alium requirere» as follows: «It had been sworn on the holy relics that the emperor would seek another kingdom to defend.» In spite of the ungrammatical Latin, it appears clear that Louis II is being asked to defend the *regnum* and *alium requirere*. Given that in line 8 Adelferius defines the principality of Benevento as *regnum* and that the Saracens were besieging Salerno, it is probable that Louis II was asked to defend the principality of Benevento without trying to take possession of it.

[203] Erchempert, *Ystoriola Longobardorum Beneventum degentium*, ch. 35.

[204] *Rythmus de captivitate Lhuduici imperatoris*, lines 5-9.

tried. Moreover, the emperor had been recognized as innocent and Sawdān, who had dared to scoff at Louis II's imperial status, had been severely punished. The sovereign, therefore, had no cause to bear any grudge against the Beneventans and could continue his fight to liberate southern Italy from the Muslims.

The manuscripts and the previous editions[205]

The HLCG is preserved in a manuscript dating to the eleventh/twelfth century: codex no. 84 of Gotha's Forschungsbibliothek (Germany), fols. 335^v-337^v (hereafter G). The work is in 2 columns, composed of 39 lines each; it begins on line 35 of the second column of fol. 335^{v206} and ends on the line 24 of fol. 337^v.[207] In G the chronicle was copied by only a single scribe. In the spaces between the lines there are some corrections by another hand, probably coeval to the manuscript. Considering the rough Latin of the author and that G is not contemporary with the chronicler, I have decided to take into account the corrections only in the presence of mistakes that impede the comprehension of the text. For example, *mine* for *nomine*,[208] *exvt* for *exivit*,[209] *Pania* for *Pannonia*,[210] *relinques* for *relinquens*,[211] *venerum* for *venenum*,[212] and *examinati* for *exanimati*.[213] Moreover I have corrected *Cleps* to *Clephs*,[214] since this Lombard king is known as Cleph. In the case of the Frankish sovereign Chlothar the name was miscopied and so I have changed *flotharius* to *Clotharius*.[215]

Stefano Maria Cingolani has argued that the word *serpentibus*, employed at the beginning of the HLCG, «Asserunt antiqui parentes Langobardorum [...] deinter serpentibus parentes eorum breviati exissent, sanguinea et aspera progeines et sine lege», is a mistake for *spernentibus*. Cingolani states that, if one accepts the reading *serpentibus*, the passage would refer to an episode of Lombard history that is not mentioned in other texts and is unparalleled in Germanic legends. He therefore believes that the best solution is to correct *serpentibus* to *spernentibus*. The latter term would refer to the small number of Lombards, explained by the fact they were only one part of a people.[216]

This hypothesis is interesting, yet it is necessary to observe that, first, the primary sources available to us are so scanty that the fact that no other work reports the snakes episode does not constitute a valid reason for maintaining the corruption of the text. Moreover, I believe that *breviati* is not related to *serpentibus*. If one considers that *exire* might also mean «to originate from», the sentence can be translated as «The ancient

---

[205] In this volume I have used a revised version of the Latin texts edited in *Testi storici e poetici*.
[206] In this part of the folio there is no indication that a new text begins.
[207] In this folio there are no other texts.
[208] HLCG, ch. 2.
[209] HLCG, ch. 3.
[210] HLCG, ch. 5.
[211] HLCG, ch. 5.
[212] HLCG, ch. 6.
[213] HLCG, ch. 11.
[214] HLCG, ch. 7.
[215] HLCG, ch. 5.
[216] Cingolani, *Le storie dei Longobardi*, pp. 49-53.

forefathers of the Lombards assert that [...] their forefathers, a rough and bloody and lawless progeny, and of small number, originated from snakes.»

The main difference between the previous editions and this one concerns a change in the punctuation, suggested by the different meaning one must attribute to the term *fargetum*, a corruption of *farigaidus*, used in the *Origin of the Lombard People*, from which the author of the HLCG probably copied some passages. Believing that these words derived from *vergessen*, the previous editors gave the following reading: «regnavit filius ipsius nomine Walteri annis VII. Fargaetum: isti omnes Adelingi fuerunt.»[217] Annalisa Bracciotti, the editor of the *Origin of the Lombard People*, has challenged this interpretation pointing out that *farigaidus* is an adjective meaning «lacking in descendants.» This translation is supported by both a linguistic analysis and the particular that, up to that part, the text mentions kings succeeding their fathers, which had not happened after the death of Waltari, evidently because he had no sons. The chronicler therefore felt the need to emphasize this detail.[218] The corrupted word *fargetum* obviously has the same meaning. On the basis of these observation, the correct reading of this sentence is: «regnavit filius ipsius nomine Walteri annis VII, fargaetum. Isti omnes Adelingi fuerunt.»[219]

In G the HLCG is not divided into chapters; I have added them in order to facilitate quotations. The chapter numbering is however different from those of the previous editions:

Historia Langobardorum codicis Gothani, in *Le leggi dei Longobardi. Storia, memoria e diritto di un popolo germanico*, eds. C. Azzara and S. Gasparri, Roma 2005, 2nd ed., pp. 317-329.

Historia Langobardorum codicis Gothani, ed. G. Waitz. *Monumenta Germaniae Historica* (hereafter MGH), *Scriptores rerum Langobardicarum et Italicarum saec. VI-IX*, Hannover 1878, pp. 7-11.

The *Historia* by Andreas of Bergamo survives in two manuscripts: the Sangallensis 317, fols. 78ʳ-86ᵛ, of the Kantonsbibliothek-Vadiana (Saint Gall, Switzerland) (hereafter V) dating to the end of the ninth century, and the Sangallensis 620, pp. 255-272, of the Stiftsbibliothek (Saint Gall), composed at the end of the twelfth century (hereafter B). In B Andreas of Bergamo's work is written on the margins of the folios containing Paul the Deacon's *History of the Lombards*.

There are no conjunctive errors between V and B, yet, because of the location in which the manuscripts are preserved, the fact that in both V and B the scribes wrote *vix* instead of *vis*,[220] and that V and B have the same lacunas[221] as well as the same words added interlineally,[222] it is likely that B derives from V.[223]

---

[217] See ch. 4, of the editions by Waitz and Azzara.

[218] *Origo gentis Langobardorum*, p. 202. Marcello Meli agrees with this point. Meli, *Eco scandinave*, p. 349.

[219] HLCG, ch. 4.

[220] V, fol. 85ᵛ. B, p. 271. Cf. Andreas of Bergamo, *Historia*, ch. 20.

[221] V, fol. 84ʳ: «iuncti sunt in loco [...].» B, p. 270.

[222] For example: V, fol. 79ᵛ: «et posuit in edicto capituli octo.» Cf. B, p. 261. B, fol. 81ᵛ: «non post multos dies.» Cf. B, p. 264. In the margin of V, fol. 86ʳ, beside «qui imperavit,» someone has added for how many years Louis II had ruled. In B, p. 272, this detail is missing, but, after «qui imperavit,» two lines have been erased.

[223] Of this opinion is also La Placa, *Andrea di Bergamo*, p. 67, note 30.

It is however necessary to point out that B is not an exact replica of V. There are, in fact, some corrections and changes, probably made by the copyist of B to render the text more clearly. For example, *Adilgis*[224] for *Adelchis*,[225] *Irmirgarda*[226] for *Ermengarda*,[227] *caput*[228] for *capud*,[229] and *vites*[230] for *vitae*.[231]

V: «tanta quidem dignitatem cantores ibi fecerunt, ut per totam Franciam Italiamque pene multe civitates ornamentum aecclesie usque hodie consonant.»[232] B: «tanta quidem dignitatem cantores ibi fecerunt, ut per totam Franciam Italiamque Alamannniam pene multae civitates ornamentum aecclesie usque hodie consonant.»[233]

V: «Erat quidam ex ipsis cui iam munera Caroli excecaverat cor.»[234] B: «Erant quidam ex ipsis quorum iam munera Karoli excecaverant cor.»[235]

V: «Eamus eorum fidelitate; bene nobis erit.»[236] B: «Eamus, eorum fidelitati nos commendemus; bene nobis erit.»[237]

V: «Karolus... Pipinus suus filius regendum Italia concessit.»[238] B: «Karolus... Pipino filio suo Italiam regendam concessit.»[239]

V: «Iste incipit vocare imperator ex Francorum genere.»[240] B: «Iste incipit vocari imperator ex Francorum genere.»[241]

V: «mandans ei quasi pacis gratia ad se venire.»[242] B: «Mandans ei quasi causa pacis ad se venire.»[243]

V: «Diligebat lectores, cantores et cunctis servientibus Deo ministrantibus aecclesiae.»[244] B: «Diligebat lectores, cantores et cunctos servientes Deo et ministrantes ecclesiae.»[245]

V: «Quid debet facere homo de inimicum suum?»[246] B: «Qui debet homo facere de inimico suo?»[247]

---

[224] B, p. 262.
[225] V, fol. 80ʳ.
[226] B, p. 264.
[227] V, fol. 81ʳ.
[228] B, p. 263.
[229] V, fol. 80ᵛ.
[230] B, p. 266.
[231] V, fol. 83ʳ.
[232] V, fol. 80ʳ.
[233] B, p. 262.
[234] V, fol. 80ᵛ.
[235] B, p. 263.
[236] V, fol. 80ᵛ.
[237] B, p. 263.
[238] V, fol. 80ᵛ.
[239] B, p. 263.
[240] V, fol. 80ᵛ.
[241] B, p. 264.
[242] V, fol. 81ʳ.
[243] B, p. 264.
[244] V, fol. 81ʳ.
[245] B, p. 264.
[246] V, fol. 81ᵛ.
[247] B, p. 265.

V: «inter ipsis tres germanis...»[248] B: «inter ipsos tres germanos...»[249]

V: «iungentes se ubi...»[250] B: «iungentes in loco...»[251]

V: «tanta quidem nivem Italia cecidit...»[252] B: «tanta nix in Italia cecidit...»[253]

V: «in finibus Beneventana.»[254] B: «in fines Beneventanas.»[255]

V: «reliqui fuga vis evaderunt.»[256] B: «reliqui fuga vix evaserunt.»[257]

A significant omission in B is the paragraph in which, after the summary of Paul the Deacon's *History of the Lombards*, Andreas of Bergamo explains that he learned the following events from some letters and elders.[258]

In B some episodes are moreover recorded in an order different from that in V. The latter mentions the elimination of Hupert, who rebelled against Louis II, the description of the damages caused by a long period of cold weather, Louis II's expedition against the Muslim Amalmasser, and the conversion of the king of the Bulgarians to Christianity.[259] In B these events are narrated in the following sequence: cold weather, conversion of the Bulgarian sovereign, Hupert's uprising, and Louis II's campaign.[260] It is not clear why this change was made in B. The reversed sequence of Louis II's expedition and the conversion of the king of the Bulgarians could be due to the decision to describe Louis II's campaigns in southern Italy all together without any digression. In V, the narration of the clashes between Louis II's army and the Muslims in the South of Italy appears after the account the Bulgarian ruler's baptism.

The changes made in B were not always carried out accurately. For example, in the account of the imperial troops' victory against the Saracens near the river Volturno, V states: «Sarracini devicti et debellati sunt multitudo innumerabiles; quia quod gladius non interemit, in fluvio Vulturno negati sunt; reliqui fuga vis evaderunt.»[261] B, on the other hand, reports: «Sarracini devicti et debellati sunt multitudo innumerabilis. In fluvio Vulturno necati sunt. Reliqui fuga vix evaserunt, quia quod gladius non interemit in fluvio Vulturno necati sunt.»[262]

The main difference between B and V is nevertheless constituted by the particular that, while in the former there is a summary of Paul the Deacon's *History of the Lombards*, in the latter the abridgment of the Lombard historian's work begins with

---

[248] V, fol. 82^r.
[249] B, p. 266.
[250] V, fol. 82^r.
[251] B, p. 266.
[252] V, fol. 83^r.
[253] B, p. 267.
[254] V, fol. 84^v.
[255] B, p. 270.
[256] V, fol. 85^r.
[257] B, p. 270.
[258] Andreas of Bergamo, *Historia*, ch. 2: «et quorum hic super continent eorum historiae minime ad nostram pervenit notitiam, sed in quantum per seriem litterarum seu per antiquos homines potui veraciter scire, hic scrivere delectatus sum.»
[259] Andreas of Bergamo, *Historia*, chs. 14-16.
[260] B, pp. 267-268.
[261] V, fol. 85^r.
[262] B, p. 270.

the motives leading the Byzantine commander Narses to invite the Lombards to invade Italy. It is possible that the first folios of V went missing, yet one must not completely rule out the possibility that Andreas of Bergamo wished to summarize the *History of the Lombards* only from their coming to Italy. This hypothesis is supported by the detail that V starts with a complete sentence, and not a sentence fragment as would be more likely if preceding folios were missing.

The prologue in B is not very helpful as it is not clear whether it is Andreas of Bergamo or the copyist of B who addresses the readers. «Quidam Andreas scribit hanc adbrevatio. Longobardorum gesta unum volumen, sex tamen libros, a Paulo viro philosopho contesta et per ordinem narrata invenimus. Exinde pauca de multis in hac adbrevatione contexere nisi sumus et sub eadem hystoriola in quantum Deo auxiliante summatimque sermonem exinde adtrahere conati sumus scribere.»[263]

It is worth noting that in this prologue the first person plural is used, while in the other parts of the *Historia* in which the author makes some observations – mentioned also in V – he employs the first person singular.[264] This difference does not necessarily represent a proof that Andreas of Bergamo did not write the first part of the summary. It is, in fact, possible that the copyist made some changes in this part of the work or Andreas of Bergamo utilized both the first person singular and the first person plural. Since in B it is not stated that such a section was added to the original text, I have decided to include it in this edition.[265] B and V are also different in the way they end. Because of the loss of some folios, B finishes with Empress Angelberga inviting Charles the Bald and Louis the German to go to Italy after Louis II's death.[266]

In light of the above observations, the text reported in V seems to be closer to the original and therefore this edition will be based on it.

V is not the autograph. It was written by six different hands, dating to the end of the ninth century, the first five from northern Italy and the sixth from Saint Gall.[267] The latter detail indicates that Andreas of Bergamo's chronicle arrived in Saint Gall in a period coeval to the author. As has already been emphasized, the last part of the *Historia* is a brief survey of the events following Charles the Bald's imperial crowning, whereas Charles's return to France after the coronation is not recorded.[268] The detail that this final section was written by a hand from Saint Gall suggests that it was composed by a different author, who was not well informed about those episodes. Yet one should not exclude the possibility that Andreas himself took his work to Saint Gall, where he perhaps finished it and had it copied. The slip about Charles the Bald could therefore be due to the chronicler's having composed the final part several years after that episode.

In V one can notice several erasures, corrections, and additions between the lines, which often emend words misspelled by the copyists. Since V is coeval to the author, it

---

[263] B, p. 255.

[264] Andreas of Bergamo, *Historia*, chs. 2 and 22.

[265] The previous editor of Andreas of Bergamo's *Historia* added it as well.

[266] Cf. Andreas of Bergamo, *Historia*, ch. 23.

[267] La Placa, *Andrea di Bergamo*, pp. 68 and 69-70, note 43. This scholar adds that Bernard Bischoff communicated the results of this analysis to her by letter.

[268] Andreas of Bergamo, *Historia*, ch. 24.

is possible that Andreas had his notes copied and then made the corrections himself. As the chronicler's Latin is quite rough, in this edition I have decided to intervene only when there are clear slips that render problematic the understanding of the text.

For example, I have made the following corrections: *coronica* to *cronica*,[269] *su potestatem* to *sub potestatem*,[270] *ad Langubardis* to *ab Langubardis*,[271] «superscripta summationem... relega tota historia» to «superscripta summationem... relegat tota historia,»[272] «si contenis te, quasi sanctus Ambrosius sis» to «sic contenis te, quasi sanctus Ambrosius sis,»[273] *iuge* to *coniuge*,[274] *scilicae* to *scilicet*,[275] «reliqui fuga vis evaderunt» to «reliqui fuga vix evaderunt,»[276] «vix illorum fuit» to «vis illorum fuit,»[277] *sorcerdotes* to *sacerdotes*.[278] As for the names, I have corrected *Cleb* to *Clef*,[279] because this Lombard king was known as Clef/Cleph.

In V there are two erasures in which it is still possible to read the text. They are both in the section in which Andreas describes the aftermath of the Fontenoy battle. «Unde (usque hodie) sic discipata est nobilitas Aquitanorum, que etiam Nortemanni eorum possedant terrae nec qui eorum fortia resistat, (sed etiam tributa reddunt).»[280] The words in parentheses are the deleted parts. The second one, especially, emphasizes a particularly inglorious detail and therefore it is likely that those words were deleted not by the author, but by someone who preferred to pass over that detail in silence. For this reason, I have decided to report them.[281] The fact that these erased words do not appear in B[282] might indicate that they were deleted before the end of the twelfth century, when the latter codex was written.

In V two corrections made on erased text are relevant since they both concern the Lombard King Desiderius's daughter, who was repudiated by Charlemagne and whose name is never mentioned in the sources coeval to her lifetime. Andreas of Bergamo reports that her name was *Berterad*.[283] Among the erased letters it is possible to read *ga*, and George Waitz, the previous editor of this work, has hypothesized that the erased name was *Gerberga*. He has maintained that the correction was made by a hand different from all the others. Gabriela La Placa has contested this and has pointed out that the name *Berterad* was written by the first of the multiple hands found in V.[284] I have therefore decided not to edit it out.[285]

---

[269] Andreas of Bergamo, *Historia*, ch. 1.
[270] Andreas of Bergamo, *Historia*, ch. 1.
[271] Andreas of Bergamo, *Historia*, ch. 1.
[272] Andreas of Bergamo, *Historia*, ch. 2.
[273] Andreas of Bergamo, *Historia*, ch. 11.
[274] Andreas of Bergamo, *Historia*, ch. 15.
[275] Andreas of Bergamo, *Historia*, ch. 19.
[276] Andreas of Bergamo, *Historia*, ch. 19.
[277] Andreas of Bergamo, *Historia*, ch. 20.
[278] Andreas of Bergamo, *Historia*, ch. 22.
[279] Andreas of Bergamo, *Historia*, ch. 1.
[280] Andreas of Bergamo, *Historia*, ch. 13.
[281] The previous editor did the same thing.
[282] Cf. B, pp. 266-267.
[283] V, fol. 79ᵛ. Andreas of Bergamo, *Historia*, ch. 3.
[284] La Placa, *Andrea di Bergamo*, pp. 69-70.
[285] Janet Nelson and Stefano Gasparri, who do not know La Placa's study, maintain that Desiderius's daughter's name was Gerberga. Nelson, *Making a Difference*, p. 183; Gasparri, *I Longobardi tra oblio e memoria*, pp. 266-269.

The previous edition is Andreae Bergomatis *Historia*, ed. G. Waitz. MGH, *Scriptores rerum Langobardicarum et Italicarum*, pp. 220-230.

In both V and B Andreas of Bergamo's chronicle is not divided into chapters; I have added them to this edition to facilitate citations. The chapter numbering is however different from that of the previous edition.

The *De Pippini regis victoria Avarica* is preserved in only one manuscript dating between the end of the eighth and the beginning of the ninth century: Codex Dietianus, B, Sant, 66 of Berlin's Staatsbibliothek (hereafter D), pp. 127-128. This work, which begins on the fourteenth line of page 127 and finishes at the end of page 128, was written in D, probably in northern Italy, on blank folios of a manuscript composed in «a Frankish area.»[286]

That the codex is contemporary with the author suggests that the rough Latin of the text is attributable to the author rather than to mistakes committed by the copyist.[287] For this reason, I have decided to follow the readings of D literally.

The most recent edition is *De Pippini regis victoria Avarica*, ed. E. Duemmler. MGH, *Poetae Latini aevi Carolini* I, Berlin 1881, pp. 116-117. A revision of this edition was added in the appendix of Einhard, *Vita Karoli Magni*, ed. O. Holder-Egger, MGH, *Scriptores rerum Germanicarum in usum scholarum separatim editi*, Hannover 1911, pp. 42-43. There is an English translation of this work in *Poetry of the Carolingian Renaissance*, pp. 186-191, which also contains the Latin text as edited in MGH.

The *Rythmus de captivitate Lhuduici imperatoris* is conserved in a late-ninth-century codex, number XC, fols. 76^r-77^v, of the Biblioteca Capitolare, Verona (Italy) (hereafter C). It has been hypothesized that this work was written on some blank folios.[288] The fact that C is contemporary with the author and that the latter seems not to have a good knowledge of the Latin language (the Latin of this work has been defined «vulgar Latin»=«latino popolare»)[289] has induced me not to correct the text in C.

The previous editions of this text are in Carmen Russo Mailler, *La politica meridionale di Ludovico II e il «Rythmus de captivitate Ludovici imperatoris»*, in «Quaderni Medievali», XIV (1982), pp. 18-19, and in MGH, *Poetae latini aevi carolini* III, 2, Berlin 1896, pp. 404-405 (ed. L. Traube).

In the title of this edition Emperor Louis II's name has been changed into *Lhuduicus*, since this is how his name is spelled in the text.[290]

---

[286] Bischoff, *The Court Library*, pp. 68-70. On this manuscript, see also the observations of Villa, *I classici*, pp. 494-497, and McKitterick, *Charlemagne*, pp. 365-367.

[287] Peter Godman believes that the vulgarisms in this and other similar texts «are not marks of ignorance, but the sign of a cultivated author's conscious attempt to compose a Latin intelligible to fellow clerics as their spoken *lingua franca*.» *Poetry of the Carolingian Renaissance*, p. 31. Rosamond McKitterick, on the other hand, thinks that the author used this kind of Latin on purpose as his work was intended for a lay audience. McKitterick, *The Carolingians*, pp. 230-231.

[288] Meersseman, *Il codice XC*, p. 23.

[289] Dronke, *Generi letterari della poesia ritmica altomedievale*, p. 176.

[290] *Rythmus de captivitate*, line 3.

Acknowledgments

I wish to thank Giuseppe Petralia and Paolo Rossi for accepting to publish this volume in their book series, the staff at Pisa University Press for their editorial assistance, and Robert Berkhofer, Roberto Pesce, Antony Shugaar, and Michael Brinks for their valuable help. Moreover, I wish to express my gratitude to Gian Carlo Alessio, Rozanne Elder, Samantha Kelly, and my research assistants Caitlin Murphy and Adam Matthews, who read the entire manuscript.

The preparation of this book has been funded by the Gerda Henkel Foundation. The Burnham – MacMillan History Department Endowment of Western Michigan University covered a part of the publication costs. I thank these institutions for their support.

PRIMARY SOURCES

Ado of Vienne, *Chronicon*, ed. G. Pertz. MGH, *Scriptores* II, Hannover 1829, pp. 315-323.

Agnellus of Ravenna, *Liber pontificalis ecclesiae Ravennatis*, ed. D. Mauskopf Deliyannis. *Corpus Christianorum. Continuatio Mediaevalis* 199, Turnhout 2006.

Ahistulfi Leges, in *Le leggi dei Longobardi*, pp. 279-291.

Andreae Bergomatis *Historia*, ed. G. Waitz. MGH, *Scriptores rerum Langobardicarum et Italicarum*, pp. 220-230.

Angelbert, *Versus de Bella quae fuit acta Fontaneto*, ed. E. Dümmler. MGH, *Poetae latini aevi karolini* II, Berlin 1884, pp. 138-139.

Annales de Saint Bertin, eds. F. Grat, J. Vielliard, S. Clémencet, Paris 1964.

Annales Fuldenses sive Annales regni Francorum orientalis, eds. G. Pertz and F. Kurze. MGH, *Scriptores rerum Germanicarum in usum scholarum separatim editi*, Hannover 1891.

Annales qui dicuntur Einhardi, in *Annales regni Francorum et Annales qui dicuntur Einhardi*.

Annales regni Francorum, in *Annales regni Francorum et Annales qui dicuntur Einhardi*, ed. F. Kurze. MGH, *Scriptores rerum Germanicarum in usum scholarum separatim editi*, Hannover 1895.

Annales Vedastini, ed. B. Von Simson. MGH, *Scriptores rerum Germanicarum in usum scholarum separatim editi*, Hannover 1909.

Annales Xantenses, ed. B. Von Simson. MGH, *Scriptores rerum Germanicarum in usum scholarum separatim editi*, Hannover 1909.

Astronomer, *Vita Hludowici imperatoris*, in Thegan, *Gesta Hludowici imperatoris* – Astronomer, *Vita Hludowici imperatoris*, ed. E. Tremp. MGH, *Scriptores rerum Germanicarum in usum scholarum separatim editi* LXIV, Hannover 1995, pp. 279-555.

Benzo of Alba, *Ad Heinricum IV imperatorem libri VII*, ed. G. H. Pertz. MGH, *Scriptores* XI, Hannover 1854, pp. 591-681.

Capitularia regum Francorum, II, eds. A. Boretius and V. Krause. MGH, *Legum sectio II*, Hannover 1897.

Chronicon Salernitanum: A Critical Edition with Studies on Literary and Historical Sources and on Language, ed. U. Westerbergh, Stockholm 1956.

Codex Carolinus, ed. W. Gundlach. MGH, *Epistolae Merovingici et Karolini aevi*, I: *Epistolae* III, Berlin 1892, pp. 469-657.

Codex diplomaticus civitatis et ecclesiae Bergomatis, ed. M. Lupi, 2 vols., Bergamo, 1784.

Constantine VII Porphyrogenitus, *De administrando imperio*, eds. G. Moravcsik and J. H. Jenkins, Washington, DC, 1967.

Cronaca della dinastia di Capua, ed. N. Cilento, in Id., *Italia meridionale longobarda*, Milano-Napoli 1971, 2nd ed., pp. 297-346.

Cronaca di Novalesa, ed. G. C. Alessio, Torino 1982.

Cronicae Sancti Benedicti Casinensis, ed. L. A. Berto. Edizione nazionale dei testi mediolatini 15. Serie II 7, Firenze 2006.

De Pippini regis victoria Avarica, ed. E. Duemmler. MGH, *Poetae Latini aevi Carolini* I, Berlin 1881, pp. 116-117.

De Pippini regis victoria Avarica, in Einhard, *Vita Karoli Magni*, ed. O. Holder-Egger. MGH, *Scriptores rerum Germanicarum in usum scholarum separatim editi*, Hannover 1911, pp. 42-43.

Edictum Rothari, in *Le leggi dei Longobardi*, pp. 13-127.

Einhard, *Vita Karoli Magni*, ed. O. Holder-Egger. MGH, *Scriptores rerum Germanicarum in usum scholarum separatim editi*, Hannover 1911.

Erchempert, *Piccola storia dei Longobardi di Benevento / Ystoriola Longobardorum Beneventum degentium*, ed. L. A. Berto, Napoli 2013.

Gesta episcoporum Neapolitanorum, ed. G. Waitz. MGH, *Scriptores rerum Langobardicarum et Italicarum saec. VI-IX*, Hannover 1878, pp. 398-466.

Grimualdi Leges, in *Le leggi dei Longobardi*, pp. 129-135.

John the Deacon, *Istoria Veneticorum*, ed. L. A. Berto. Fonti per la Storia dell'Italia medievale, Istituto Storico Italiano per il Medio Evo, Bologna 1999.

Historia Langobardorum codicis Gothani, ed. G. Waitz. MGH, *Scriptores rerum Langobardicarum et Italicarum saec. VI-IX*, Hannover 1878, pp. 7-11.

Historia Langobardorum codicis Gothani, in *Le leggi dei Longobardi*, pp. 317-329.

Le leggi dei Longobardi. Storia, memoria e diritto di un popolo germanico, eds. C. Azzara and S. Gasparri, Roma 2005, 2nd ed.

Libellus de imperatoria potestate in urbe Roma, in *Il Chronicon di Benedetto monaco di S. Andrea del Soratte e il Libellus de imperatoria potestate in urbe Roma*, ed. G. Zucchetti, Fonti per la Storia d'Italia, Roma 1920, pp. 191-210.

Livtprandi Leges, in *Le leggi dei Longobardi*, pp. 137-235.

E. A. Lowe, *Die ältesten Kalendarien aus Monte Cassino*, Munich 1908.

Lupus Protospatharius, *Annales*, ed. G. Pertz. MGH, *Scriptores* V, Hannover 1844, pp. 51-63.

Nithard, *Historie des fils de Louis le Pieux*, ed. Ph. Lauer. Les Classiques de l'histoire de France au Moyen Age, Paris 1926.

Origo gentis Langobardorum, ed. A. Bracciotti, Roma 1998.

Paul the Deacon, *Historia Langobardorum*, eds. L. Bethmann and G. Waitz. MGH, *Scriptores rerum Langobardicarum et Italicarum saec. VI-IX*, Hannover 1878, pp. 12-187.

Le pergamene degli archivi di Bergamo a. 740-1000, ed. M. Cortesi, Bergamo 1988.

Poetry of the Carolingian Renaissance, ed. P. Godman, Norman 1985.

Ratchis Leges, in *Le leggi dei Longobardi*, pp. 233-247.

Regino of Prüm, *Chronicon cum continuatione Treverensi*, ed. F. Kurze. MGH, *Scriptores rerum Germanicarum in usum scholarum separatim editi*, Hannover 1890.

Rythmus de captivitate Ludovici imperatoris, ed. L. Traube. MGH, *Poetae latini aevi carolini* III, 2, Berlin 1896, pp. 404-405.

Rythmus de captivitate Ludovici imperatoris, in C. Russo Mailler, *La politica meridionale di Ludovico II e il «Rythmus de captivitate Ludovici imperatoris»*, in «Quaderni Medievali», XIV (1982), pp. 18-19.

Sedulius Scotus, *Carmina*, ed. L. Traube. MGH, *Poetae latini aevi karolini* III, Berlin 1896, pp. 151-238.

Testi storici e poetici dell'Italia carolingia, ed. L. A. Berto. Medioevo Europeo 3, Padova 2002.

Thegan, *Gesta Hludowici imperatoris*, in Thegan, *Gesta Hludowici imperatoris* – Astronomer, *Vita Hludowici imperatoris*, ed. E. Tremp, MGH, *Scriptores rerum Germanicarum in usum scholarum separatim editi* LXIV, Hannover 1995, pp. 167-277.

SECONDARY SOURCES

G. Albertoni, *L'Italia carolingia*, Roma 1997.

A. Ambrosioni, *Gli arcivescovi nella vita di Milano*, in *Milano e i Milanesi prima del Mille (VIII-X secolo)*, Spoleto 1986, pp. 85-118.

Andreas of Bergamo, in *Wikipedia*, https://en.wikipedia.org/wiki/Andreas_of_Bergamo (accessed on Februay 25, 2016).

M. P. Andreolli, *Una pagina di storia longobarda: 'Re Ratchis'*, in »Nuova Rivista Storica«, L (1966), pp. 281-327.

G. Arnaldi, *Berengario I*, in *Dizionario biografico degli Italiani*, 9, Roma 1967, pp. 1-26.

G. Arnaldi, *Natale 875: Politica, ecclesiologia e cultura del papato altomedievale*, Roma 1990.

G. Arnaldi, *Annali, cronache, storie*, in *Lo spazio letterario nel Medioevo*, I: *Il Medioevo latino. 2. La produzione del testo*, Roma 1993, pp. 463-513.

C. Azzara, *Venetiae: Determinazione di un'area regionale fra antichità e alto Medioevo*, Treviso 1994.

U. Balzani, *Le cronache italiane nel Medio Evo*, Milano 1900, 2nd ed.

R. Balzaretti, *Spoken Narratives in Ninth-Century Milanese Court Records*, in *Narrative and History in the Early Medieval West*, eds. E. M. Tyler and R. Balzaretti, Turnhout 2006, pp. 11-37.

A. Barbero, *Charlemagne: Father of a Continent*, Berkeley 2004.

L. A. Berto, *Remembering Old and New Rulers: Lombards and Carolingians in Carolingian Italian Memory*, in «Medieval History Journal», XIII, 1 (2010), pp. 23-53.

M. G. Bertolini, *Andrea da Bergamo*, in *Dizionario biografico degli Italiani*, 4, Roma 1966, pp. 79-80.

M. G. Bertolini, *Angilberto*, in *Dizionario biografico degli Italiani*, 3, Roma 1961, pp. 260-263.

O. Bertolini, *Adelchi, re dei Longobardi*, in *Dizionario biografico degli Italiani*, 1, Roma 1960, pp. 258-259.

O. Bertolini, *Carlomagno e Benevento*, in *Karl der Grosse. Lebenswek und Nachleben*, I: *Persönlichkeit und Geschichte*, ed. H. Beumann, Düsseldorf 1965, pp. 609-671.

O. Bertolini, *La data dell'ingresso dei Longobardi in Italia*, in Id., *Scritti scelti di storia medievale*, 2 vols., Livorno 1968, vol. I, pp. 19-61.

R. R. Bezzola, *Les origines et la formation de la littérature courtoise en Occident 500-1220*, I: *La tradition impériale de la fin de l'Antiquité au XIe siècle*, Paris 1944.

B. Bischoff, *The Court Library of Charlemagne*, in Id., *Manuscripts and Libraries in the Age of Charlemagne*, Cambridge 1994, pp. 56-75.

E. Boshof, *Ludwig der Fromme*, Darmstadt 1996.

P. Cammarosano, *Nobili e re: L'Italia politica dell'alto medioevo*, Roma-Bari 1998.

L. Capo, *La polemica longobarda sulla caduta del regno*, in «Rivista Storica Italiana», CVIII, 1 (1996), pp. 5-35.

L. Capo, *Il «Liber Pontificalis», i Longobardi e la nascita del dominio territoriale della Chiesa romana*, Spoleto 2009.

N. Christie, *The Lombards: The Ancient Longobards*, Oxford 1995.

N. Cilento, *Adelchi (Adelgiso)*, in *Dizionario biografico degli Italiani*, 1, Roma 1960, p. 259.

S. M. Cingolani, *Le storie dei Longobardi: Dall'Origine a Paolo Diacono*, Roma 1995.

E. Colonna, *Figure femminili in Liutprando di Cremona*, in «Quaderni medievali», XIV (1982), pp. 29-60.

M. Coumert, *Origines des Peuples: Les récits du Haut Moyen Âge occidental (550-850)*, Paris 2007.

E. R. Curtius, *European Literature and the Latin Middle Ages*, New York 1953.

S. Del Bello, *Indice toponomastico altomedievale del territorio di Bergamo: Secoli VII-IX*, Bergamo 1986.

P. Delogu, *Strutture politiche e ideologia nel regno di Ludovico II*, in «Bullettino dell'Istituto storico italiano per il Medio Evo», LXXX (1968), pp. 137-189.

P. Delogu, *Lombard and Carolingian Italy*, in *The New Cambridge Medieval History*, II: *c. 700-c. 900*, ed. R. McKitterick, Cambridge 1995, pp. 290-319.

Ph. Depreux, *Das Königtum Bernhards von Italien und sein Verhältnis zum Kaisertum*, in «Quellen und Forschungen aus italieneschen Archiven und Bibliotechen», LXXII (1992), pp. 1-25.

Ph. Depreux, *Tassilon III et le roi des Francs: examen d'une vassalité controuversée*, in «Revue historique» CCLCIII (1995), pp. 23-73

P. Dronke, *Generi letterari della poesia ritmica altomedievale*, in *Poesia dell'alto Medioevo europeo: Manoscritti, lingua e musica dei ritmi latini*, ed. Franco Stella, Firenze 2000, pp. 172-185.

N. Everett, *Literacy in Lombard Italy, c. 568-774*, Cambridge 2003.

E. Fabbro, *Charlemagne and the Lombard Kingdom That Was: The Lombard Past in Post-Conquest Italian Historiography*, in «Journal of the CHA» XXV, 2 (2014), pp. 1-26.

G. Fasoli, *Carlo Magno nelle tradizioni storico-leggendarie italiane*, in *Karl der Grosse. Lebenswek und Nachleben*, IV: *Das Nachleben*, eds. W. Braunfels and P. E. Schramm, Düsseldorf 1967, pp. 348-363.

I. Fees, *Eberardo, marchese del Friuli*, in *Dizionario biografico degli Italiani*, 42, Roma 1993, pp. 252-255.

V. Fumagalli, *Il regno italico*, Torino 1978.

V. Fumagalli, *Landscapes of Fear: Perceptions of Nature and the City in the Middle Ages*, Cambridge 1994.

M. Ferrari, *Manoscritti e cultura*, in *Milano e i Milanesi prima del Mille (VIII-X secolo)*, Spoleto 1986, pp. 241-275.

F. Gabrieli, *Storia, cultura e civiltà degli Arabi in Italia*, in *Gli Arabi in Italia: Cultura, contatti e tradizioni*, eds. F. Gabrieli and U. Scerrato, Milano 1979, pp. 13-269.

S. Gasparri, *I duchi longobardi*, Roma 1978.

S. Gasparri, *La cultura tradizionale dei Longobardi: Struttura tribale e resistenze pagane*, Spoleto 1983.

S. Gasparri, *Il ducato e il principato di Benevento*, in *Storia del Mezzogiorno*, part II: *Il Medioevo*, 2 vols., Napoli 1988, vol. I, pp. 83-146.

S. Gasparri, *Prima delle nazioni: Popoli, etnie e regni fra Antichità e Medioevo*, Roma 1997.

S. Gasparri, *Il passaggio dai Longobardi ai Carolingi*, in *Il futuro dei Longobardi: L'Italia e la costruzione dell'Europa di Carlo Magno. Saggi*, eds. C. Bertelli, G. P. Brogiolo, Milano 2000, pp. 25-43.

S. Gasparri, *I Longobardi tra oblio e memoria*, in *Studi sul Medioevo per Girolamo Arnaldi*, eds. G. Barone, L. Capo, S. Gasparri, Roma 2001, pp. 237-277.

S. Gasparri, *The Fall of the Lombard Kingdom: Facts, Memory and Propaganda*, in *774: Ipotesi su una transizione*, ed. by S. Gasparri, Turnhout 2008, pp. 41-65.

S. Gasparri, *Italia longobarda. Il regno, i Franchi, il papato*, Roma-Bari 2012.

W. Goffart, *The Narrators of Barbarian History (A. D. 550-800): Jordanes, Gregory of Tours, Bede, and Paul the Deacon*, Princeton 1988.

Th. Granier, *La captivité de l'empereur Louis II à Bénévent (13 août-17 septembre 871) dans les sources des IXe-Xe siècles: l'écriture de l'histoire, de la fausse nouvelle au récit exemplaire*, in *Faire l'événement au Moyen Âge*, eds. C. Carozzi and H. Taviani-Carozzi, Aix-en-Provence 2007, pp. 13-39.

N. Gray, *The Paleography of Latin Inscriptions in the Eighth, Ninth and Tenth Centuries in Italy*, in «Papers of the British School at Rome», n.s. 3, XVI (1948), pp. 38-167.

B. Guenée, *Histoire et Culture historique dans l'Occident médiéval*, Paris 1980.

J. Heidecker, *The Divorce of Lothar II: Christian Marriage and Political Power in the Carolingian World*, Ithaca 2010.

A. J. Kosto, *Hostages in the Carolingian World (714-840)*, in «Early Medieval Europe» XI, 2 (2002), pp. 123-147.

H. Krahwinkler, *Friaul im Frühmittelalter Geschichte einer Region vom Ende des fünften bis zum Ende des zehnten Jahrhunderts*, Wien-Köln 1992.

B. Kreutz, *Before the Normans: Southern Italy in the Ninth and Tenth Centuries*, Philadelphia 1991.

G. La Placa, *Andrea di Bergamo e l'«abbrevatio de gestis Langobardorum»: note biografiche e testuali*, in «Maia. Rivista di letterature classiche» XLVI (1994), pp. 61-72.

C. La Rocca and L. Provero, *The Dead and their Gifts: The Will of Eberhard, Count of Friuli, and his Wife Gisela, Daughter of Louis the Pious (863-864)*, in *Rituals of Power: From Late Antiquity to the Early Middle Ages*, eds. F. Theuws and J. L. Nelson, Leiden 2000, pp. 225-280.

B. Lewis, *The Political Language of Islam*, Chicago 1988.

B. Luiselli, *Storia culturale dei rapporti fra mondo romano e mondo germanico*, Roma 1992.

F. Manacorda, *Ricerche sugli inizii della dominazione dei Carolingi in Italia*, Roma 1968.

R. McKitterick, *The Carolingians and the Written Word*, Cambridge 1989.

R. McKitterick, *History and Memory in the Carolingian World*, Cambridge 2004.

R. McKitterick, *Charlemagne: The Formation of a European Identity*, Cambridge 2008.

S. MacLean, *Kingship and Politics in the Late Ninth Century: Charles the Fat and the End of the Carolingian Empire*, Cambridge 2003.

G. G. Meersseman, *Il codice XC della Capitolare di Verona*, in «Archivio Veneto» CIV (1975), pp. 11-44.

M. Meli, *Eco scandinave nella «Historia Langobardorum» di Paolo Diacono*, in *Paolo Diacono: Uno scrittore tra tradizione longobarda e rinnovamento carolingio*, ed. P. Chiesa, Udine 2000, pp. 333-353.

P. Molinelli, *Riflessi di un mondo plurilingue e multiculturale nel «Chronicon» di Andrea da Bergamo (IX secolo)*, in *Il plurilinguismo nella tradizione letteraria latina*, ed. R. Oniga, Roma 2003, pp. 255-272.

M. Montanari, *L'alimentazione contadina nell'alto Medioevo*, Napoli 1979.

J. Moorhead, *Ostrogothic Italy and the Lombard Invasions*, in *The New Cambridge Medieval History*, I: *c. 500-c. 700*, ed. P. Fouracre, Cambridge 2005, pp. 140-162.

C. G. Mor, *La storiografia italiana del sec. IX da Andrea di Bergamo ad Erchemperto*, in *Atti del II congresso internazionale di studi sull'alto Medioevo*, Spoleto 1953, pp. 241-247.

P. Moro, *«Quam horrida pugna»: Elementi per uno studio della guerra nell'alto medioevo italiano (secoli VI-X)*, Venezia 1995.

G. Musca, *L'emirato di Bari*, Bari 1967, 2nd ed.

L. Nees, *Charles the Bald and the «cathedra Petri»*, in *Charles the Bald: Court and Kingdom*, eds. M. T. Gibson and J. L. Nelson, Aldershot 1990, 2nd ed., pp. 340-347.

J. L. Nelson, *Charles the Bald*, London-New York 1992.

J. L. Nelson, *Making a Difference in Eighth-Century Politics: The Daughters of Desiderius*, in *After Rome's Fall: Narrators of Early Medieval History. Essays Presented to Walter Goffart*, ed. C. Murray, Toronto 1998, pp. 171-190.

Th. F. X. Noble, *The Revolt of King Bernard of Italy in 817: Its Causes and Consequences*, in «Studi Medievali» XV, 1 (1974), pp. 315-326.

Th. F. X. Noble, *The Republic of St. Peter: The Birth of the Papal State, 680-825*, Philadelphia 1984.

G. Noyé, *La Calabre entre Byzantins, Sarrasins et Normands*, in *Cavalieri alla conquista del Sud: Studi sull'Italia normanna in memoria di Leon-Robert Ménager*, eds. E. Cuozzo and J.-M. Martin, Roma-Bari 1998, pp. 90-116.

J. Jarnut, *Bergamo 568-1098: Verfassungs-, Sozial- und Wirtschaftsgeschicte einer lombardischen Stadt in Mittelalter*, Wiesbaden 1979.

J. Jarnut, *Geschichte der Langobarden*, Stuttgart 1982.

J. Jarnut, *Kaiser Ludwig der Fromme und König Bernhard von Italien. Der Versuch einer Rehabilitierung*, in «Studi Medievali» XXX, 2 (1989), pp. 637-648.

J. Jarnut, *I Longobardi nell'epoca precedente all'occupazione dell'Italia*, in *Langobardia*, eds. S. Gasparri and P. Cammarosano, Udine 1990, pp. 3-33.

G. Ortalli, *Il ducato e la «civitas Rivoalti»: tra carolingi, bizantini e sassoni*, in *Storia di Venezia*, I: *Origini-Età ducale*, eds. L. Cracco-Ruggini, M. Pavan, G. Cracco, G. Ortalli, Roma 1992, pp. 725-790.

R. Pitkäranta, *Zur Sprache des Andreas von Bergamo*, in «Arctos» XIII (1979), pp. 129-149.

W. Pohl, *Die Awaren. Ein Steppenvolk in Mitteleuropa. 567-822 n. Chr.*, München 1988.

W. Pohl, *Memory, Identity and Power in Lombard Italy*, in *The Uses of the Past in the Early Middle Ages*, eds. Y. Hen and M. Innes, Cambridge 2000, pp. 9-28.

W. Pohl, *Invasions and Ethnic Identity*, in *Italy in the Early Middle Ages 476-1000*, ed. C. La Rocca, Oxford 2002, pp. 11-33.

W. Pohl, *La costituzione di una memoria storica: il caso dei Longobardi*, in *Studi sulle società e le culture del Medioevo per Girolamo Arnaldi*, eds. L. Gatto and P. Supino Martini, Firenze 2002, pp. 563-580.

F. Prinz, *Klerus und Krieg im früheren Mittelalter*, Stuttgart 1971.

P. Riché, *The Carolingians: A Family Who Forged Europe*, Philadelphia 1993.

C. Russo Mailler, *La politica meridionale di Ludovico II e il «Rythmus de captivitate Ludovici imperatoris»*, in «Quaderni Medievali» XIV (1982), pp. 6-27.

A. A. Settia, *Castelli e villaggi nell'Italia padana: Popolamento, potere e sicurezza fra IX e XIII secolo*, Napoli 1984.

A. A. Settia, *Potere e sicurezza nella bergamasca del secolo X*, in *Bergamo e il suo territorio nei documenti altomedievali*, ed. M. Cortesi, Bergamo 1991, pp. 45-62.

P. Skinner, *Gender and Memory in Medieval Italy*, in *Medieval Memories: Men, Women and the Past, 700-1300*, ed. E. van Houts, Harlow 2001, pp. 36-52.

P. Skinner, *Women in Medieval Italian Society 500-1200*, Harlow 2001.

The Uses of the Past in the Early Middle Ages, eds. Y. Hen and M. Innes, Cambridge 2000.

A. A. Vasil'ev, *Byzance et les Arabes*, Bruxelles 1935.

C. Villa, *I classici*, in *Lo spazio letterario del Medioevo*, I: *Il medioevo latino*, eds. G. Cavallo, C. Leonardi, E. Menestò, vol. I.1, *La produzione del testo*, Roma 1992, pp. 479-522.

A. Viscardi, *Le Origini. Storia letteraria d'Italia*, Milano 1966, 4th ed.

Ch. Wickham, *Early Medieval Italy: Central Power and Local Society 400-1000*, London 1981.

Ch. Wickham, *Lawyers' Time: History and Memory in Tenth and Eleventh Century Italy*, in Id., *Land and Power. Studies in Italian and European Social History, 400-1200*, London 1994, pp. 275-293.

I. Wood, *The Merovingian Kingdoms: 450-751*, London 1994.

PART II

HISTORIA LANGOBARDORUM CODICIS GOTHANI
HISTORY OF THE LOMBARDS OF GOTHA'S CODEX

[HISTORIA LANGOBARDORUM CODICIS GOTHANI]

[1.] Asserunt antiqui parentes Langobardorum, per Gambaram parentem suam, pro quid exitus aut movicio seu visitatio eorum fuisset, deinter serpentibus parentes eorum breviati exissent, sanguinea et aspera progeines[a], et sine lege.

In terra Italiae adventantes, fluentem lac et mel, et quod amplius est, salutem invenerunt baptismatis, et vestigia sanctae trinitatis recipientes, inter numerum bonorum effecti sunt. In illis impletum est: "Non inputatur peccatum, cum lex non esset."

Primis lupi rapaces, postea agni inter dominicum gregem pascentes; proinde tanta laus et gratia referenda est Deo, qui illos de stercore inter iustorum numerum collocavit, nisi davitica impleta prophetia: "Et de stercore erigens[b] pauperem, sedere facit eum cum principibus populi sui."

Sic suprascripta Gambara cum eisdem movita adserebat, non ut prophetaret quę nesciebat, sed phitonissa inter sibillę cognomina, dicens, eo quod illi[c] superna visitatione movissent, ut de spina rosa efficeretur[d], nesciens in qualia, nisi divinandum perspicerit.

Moviti itaque non ex necessitate aut duricia cordis aut parentum oppressione, sed ut ex alto salutem consequeretur, asserit exituros.

Mirumque est omnibus et inauditum videre, ubi non fuit meritum parentum, talis salus refulgere, qui deinter mucrones spinarum odoramenta aeclesiarum inventi sunt.

Sicut ipse misericors filius Dei antea predixerat: "Non veni vocare iustos, sed peccatores." Isti fuerunt, unde ipse salvator ad Iudęos in proverbiis dicens: "Habeo alias oves, quę non sunt ex hoc ovili et illas me oportet adduci ad aquam vivam poscendam."

[2.] Hic incipiens originem et nationem seu parentelam Langobardorum, exitus et conversationem eorum, bella et vastationes quę fecerunt reges eorum, et patrias quas vastarunt.

---

[a] progenies *Waitz Azzara*. [b] *G adds* g *to* eriens *interlineally.* eriens *Waitz Azzara*. [c] *G adds* i *above* e *of* ille. ille *Waitz Azzara*. [d] efficetur *Azzara*.

[1] *Origo gentis Langobardorum*, ch. 1, and Paul the Deacon, *Historia Langobardorum*, II, 8, narrate that Gambara was the mother of Ibor and Aio, the two young warriors who led the first migrations of the Winili/Lombards.

[2] A clear allusion to the Promised Land of the Jews. See Exod. 3: 8 and Deut. 11: 9. A similar, but less explicit, depiction of Italy can be found in Paul the Deacon, *Historia Langobardorum*, II, 8. Cf. Luiselli, *Storia culturale*, p. 723, and Cingolani, *Le storie dei Longobardi*, p. 52.

[3] Rom. 5: 13.

[4] Ps. 112: 7-8.

[5] Paul the Deacon explains that Gambara was «a woman of the keenest ability and most prudent in counsel among her people, and they trusted not a little to her shrewdness in doubtful matter,» but he does not say anything

HISTORY OF THE LOMBARDS OF GOTHA'S CODEX

1. The ancient forefathers of the Lombards assert that their exodus, movements, and journey took place through their ancestress Gambara[1] and that their forefathers, a rough and bloody and lawless progeny, of small number, originated from snakes.

They came into the land of Italy, where milk and honey flow,[2] and, what is more important, they found the salvation of baptism there. Receiving the marks of the Holy Trinity, they were included in the number of the good. In them was fulfilled the saying: "Sin is not imputed where there is no law."[3]

At first they were ravening wolves, afterwards they became lambs feeding in the Lord's flock. For this reason great praise and thanks must be given to God who raised them from the dunghill and set them in the number of the just in order to fulfill the prophecy of David: "He raised the poor man from the dunghill, and made him to sit with the princes of his people."[4]

So asserted the above-mentioned Gambara, who traveled with them, not prophesying things which she did not know, but speaking like a pythoness, which is one of the names of the Sybil, not knowing anything else than what she learned through divination. The Lombards were in fact undertaking a divine journey so that the thorn could be turned into a rose.[5]

She asserted that they had left not out of necessity, nor hardness of heart, nor because their parents were oppressive, but to obtain salvation from on high.[6]

For everybody it is a wonderful and unheard-of thing to see that, where there was no merit in their parents, such salvation shone forth that they found the perfumes of the churches among the sharp points of the thorns.

As the compassionate Son of God had preached before, "I came not to call the righteous, but sinners."[7] These were the ones of whom the Savior Himself spoke in the parables to the Jews: "I have other sheep, which are not of this fold, and it is appropriate that I take them to seek the living water."[8]

2. Here begins the origin, birth or rather descent of the Lombards, their exodus and their settlements, the wars and devastation their kings carried out, and the countries they devastated.

---

about her prophetic abilities. Paul the Deacon, *Historia Langobardorum*, I, 3. Stefano Cingolani hypothesizes that the reference in Paul the Deacon, *Historia Langobardorum*, I, 1, to other causes leading to the migration of the Winili/Lombards could be explained by the existence of another version of those events which was written down in the HLCG. Cingolani, *Le storie dei Longobardi*, p. 48. Some similarities with the HLCG can be found in the work of an eleventh-century author, Benzo of Alba, *Ad Heinricum IV imperatorem*, IV, 3. Cf. Cingolani, *Le storie dei Longobardi*, pp. 59-60.

[6] Paul the Deacon, *Historia Langobardorum*, I, 3, recounts that the Winili left their land because it was overpopulated.

[7] Matt. 9: 13.

[8] John 10: 16.

Vindilicus dicitur amnis[a] ab extremis Gallię finibus; iuxta eundem fluvio primis habitatio et proprietas eorum fuit. Primis Winili proprio nomine[b] seu et parentela; nam, ut asserit Hieronimus, postea ad vulgorum vocem Langobardi nomen mutati sunt pro eo ad barba prolixa et numquam tonsa. Hic supradictus Ligurius fluvius Albię fluvii canalis inundans et nomen finitur.

Postquam de eadem ripa, ut supra dictum est, Langobardi exierunt, sic Scatenauge Albię fluvi ripa primis novam habitationem posuerunt; sic deinde certantes Saxonię patria attigerunt, locus ubi Patespruna cognominantur; ubi sicut nostri antiqui patres longo tempore asserunt habitasse, et in multis partibus bella et pericula generarunt.

Ibique primum[c] regem levaverunt nomine Agelmund. Cum ipso de hoc loco in antea patrias ad suam partem expugnare coeperunt; unde in Beovinidis aciem et clauses seu tuba clangencium ad suam proprietatem perduxerunt.

Unde usque hodie pręsentem diem Wachoni regi eorum domus et habitatio apparet signa.

Deinde meliorem ubertatis patrię requirentes, ad Traciam provinciam transierunt, in Pannonię urbis patriam suam hereditatem afflixerunt, unde cum Abaris reluctantes seu bella plurima ardentissimo animo ipsam Pannoniam expugnaverunt. Et Abari cum illis foedus amicicię emiserunt et XX et duo annos ibi habitare perhibetur.

[3.] Illo vero tempore exivit[d] rex Odoacer de Ravenna cum exercitu Alanorum et venit in Rudilanda et pugnavit[e] cum Rugiis et occidit Fewane rege Rugorum et secum multos captivos in Italiam[f] adduxerunt.

Tunc exierunt Langobardi[g] de Pannonia et venerunt et habitaverunt in Rudilanda annos plurimos et ad suam dogmam perduxerunt.

---

[a] amnnis G. amnis *Azzara Waitz.* [b] *G adds* no *to* mine *interlineally.* [c] primis *Waitz Azzara.* [d] exivt G. exivit *Waitz Azzara.* [e] *G adds* et *above* ex *of* expugnavit. pugnavit *Waitz Azzara.* [f] Italia *Waitz Azzara.* [g] *G adds* n *to* Lagobardi *interlineally.*

---

[9] According to Paul the Deacon, *Historia Langobardorum*, I, 7, the first region the Winili moved to was Scoringa, where they met the Vandals.

[10] It is believed that Winili means «fighters.» Jarnut, *Geschichte der Langobarden*, p. 10. Gasparri, *La cultura tradizionale*, pp. 14-22, hypothesizes that this term might also stand for «mad, furious, victorious dogs» and that it would refer to some Germanic beliefs about warriors possessing superhuman characteristics.

[11] In reality, it was Isidore of Seville, who, immediately after mentioning the Lombards, talks about the river Vindilicus, indicated as the land of the Vandals. The author of HLCG confused the Winili-Lombards with the Vandals. Cingolani, *Le storie dei Longobardi*, p. 55.

[12] Paul the Deacon, too, mentions this etymology and the detail that the Lombards did not shave their beards. Paul the Deacon, *Historia Langobardorum*, I, 9. For an analysis of the name change, see Gasparri, *La cultura tradizionale*, pp. 12-27, 33-37; Cingolani, *Le storie dei Longobardi*, pp. 37-55; Coumert, *Origines des Peuples*, pp. 145-176.

[13] It is probably Paderborn. Cf. Cingolani, *Le storie dei Longobardi*, pp. 55-56, and Coumert, *Origines des Peuples*, p. 257.

Vindilicus is a river which lies on Gaul's extreme boundary; their first dwellings and possessions were near to this river.[9] At first their name was Winili,[10] which was the same as that of their ancestors, but, as Jerome[11] asserts, they later changed their name to the common word Lombards because of their long and never-shaven beards.[12] The above-mentioned river Ligurius flows into the channels of the river Elbe and loses its name.

After the Lombards left from that shore, as has been said before, they made their new home at first at Scatenauge on the banks of the river Elbe; then they went fighting into the country of the Saxons, in the place called Patespruna,[13] where, as our ancient fathers assert, they dwelt for a long time and brought war and destruction to many places.

Here, they raised over them their first king, whose name was Agelmund.[14] Under him, they left that area and began to conquer their homeland; then, they led the army against the Beovinidis[15] and seized them at the sound of trumpets.

The remains of the house and dwelling of their King Wacho can still be seen today.

Then, needing a more fertile country, they went into the province of Thrace and decided to settle in the territory of the city of Pannonia.[16] Here, striving against the Avars, the Lombards waged many wars against them with most ardent courage and conquered Pannonia. The Avars then made a treaty with them and it is recounted that the Lombards lived there for twenty-two years.[17]

3. At that time King Odovacer[18] left Ravenna with an army of Alans,[19] went to Rugiland, fought with the Rugians, and killed the King of the Rugians, Fewan, and brought many captives with him to Italy.[20]

Then the Lombards left Pannonia, went to Rugiland,[21] lived there for many years, and subjugated it.

---

[14] Agelmund is indicated as the first king of the Lombards also in the prologue of the laws issued by the Lombard King Rothari (*Edictum Rothari*, p. 14); *Origo gentis Langobardorum*, ch. 2; Paul the Deacon, *Historia Langobardorum*, I, 14, who reports that, after leaving Scoringa, the Lombards went to Mauringa and Golanda. Paul the Deacon, *Historia Langobardorum*, I, 10-13.

[15] Jörg Jarnut believes that by Beovinidis, who are mentioned in ch. 11 as well, the author meant the Bohemians, while Magali Coumert thinks that this is a reference to the Slavic population of the Winides. If so, this would be an anachronism as in that period the Slavs had not yet arrived in that region. Jarnut, *I Longobardi nell'epoca precedente*, p. 21; Coumert, *Origines des peuples*, p. 259.

[16] It corresponds roughly to present-day Hungary.

[17] Before narrating the episode concerning Odovacer, Paul the Deacon reports that the Lombards fought against the Bulgarians. After a terrible defeat in which Agelmund was killed, the Lombards elected a new king, Lamissio, who led his people to victory. Paul the Deacon, *Historia Langobardorum*, I, 16-17. It is believed that the Lombards' enemies were the Huns and that these clashes took place in about the 440s. Christie, *The Lombards*, pp. 14-16.

[18] After deposing the emperor of the western Roman Empire, Romulus Augustus, in 476, Odovacer ruled Italy until 489.

[19] Paul the Deacon, *Historia Langobardorum*, I, 19, does not mention the presence of Alans in Odovacer's army.

[20] This part is copied almost verbatim from *Origo gentis Langobardorum*, ch. 3. For description of the battles, see Paul the Deacon, *Historia Langobardorum*, I, 19.

[21] The Lombards moved to Rugiland in 488. Jarnut, *I Longobardi nell'epoca precedente*, pp. 21-23.

[4.] Ante Peronem regnavit Godoin.

Post Peronem tenuit principatum Langobardorum Claffo[a].

Et post Claffonem regnavit Tatto.

Eo tempore redierunt Langobardi in campis Filda. Fecerunt ibi annos tres. Et post haec pugnavit Tatto cum Rodulfo[b] rege Herolorum, et occidit eum, et tulit bandonem ipsius, et populum ipsius in fugam misit. Ibi praedavit omnia bona eorum. Postea Heroli regem non habuerunt.

Deinde occidit Wacho, filius Unichis, Tattone rege barbane suo cum Vinsilane. Et regnavit Wacho. Et expugnavit Heldechis, filio Tattoni; et fugit Heldechis ad Gibidos et ibi mortuus est. Iniuriam vindicandum, Gibites scandalum commiserunt cum Langobardis.

Eo tempore inclinavit Wacho Suavus sub regno Langobardorum. Wacho habuit uxores tres, Ranigundam, filiam Pisen regi Turingorum; et post ipsam accepit uxorem nomine Austrecusa, filia <regis> Gibedorum. Et habuit Wacho ex eis filias duas, nomine <unae>[c] Wisicharda, quam tradidit in matrimonio Teodeperto regi Francorum; nomine secundę Walderata quam habuit uxorem Chusubald rex Francorum. Postea accepit Wacho terciam uxorem filiam regis Herolorum nomine Silenga; de qua habuit <filium>[d] nomine Walterenem. Et mortuus est Wacho. Et regnavit filius ipsius nomine Walteri annis VII, fargaetum. Isti omnes Adelingi fuerunt.

[5.] Et post Waltarene regnavit Audoin. Mater autem Audoin nomine Menia uxor fuit Pissę regis. Audoin ex genere fuit Gausus. Ipse adduxit Langobardos in Pannoniam, et mortuus est Audoin in Pannonia[e]. Et regnavit Albuin[f], filius eius, pro eo; cui mater fuit Rodelenda.

---

[a] *G writes and underlines* Ca *before* Claffo. [b] *G corrects* Rofulfo *to* Rodulfo. Rodulfo *Waitz Azzara.* [c] unae *Waitz and Origo gentis Langobardorum, ch. 4.* [d] filium *Waitz and Origo gentis Langobardorum, ch. 4.* [e] *G adds* nno *to* Pania *interlineally.* [f] Albouin *G.* Albuin *Waitz Azzara.*

[22] The HLCG is the only source that mentions Godoin and Pero.

[23] In *Origo gentis Langobardorum*, ch. 4, and in *Edictum Rothari*, p. 14, Claffo succeeds Godeoc.

[24] According to Paul the Deacon, the Lombards «departed from Rugiland, and dwelt in open fields, which are called 'feld' in the barbarian tongue.» Paul the Deacon, *Historia Langobardorum*, I, 20. *Origo gentis Langobardorum*, ch. 4, reports «in campis Feld.» They are probably referring to Marchfeld, an area east of Vienna. Jarnut, *Geschichte der Langobarden*, p. 19.

[25] Paul the Deacon, *Historia Langobardorum*, I, 20, relates this detail as well.

[26] «And Tatto reigned [...] no longer had a king.» A similar account can be found in *Origo gentis Langobardorum*, ch. 4. After this defeat, the Heruls ceased to exist as a distinct people. Jarnut, *Geschichte der Langobarden*, pp. 20-21. For a description of this war, see Paul the Deacon, *Historia Langobardorum*, I, 20.

[27] Zuchilo in *Origo gentis Langobardorum*, ch. 4, and in Paul the Deacon, *Historia Langobardorum*, I, 21.

[28] Paul the Deacon does not mention Vinsilane.

4. Godoin reigned before Pero.[22]

Claffo held the leadership of the Lombards after Pero.[23]

And Tatto reigned after Claffo.

In that time the Lombards went back to the fields of Filda.[24] They stayed there for three years.[25] And after that Tatto fought with the King of the Heruls, Rodulf, killed him, took his banner, and put his people to flight. There he looted all their possessions. Afterwards the Heruls no longer had a king.[26]

Then Wacho, son of Unichis,[27] killed his uncle, King Tatto, with Vinsilane.[28] So Wacho reigned and defeated Heldechis, son of Tatto; and Heldechis took refuge among the Gepids and died there. The Gepids committed a shameful act against the Lombards to avenge the insult.[29]

In that time Wacho subjugated the Sueves to the rule of the Lombards.[30] Wacho had three wives: Ranigunda, daughter of the King of the Thuringians, Pisen;[31] and after her, he took a wife named Austrecusa, daughter of the King of the Gepids. From them Wacho had two daughters. The name of the first was Wisicharda whom he gave in marriage to the King of the Franks, Theudebert.[32] The name of the second was Walderada, whom the King of the Franks, Chusubald,[33] had as wife. Afterwards Wacho took a third wife, the daughter of the king of the Heruls, whose name was Silenga. From her he had a son named Walthari.[34] Wacho died and his son, named Walthari, reigned for seven years. He had no descendants.[35] All these were Adelingi.[36]

5. And Audoin reigned after Walthari. The mother of Audoin, whose name was Menia,[37] was the wife of King Pisen.[38] Audoin was of the Gausi family. He took the Lombards to Pannonia. And Audoin died in Pannonia.

His son Alboin reigned in his place. His mother was Rodelenda.

---

[29] Paul the Deacon, *Historia Langobardorum*, I, 21, says only that «for this reason the Gepids from that time incurred enmities with the Lombards.»

[30] This particular is recounted also by Paul the Deacon, *Historia Langobardorum*, I, 21.

[31] Fisud in *Origo gentis Langobardorum*, ch. 4.

[32] Theudebert (533-548).

[33] Scusuald in *Origo gentis Langobardorum*, ch. 4. In reality his name was Theudebald (548-555). See the genealogical table in Wood, *The Merovingian Kingdoms*, p. 344.

[34] These particulars can be found also in Paul the Deacon, *Historia Langobardorum*, I, 21, who, however, does not mention the name of the Thuringian king and adds that, after a while, the King of the Franks, Chusabald, began to hate his wife and therefore gave her to one of his men.

[35] *Farigaidus* in *Origo gentis Langobardorum*, ch. 4. For further information about this term, see the introduction (p. 33), and Meli, *Eco scandinave*, p. 349.

[36] Lihingi in *Origo gentis Langobardorum*, ch. 4, and in Paul the Deacon, *Historia Langobardorum*, I, 21. This dynasty was created by the Lombard king, Lethi, who had ruled at the beginning of the fifth century. Jarnut, *Geschichte der Langobarden*, p. 29.

[37] Neither the *Origo* nor Paul the Deacon mention Menia.

[38] He is the king of the Thuringians mentioned in HLCG, ch. 4.

Eo tempore pugnavit[a] Albuin[b] cum rege Gebedorum nomine Cunimundo et occidit eum Albouin in ipsa pugna; et debellati sunt Gebeti validissime vehementer. Tunc tulit Albuin rex uxorem nomine Rosemoniam, filiam Chunimundi, quem ipse occiderat; et ipse prędaverat. Ante habuit mulierem nomine Ludusenda, quae fuit filia Clothari[c] regis Francorum; de qua habuit filiam nomine Albsuinda.

Iste Albuin movit et adduxit Langobardos in Italia, invitatus ad Narside proconsule et preside Italię, qui minas Suffię reginę erat perterritus.

Eo tempore cum exire coeperunt Langobardi a Pannonia, tunc fecerunt pactum et foedus amicicię Abari cum ipsis Langobardis et cartam conscriptionis, ut usque ad annos ducentos, si eorum oporte esset Pannoniam requirere, sine omnia bella certaminis ad eorum partem ipsam terram relaxarent. Et in Italiam, in quam ipsi perrexerant, usque ad plenos ducentos annos in eorum auxilium essent parati.

Et movisse Albuin rex Langobardorum de Pannonia exercitu[d] suo valde copiosum mense aperile[e] in Pascha, indictione prima; secunda vero indictione incipiente coeperunt predare finem Italię, tercia autem factus est dominus Italię. Nam Narsis proconsul Italię, si quid eorum promiserat, relinquens[f] Italiam, ad Spaniarum provinciam est reversus.

[6.] Tunc Papiae cives et Mediolanum metropolim cum reliquę alię civitates Italiorum, videntes se vacuę, sicut a Deo fuerat predestinatum, colla sua ipsi[g] Albuin regi subicierunt.

Et cum regnasset Albuin[h] in Italia annos tres et menses sex, malo inito contra eum consilio per Rosemoniam uxorem et consilio Peredei cubicularii sui ab Elmechis spatario suo occisus est in Verona civitate.

Et volebat Helmechis regnare et non potuit propter metum Langobardorum et necem Albuini. Tunc mandavit Rosemonia festinanter Longino prefecto militi Ravenensi, ut eam in fugam susciperet ad Ravennam. Ut autem audivit Longinus haec verba, misit movere angarias[i] et tulerunt Rosemoniam et Alsuendam, filiam Albuini[l] regis, et omnem thesaurum Langobardorum secum duxerunt et Helmechis.

---

[a]   *G adds* u *to* pgnavit *interlineally.* [b] *G corrects* Alboin *to* Albuin. [c] flothari *G.* [d] *G adds* cum *interlineally. Waitz Azzara omit* cum. [e] aprile *Waitz Azzara.* [f] *G adds* n *to* reliques *interlineally.* [g] *G erases* us *after* ipsi. ipsius *Waitz Azzara.* [h] Albuit *G.* Albuin *Waitz Azzara.* [i] angareas *Waitz Azzara.* [l] Albuin *Waitz Azzara.*

[39]   Paul the Deacon, *Historia Langobardorum*, I, 27, narrates that the defeat was so great that the Gepids ceased to exist as a people.

[40]   Chlotsuinda in *Origo gentis Langobardorum*, ch. 5, and in Paul the Deacon, *Historia Langobardorum*, I, 27.

[41]   Chlothar I (511-560/561).

[42]   «And Audoin reigned [...] Albsuinda.» A similar account can be found in *Origo gentis Langobardorum*, ch. 5.

[43]   Paul the Deacon states that Narses was a *chartularius* and later became *patricius*. Paul the Deacon, *Historia Langobardorum*, II, 3.

[44]   According to Paul the Deacon, the Italians, envious of the wealth Narses had acquired, asked emperor Justin II to remove him from office, and that Empress Sophia sent Narses a message saying that, because he was a eunuch, «she would make him portion out to the girls in the women's chamber the daily tasks of wool.» Narses then asked the Lombards to invade Italy. Paul the Deacon, *Historia Langobardorum*, II, 5.

At that time Alboin fought with the king of the Gepids, whose name was Cunimund. Albuin killed him in that battle and the Gepids were very heavily defeated.[39] King Alboin then took a wife named Rosemund, daughter of Cunimund, whom he had killed; Alboin had captured her. Before her, he had a wife named Ludusenda,[40] who was the daughter of the King of the Franks, Chlothar,[41] and from whom he had a daughter named Albsuinda.[42]

Invited by the proconsul[43] and governor of Italy, Narses, who was terrorized because of queen Sophia's threats,[44] this Alboin moved the Lombards and took them to Italy.

In the time when the Lombards began to leave Pannonia, the Avars made a pact and an agreement of friendship with the Lombards and had a document written down according to which, if, for the following two hundred years, the Lombards would need Pannonia, the Avars would leave them their part of that land without any war, and for two hundred years the Avars would be ready to help the Lombards in Italy where the Lombards were going.[45]

And the King of the Lombards, Alboin, left Pannonia with his very large army in the month of April, at Easter, during the first indiction;[46] at the beginning of the second indiction, they began to sack Italy and during the third Alboin became lord of Italy. In fact, as he had promised them, the proconsul of Italy, Narses, left Italy and went back to the province of the Spains.[47]

6. Seeing that they were defenseless, the citizens of Pavia and the metropolis of Milan along with the remaining cities of the Italians submitted their necks to Alboin as it had been predestined by God.[48]

After ruling for three years and six months in Italy, Alboin was killed by his *spatharius* Helmechis in the city of Verona as a consequence of an evil plot originated by his wife Rosemund and his chamberlain Peredeus.[49]

Helmechis wanted to reign, but he could not do it for fear of the Lombards[50] and the murder of Alboin. Then Rosemund quickly sent word to the military prefect of Ravenna, Longinus, asking him to help her flee to Ravenna. As Longinus heard these words, he sent some boats which took Rosemund, Alsuenda, King Alboin's daughter, and Helmechis, and, they also took all the treasure of the Lombards with them.

For the different ways Narses's invitation has been interpreted, see Christie, *The Lombards*, pp. 60-63, and Moorhead, *Ostrogothic Italy and the Lombard Invasions*, p. 152.

[45] Paul the Deacon relates the existence of a pact between the Lombards and the Avars, but he only reports that the former left Pannonia to the latter and «if at any time it should be necessary for the Lombards return they should take back their own fields.» Paul the Deacon, *Historia Langobardorum*, II, 7.

[46] Paul the Deacon, *Historia Langobardorum*, II, 7, states that the Lombards left Pannonia in 568.

[47] This detail is not mentioned by Paul the Deacon, who recounts that Narses died shortly after going to Rome from Campania and that his body and his riches were carried to Constantinople. Paul the Deacon, *Historia Langobardorum*, II, 11.

[48] According to Paul the Deacon, *Historia Langobardorum*, II, 26-27, Pavia held out for three years.

[49] Paul the Deacon recounts that Rosemund wanted to kill Alboin because he forced her to drink from a cup fashioned out of her father's skull. Following Helmechis's suggestion, she convinced Peredeus to participate in the murder of the king, by taking the place of the girl who was Peredeus's lover one night and, after Peredeus made love to her, Rosemund threatened to reveal all to Alboin if he refused to do what she asked. Helmichis then killed the king of the Lombards. Paul the Deacon, *Historia Langobardorum*, II, 28.

[50] Paul the Deacon, *Historia Langobardorum*, II, 29, reports that the Lombards wanted to kill Helmechis.

Unde plures annos scisma et bella inter Langobardos et Romanos fuerunt. Tunc, ut per fẹmeneum[a] primum exordium accidit mala suasio peccati, inde usque ad prẹsentem diem feminalis tenet consuetudo peccandi, suasit ipsa Rosemonia Longino militi, sicut prius ab Elmechis, ut et ipsa occideret Helmechis et Longino esset uxor. Inito isto consilio, temperavit venenum[b] Rosemonia et dedit Helmechis. Cumque gustasset, intellexit, quod malignum biberat. Precepit ut et ipsa Rosemonia cum eo biberet[c] invita et mortui sunt ambo. Tunc Longinus prefectus tulit omnes thesauros Langobardorum et Albsuendam, filia Albuin regis, iussit ponere in naves et transmisit eam Constantinopolim ad imperatorem suum.

[7.] Eo tempore levaverunt Langobardi sibi regem nomine Clephs[d] de genere Peleos; et regnavit annos duos et menses sex et mortuus est.

Et iudicaverunt iudices Langobardorum sine rege Italiam annos XII. Post haec levaverunt sibi regem nomine Autarenem, filium Cleffonis; et accepit Autaren uxorem nomine Teodelenda, filia Garibaldi et Walderadẹ.

Et venit cum Teodelenda frater eius nomine Gundwald et ordinavit eum Authari rex ducem in civitatem Austinse. Et regnavit annis septem et mortuus est.

Et venit Agilwald dux Turigorum de Taurini, et iunxit Teodelindẹ reginẹ et factus est rex Langobardorum et occidit tres duces rebellos[e] suos, Zangrulf de Verona, Mimolfo de insula sancti Iuli et Gaidulfo de Bergamo et alios plures rebellos[f] suos.

Et genuit Aioald rex de Teodelinda filia nomine Gudebergam et filio nomine Adelwald.

Et regnavit Agilwaldo annos XX et V.

Adelwald, filius eius, regnavit annos X[g].

Arioaldus regnavit annos decem.

---

[a] G adds i *above the second* e of fẹmeneum. fimeneum *Waitz Azzara.* [b] G adds n *above* r *of* venerum. [c] G adds i *above the second* e *of* biberet. biberit *Waitz Azzara.* [d] Cleps G *Waitz Azzara.* [e] G adds e *above* o *of* rebellos. [f] G adds e *above* o *of* rebellos. [g] decem *Waitz Azzara.*

[51] Paul the Deacon does not make this statement, while the chronicler Agnellus of Ravenna takes Rosemund's behavior as his starting point to warn husbands about their wives, suggesting that they should never provoke their wrath. Agnellus of Ravenna, *Liber pontificalis*, ch. 97.

[52] This sentence is not clear because of the author's weak knowledge of the Latin language. For this reason, I have decided to follow the version narrated by *Origo gentis Langobardorum*, ch. 5, and Paul the Deacon, *Historia Langobardorum*, II, 31.

[53] «Rosemund was persuaded [...] to his emperor.» Cf. *Origo gentis Langobardorum*, ch. 5. Paul the Deacon adds that Peredeus too was taken to Constantinople where his eyes were plucked out because the emperor feared him. Imitating Samson, Peredeus was later able to avenge his injuries by killing two Byzantine nobles. Paul the Deacon, *Historia Langobardorum*, II, 31.

So there were schisms and wars between the Lombards and the Romans for many years. Then, as the evil inclination to sin had a female origin, the same reason for which women have had the habit of sinning up to the present day,[51] Rosemund was persuaded by the commander Longinus,[52] as she was previously by Helmechis, to kill Helmechis and be wife to Longinus. Rosemund took this advice, prepared some poison, and gave it to Helmechis. As he tasted it, he understood that he had drunk an evil thing. He then had Rosemund drink with him and they both died. Then the prefect Longinus took all the treasures of the Lombards and Albsuinda, King Alboin's daughter, and ordered that Albsuenda be put on a ship and sent to Constantinople to his emperor.[53]

7. In that time the Lombards elected as king Cleph of the Pelei lineage.[54] He reigned for two years and six months and died.[55]

The judges[56] of the Lombards ruled Italy without a king for twelve years.[57] After that, they elected a king named Authari, son of Cleph.

Authari took a wife named Theodelinda, daughter of Garibald and Walderada.[58]

And with Theodelinda came her brother, named Gundwald, and King Authari appointed him as duke of the city of Asti. He reigned for seven years and died.

The Duke of the Thuringians, Agilwald, came from Turin,[59] married queen Theodelinda, was elected king of the Lombards, and killed three rebellious dukes, Zangrulf of Verona, Mimulf of the island of St. Iulius,[60] and Gaidulf of Bergamo, and many other rebels.

King Aioald[61] engendered from Theodelinda a daughter named Gudeberga[62] and a son named Adelwald.[63]

Agilvald reigned for twenty-five years.[64]

His son Adelwald reigned for ten years.[65]

Arioald reigned for ten years.[66]

---

[54] Paul the Deacon does not mention this detail. At the beginning of King Rothari's edict (*Edictum Rothari*, p. 14), it is said that Cleph belonged to the Beleos family.

[55] One year and six months in Paul the Deacon, *Historia Langobardorum*, II, 31. Cleph (572-574).

[56] i. e. dukes.

[57] Ten years in Paul the Deacon, *Historia Langobardorum*, II, 32.

[58] «In that time [...] Walderada.» The same account is in *Origo gentis Langobardorum*, ch. 6. Garibald was the king of the Bavarians. Paul the Deacon does not mention Walderada. Paul the Deacon, *Historia Langobardorum*, III, 30.

[59] Agilulf in Paul the Deacon, *Historia Langobardorum*, III, 30. He was duke of Turin.

[60] Island in Lake Orta.

[61] i. e. Agilwald.

[62] Gundiperga in Paul the Deacon, *Historia Langobardorum*, IV, 47.

[63] Adaloald in Paul the Deacon, *Historia Langobardorum*, IV, 25.

[64] Agilulf (590-616).

[65] Adaloald (616-626).

[66] Arioald (626-636).

[8.] Rothari regnavit annos sedecim.

Per quem leges et iusticiam Langobardis est inchoate. Et per conscriptionem primis iudices percurrerunt; nam antea per cadarfada et arbitrio seu ritus fierunt causationes.

Istius Rothari regis temporibus[a] ortum est lumen in tenebris per quem supradicti Langobardi ad cannonica[b] tenderunt certamina et sacerdotum facti sunt adiutores.

[9.] Rodoald regnavit menses sex.

Aribertus regnavit annis VIIII.

Grimwald regnavit annos VIIII.

Berthari regnavit annis X et VII.

Cunibert regnavit annis XIII.

Liupert regnavit annos duos.

Aribert regnavit annos XII.

Ansprado regnavit menses tres.

Liutprando regnavit annos XXXI et menses VII.

Hildeprand regnavit menses VII.

Ratgis regnavit[c] annos IIII et menses VIIII.

Aistulfus regnavit annos VIII[d].

Desiderius cum filio suo Adelchis regnaverunt annos decem et VII et menses tres.

[10.] Hic finitum est regnum Langobardorum et incoavit regnum Italię per gloriosissimum Carolum regem Francorum; qui adiutor et defensator domni Petri principis apostolorum ab Italia perrexerat eius iusticiam requirendam[e].

Nam nulli lucri cupiditas peragrare, sed bono pius et misericors factus est adiuvator; et sicut poterat omnia demollire, factus est clemens indultor. Et paternę patrię leges Langobardis misertus concessit et suas, ut voluit, quę necessariae erant Langobardis, adiunxit. Et innumerabilibus viris, qui eidem culparunt incessanter, culpas dimisit. Pro quod illi omnipotens Deus centies multiplicavit ubertates.

---

[a]   *G adds* temporibus *in the margin of the folio.* [b] cannonicam *Waitz Azzara.* [c] regnnavit *G.* [d] 7 *Waitz.* VII *Azzara.* [e] requirendum *Waitz Azzara.*

[67]   Rothari (636-652).
[68]   In 643 Rothari had the Lombard laws written down. See *Edictum Rothari*, pp. 13-113.
[69]   In King Liutprand's legislation, similar terms, *cawerfeda* and *cawerfida*, are used. *Liutprandi Leges*, chs. 77, 133.
[70]   Rodoald (652-653).
[71]   Aribert (653-661).
[72]   Grimoald (662-671). Before Grimoald, Perctarit and Godepert, Aribert's sons, reigned from 661 to 662.
[73]   Perctarit (672-688).
[74]   Cunibert (688-700).

8. Rothari reigned for sixteen years.[67]

Thanks to him, laws and justice began for the Lombards. And for the first time the judges used written laws.[68] Previously, all causes were decided by *cadarfada*, that is either by arbitration or by custom.[69]

In the period of King Rothari, light arose in the darkness and, because of it, the aforesaid Lombards devoted themselves to the canonical disputes and became helpers of the priests.

9. Rodoald reigned for six months.[70]

Aribert reigned for nine years.[71]

Grimoald reigned for nine years.[72]

Berthari reigned for seventeen years.[73]

Cunibert reigned for thirteen years.[74]

Liupert reigned for two years.[75]

Aribert reigned for twelve years.[76]

Ansprad reigned for three months.

Liutprand reigned for thirty-one years and seven months.[77]

Hildeprand reigned for seven months.[78]

Ratchis reigned for four years and nine months.[79]

Aistulf reigned for eight years.[80]

Desiderius reigned with his son Adelchis for seventeen years and three months.[81]

10. Here the kingdom of the Lombards ended and the kingdom of Italy[82] began with the most glorious Charles, king of the Franks. As helper and defender of the lord Peter, the prince of the apostles, he had gone to Italy to demand justice for him.[83]

The desire of gain had not caused Charles to go, but he became Peter's helper as he was good, pious, and compassionate. Though he might have destroyed everything, he became clement and indulgent. Because he was merciful, he bestowed on the Lombards the laws of their homeland, adding some when he believed they were necessary for the Lombards. He forgave the wrongdoings of innumerable men who had incessantly acted against him.[84] For this reason the Almighty God multiplied his riches a hundredfold.

---

[75] Liupert (700-701).
[76] Aribert II (701-712).
[77] Liutprand (712-744).
[78] Hildeprand (744).
[79] Ratchis (744-749).
[80] Aistulf (749-756).
[81] Desiderius (756-774).
[82] In this period the kingdom of Italy only included present-day North Italy and Tuscany.
[83] Charlemagne ended the kingdom of the Lombards by conquering their capital, Pavia, in 774.
[84] For Charlemagne's policy in Italy, see the introduction (section 1: *Carolingian Italy*).

Postquam Italiam coepit, Spaniam suos terminos posuit; deinde Saxoniam perdomuit. Post Baivariam[a] dominator existet et super innumerabiles gentes eius timor irruit.

Ad ultimum vero, ut dignus fuit, imperii honor adeptus est coronam imperii, dignitates Romanę potestatis accepit, factus est domni Petri apostoli subditissimus filius et eius facultates ab inimicis defensabat.

[11.] Post hęc autem omnia regnum Italię tradidit magno et glorioso filio suo domno Pippino magno regi et sicut omnipotens Deus patri[b] concessit fortitudinis gratiam, ita et in filio habundavit.

Per quem Tratia provincia una cum Abaris ad Francorum servitutem est redacta. Illi qui ab inicio malorum stirpe progeniti inimici ęcclesiarum, persecutores christianorum semper fuerunt, per isto, ut diximus, domno Pippino seu et patri suo solatium supradicti Abari sunt evacuati et superati et sanctae aecclesię defensatę et multa vasa sanctorum, quae illi crudeles et impii rapuerunt, per istum defensatorem sunt ad propriam reversa.

Deinde Beneventana provincia, ut digni fuerunt, suę prevaricationis sacramenti, cives eorum igne sunt exanimati[c] et consumpti et populus eorum capitalem subierunt sentenciam.

Post haec et Beowinidis cum exercitu suo perrexit eamque vastavit et populos terrę eius predavit et captivos adduxit.

Igitur Corsicam insulam a Mauris oppressam suo iussu eiusque exercitus liberavit.

Praesentem diem per eius adiutorium splenduit Italia, sicut fecit antiquissimis diebus. Leges et ubertas et quietudinem habuit per domni nostri merita, prestante domino nostro Ihesu Christo. Amen.

[a]   Bavariam *Waitz Azzara.* [b]   *G erases* s *after* patri. patris *Waitz Azzara.* [c]   examinati G. exanimati *Waitz Azzara.*

[85]   In reality, Charlemagne's attempt in 778 to expand his dominion to Spain was unsuccessful. During the retreat, the Basques destroyed the rearguard of his army at Roncesvalles in the Pyrenees. In the following years his son Louis the Pious was able to conquer some territories corresponding roughly to present-day Catalonia. Riché, *The Carolingians*, pp. 115-116; Barbero, *Charlemagne*, pp. 57-61.

[86]   The war to subdue Saxony was the longest and the most difficult of all the wars Charlemagne fought. Riché, *The Carolingians*, pp. 102-107; Barbero, *Charlemagne*, pp. 44-53.

[87]   Charlemagne annexed Bavaria when the Duke of the Bavarians, Tassilo, attempted to free himself of Frankish tutelage. Riché, *The Carolingians*, pp. 101-102; Barbero, *Charlemagne*, pp. 63-65.

[88]   Pope Leo III crowned Charlemagne emperor on Christmas day 800.

After taking Italy, he set the boundaries of his territories in Spain;[85] then he subdued Saxony.[86] Afterwards he became lord of Bavaria,[87] and the fear of him came upon innumerable peoples.

But at last, because he was worthy of the imperial office, he acquired the imperial crown, obtained all the dignities of Roman power, became the most dutiful son of lord Peter, the apostle, and defended Peter's properties from his enemies.[88]

11. After all these things, he handed over the kingdom of Italy to his great and glorious son, lord Pippin, the great king, and, as the Almighty God granted the father the gift of fortitude, so did it abound in the son.[89]

Through Pippin the province of Thrace and the Avars were brought into subjection to the Franks. As we have said, to his own great comfort and that of his father, the lord Pippin expelled and overcame the aforementioned Avars, who, sprung from a stock that is the root of all evil, had always been enemies of the churches and persecutors of the Christians. The holy churches were defended and many holy vessels, which those cruel and impious men had carried off, were brought back home by the same defender.[90]

Then, as they deserved for breaking their oath, the inhabitants of the Beneventan province underwent the capital sentence and their cities were destroyed and burned down.[91]

After this, Pippin also went against the Beowinidis with his army, ravaged their land, despoiled the people of that land and carried them captive back with him.

Then, by his order, his army liberated the island of Corsica which was oppressed by the Moors.[92]

At the present day, thanks to his help, Italy shines as she did in the most ancient days. She has laws, abundance, and quietness thanks to the merits of our lord and the will of our Lord Jesus Christ. Amen.

[89] Pippin became king of the Lombards in 781 at about the age of four and ruled the kingdom of Italy until his death in 810. Barbero, *Charlemagne*, pp. 37-38.

[90] Pippin's victorious campaign against the Avars, who lived in an area corresponding roughly to present-day Hungary, occurred in 796. Charlemagne's biographer Einhard emphasized that in the war against the Avars the Franks obtained a huge booty. Einhard, *Vita Karoli Magni*, ch. 13. For a description of this expedition, see the poem *King Pippin's Victory over the Avars* in this volume.

[91] Charlemagne and his son Pippin tried to subdue the Lombard principality of Benevento several times, but never succeeded. Cf. Bertolini, *Carlomagno e Benevento*; Gasparri, *Il ducato e il principato di Benevento*, pp. 110-112.

[92] According to the *Annales regni Francorum*, this expedition occurred in 806. The Muslims however continued to be a serious threat to the inhabitants of Corsica. The Frankish Annals describe Moorish raids in 807 and 809 and narrate that the Muslims reoccupied the island in 810.

ANDREAE BERGOMENSIS HISTORIA
ANDREAS OF BERGAMO, HISTORY

[ANDREAE BERGOMENSIS HISTORIA]

[1.] <Longobardorum[a] gesta, unum volumen, sex tamen libros, a Paulo viro philosopho contesta et per ordinem narrata invenimus. Exinde pauca de multis in hac adbrevatione contexere nisi sumus et sub eadem hystoriola in quantum Deo auxiliante summatimque sermonem exinde adtrahere conati sumus scribere.

In septentrionali plaga Europae, in finibus Germaniae fere, insula est nomine Scatinavia. In qua propter multitudinem populorum legimus populum illum in tres partes esse sorte divisum; et pars tercia, cui sors cecidit, Winoli vocati sunt. Positis super se ducibus Hibor et Agio germanis cum matre Gambara, egressi de Scatinavia, venerunt in regionem quae appellatur Scoringa. Ubi per aliquot[b] annos consederunt. Erant ipsi Winoli iuvenili etate, barba florida et pro quod plures videntibus estimarentur, etiam eorum feminae crine solutae erga faciem ad similitudinem barbae composuerunt. Unde post hoc Longobardi dicti sunt. Ubi super Wandalos primam victoriam ceperunt.

Pro famis labore de Scoringa egredientes, in Mauringam ingressi sunt. Deinde in Gotholanda venerunt, ubi aliquantum temporis commorati sunt. Mortuis interea Ibor et Agione, constituerunt super se Longobardi primum regem, Agimund nomine. Hic rexit Longobardos annos XXXIII. Deinde venerunt ad quoddam flumen ubi Lamisio cum una amazone pugnavit et vicit.

Transierunt eundem flumen. Cum ad ulteriores terras pervenissent, ubi quasi fidentes per negligentiam resoluti, noctu, dum cuncta quiescerent, super eos Bulgares irruentes, plures ex eis occiderunt, etiam regem Agilmund interimunt.

Congregati qui remanserunt Lamisionem super se regem constituunt et super Bulgares vindicta ulcisci cupiebant. Sicut et fecerunt. Ex illo iam tempore Longobardi audatiores effecti sunt.

Defuncto Lamisione, regnavit pro eo Lethu annis XL. Eodem[c] mortuo reliquit regnum Hildeoc, filio suo. Hoc quoque defuncto, Godioc regnum suscepit. Venerunt exinde in Rugulanda et ibi aliquanti temporis commorati sunt, quia fertilis erat. Mortuo Godioc, successit Claffo, filius suus. Eo defuncto, Tato, eius filius, ascendit ad regnum. Egressi de Rugulanda, habitaverunt in campis patentibus per annos tres. Ubi pugnaverunt contra Herulos, victoria patrata. Et sic omnis Herulorum virtus concidit, ut ex illo tempore ultra super se regem omnino non haberent. Mortuo Tatone, Wacho regnavit. Qui[d] super Suabos irruit eosque suo dominio subiugavit. Defuncto igitur Wachone, Walthari, suo filio, regnum reliquit. Hoc quoque defuncto, regnavit pro eo Audoin.

---

[a]   Quidam Andreas scribit hanc adbrevatio. Longobardorum *B*. [b] *B adds* o *to* aliqut *interlineally*. [c] Eidem *Waitz*. [d] *B adds* regnavit. Qui *interlineally*.

[1]   Paul the Deacon, *Historia Langobardorum*, I, 1.
[2]   Paul the Deacon, *Historia Langobardorum*, I, 2. The passage is not clear as Andreas of Bergamo summarizes too much. According to Paul the Deacon, because Scandinavia was overpopulated, the inhabitants were divided into three parts and it was determined by lot who had to leave the island.

ANDREAS OF BERGAMO, HISTORY

1. We found the deeds of the Lombards collected and narrated in an orderly way by the learned Paul in a volume subdivided into six books. In this summary we have then tried to put together a few of those many events and, as much as God has helped us, we have attempted to write them briefly in this little history.

In the northern region of Europe, on the boundaries of Germany, there is an island called Scandinavia.[1] We read that on that island the population was divided into three parts by lot because of the great multitude of peoples; those of the third part, chosen by lot, were called Winili.[2] Having elected as their leaders the brothers Ibor and Aio and their mother Gambara,[3] they left Scandinavia and arrived in a region that is called Scoringa, where they lived for some years.

The Winili were young and had flowing beards, and, in order to appear numerous to those who saw them, even their women untied their hair and arranged it on their faces like a beard. For this reason they were thereafter called Lombards.[4] In that place they obtained their first victory against the Vandals.[5]

Because of a famine, they left Scoringa and entered Mauringa. Then they went to Gotholand,[6] where they remained for a while. As Ibor and Aio had meanwhile died, the Lombards established over them their first king; his name was Agilmund. He ruled the Lombards for thirty-three years.[7] They then went to a certain river where Lamissio battled an Amazon and defeated her.[8]

The Lombards crossed that river and arrived in the lands beyond it. There, as they had become too confident and were negligently relaxed, the Bulgarians attacked them at night while everybody was sleeping, slaying many of them and killing King Agilmund as well.

The survivors gathered and established Lamissio as king over them. They wished to revenge themselves against the Bulgarians. So they did. From that time onwards the Lombards became more audacious.[9]

After Lamissio's death, Lethu reigned in his place for forty years. When he died, he left the kingdom to his son Hildeoc. He having died too, Godioc took up the kingdom.[10] The Lombards then went to Rugiland, where they remained for a while because it was fertile.[11] At Godioc's death, his son Claffo succeeded him. He having died, Claffo's son Tato rose to kingship. After leaving Rugiland, the Lombards lived for three years in the

---

[3] Paul the Deacon, *Historia Langobardorum*, I, 3.
[4] «Langobardi» derives from «lang bart» which means «long beard.»
[5] Paul the Deacon, *Historia Langobardorum*, I, 7-10.
[6] Golanda in Paul the Deacon, *Historia Langobardorum*, I, 13.
[7] Paul the Deacon, *Historia Langobardorum*, I, 7-14.
[8] Paul the Deacon, *Historia Langobardorum*, I, 15.
[9] Paul the Deacon, *Historia Langobardorum*, I, 16-18.
[10] Paul the Deacon, *Historia Langobardorum*, I, 18.
[11] Paul the Deacon, *Historia Langobardorum*, I, 19.

Hic habebat filium, Alboin nomine. Qui, cum Gepidi super Longobardos irruerent, magna eos strage stravit. Mortuo Audoin, Alboin, filius suus, in regno successit. Qui sibi in coniugio sociavit Clodisindam, filiam Lotharii regis Francorum. Et cum Avaris perpetuam pacem fecit. Et Cunimund regem Gepidorum superavit; et tantam adepti sunt predam, ut iam ad amplissimas pervenirent divitias. Gepidi vero a Longobardis subiecti sunt. Lombardi vero in Pannonia habitaverunt et longe lateque nomen eorum percrebuit.

Narsis, qui tunc preerat Rome Italieque, bellum adversus Totilam regem Gothorum preparans, legatos ad Alboin dirigit, ut ei contra Gothos auxilium ministraret[a]. Tunc Alboin electam manum per mare Adriaticum dirigit. Qui in Italiam transvecti, sociati Romanis, pugnam inierunt cum Gothis. Quibus ad internitionem pariter cum Totila rege suo deletis, Longobardi honorati multis muneribus victores ad propria remearunt. Omni tempore quo Longobardi in Pannonia residerunt Romanis adiutores fuerunt.>

Narsis[b] patritius Romanorum bella sustinuit[c] et eos semper defendit. Invidia Romani contra eum pertulit; ad Iustinianum[d] imperatorem acusaverunt[e]. Qui et ipse augustus et Sophia, uxor eius, mandans ei, quia eunuchus erat, ut ad se veniret et lanas in genitio per pensione dividere. Narsis vero patritius sic ei mandans, non tantum[f] se lana dividere, sed etiam talem telam orditurum, quale ipsa dum viveret deponere non possit.

Legatos Narsis ad Langobardos mittens et pommorum genera vel reliqua dignitate transmittens, ut animos eorum amabilis facerent, quatenus in Italia[g] venirent et plena eas absque pugna perciperent.

Langobardi mox ut audiunt, gavisi sunt gaudio. Panonia vero amicis suis Avarorum gens comendaverunt, que possessas habebant per annos XLII. Cum uxoribus et natis et omnia quae habebant exientes de Panonia mense aprile, per indictione prima, alium die post Pasca Domini, qui fuit kalendis aprilis, cum iam Domini incarnatione anni quingenti sexaginta octo essent evoluti. Igitur Langobardi introierunt Italia per Foroiulanorum terminum.

[a] nimistraret B. ministraret *Waitz.* [b] *In V, Andreas's work starts from this word.* [c] sustituit V. sustinuit *Waitz.* [d] *V corrects* Iustitianum *to* Iustinianum. [e] *V corrects* acusant *to* acusaverunt. [f] *V writes* tam *with an abbreviation mark above* m. tantum *Waitz.* [g] *V adds* lia *to* Ita *interlineally.*

[12] Paul the Deacon, *Historia Langobardorum*, I, 20.
[13] Paul the Deacon, *Historia Langobardorum*, I, 21.
[14] Paul the Deacon, *Historia Langobardorum*, I, 22.
[15] Paul the Deacon, *Historia Langobardorum*, I, 23.
[16] The correct name is Clothar.
[17] Paul the Deacon, *Historia Langobardorum*, I, 27. In reality Paul the Deacon says that the name of Alboin became famous everywhere.
[18] Paul the Deacon, *Historia Langobardorum*, II, 1.

open plains, where they fought and obtained victory against the Heruls. The power of the Heruls declined to such a degree that thereafter they had no king over them any more.[12] At Tato's death, Wacho reigned. He attacked the Sueves and subjugated them to his dominion.[13] When Wacho passed away, he left the kingdom to his son Walthari. He having died too, Audoin reigned in his place.[14]

Audoin had a son named Alboin. As the Gepids had attacked the Lombards, Alboin routed them with great carnage.[15] At Audoin's death, his son Alboin succeeded him in the kingdom. He married Clothsuinda, daughter of the King of the Franks, Lothar.[16] He made an everlasting peace with the Avars and defeated the King of the Gepids, Cunimund. The Lombards acquired so much loot that they were greatly enriched. The Gepids were subjugated by the Lombards. The Lombards then settled in Pannonia and their fame greatly grew far and wide.[17]

Narses, who was then ruling Rome and Italy and was preparing the war against the King of the Goths, Totila, sent ambassadors to Alboin so that he would help him against the Goths. Alboin then sent a select contingent across the Adriatic Sea. As they arrived in Italy, the Lombards joined the Romans and began to fight against the Goths. When the Goths as well as their King Totila were exterminated, the Lombards, honored with many gifts, returned as victors to their homeland. The Lombards helped the Romans for all the period they lived in Pannonia.[18]

Patrician Narses fought the wars of the Romans and always defended them.[19] The Romans were envious of him and accused him to Emperor Justinian.[20] The Augustus and his wife Sophia sent Narses a message saying that, because he was a eunuch, they would make him come to them and have him work wool in the gynaeceum. Patrician Narses answered her that he would not only work wool for Sophia, but he would also weave her such a web that she could not lay it down as long as she lived.[21]

Narses sent the Lombards messengers and different kinds of fruit and other riches in order to make them eager to come to Italy, which was well supplied with them, and to conquer Italy without fighting.[22]

As soon as they heard that, the Lombards rejoiced greatly and gave Pannonia,[23] which they had owned for forty-two years, to their friends, the people of the Avars.[24] They left Pannonia with their wives, children, and everything they had in the month of April, in the first indiction, on the day after Easter, that was the kalends of April, when 568 years already passed from the incarnation of the Lord.[25] The Lombards entered Italy through the territory of the Friulans.

---

[19] Narses led the Byzantine troops during the last phase of the war in Italy between the Byzantines and the Ostrogoths.

[20] During this period the emperor was Justin II (565-578). Justinian ruled from 527 to 565.

[21] Cf. Paul the Deacon, *Historia Langobardorum*, II, 5, who narrates that the emperor replaced Narses with Longinus.

[22] Cf. Paul the Deacon, *Historia Langobardorum*, II, 5, who does not mention the last detail.

[23] Pannonia corresponds approximately to present-day Hungary.

[24] Cf. Paul the Deacon, *Historia Langobardorum*, II, 8. Paul the Deacon writes Huns, a definition that several medieval authors used for the Avars.

[25] Some scholars believe that the Lombards entered Italy in 569. See, for example, Bertolini, *La data dell'ingresso dei Longobardi in Italia*, pp. 19-61.

Alboin nepoti sui Gisolfi Foroiuli concessit et reliquos[a] nobiles Langobardi. His diebus Langobardi Italia invaserunt, Vincentiam Veronamque et reliquas Veneciarum[b] civitates cepit et per tres annos Ticino possedit. Interim Alboin invasit omnia usque ad Tuscia preter Romam et Ravennam.

Ticinensis vero per tres annos se continentes, per obsides quas dederunt, iam videntes suorum fortia circa se subiugata, Langubardi se tradiderunt.

Pauca vero de multa dicam.

Rex Alboin postquam in Italia tres annos et sex menses regnavit, insidię sue coniuge interemptus est.

Langobardi ex comuni consilio Clef[c] nobilissimum in urb[d] Ticinenssium sibi regem constituerunt. Regnavit anno uno mensibus sex. A puero de suo obsequio gladio iugulatus est.

Post cuius mortem Langobardi per annos X regem non habuerunt, sed sub[e] potestatem ducibus fuerunt.

Post autem annos X elegerunt Autari, Clefoni filius. Autari vero duxit uxorem, Teudelinda nomine, filia Garibaldi Baioariorum rex, sancta et nobilissima. Ipsa edificavit aecclesia sancti Iohanni sita Moditia.

Rex Autari aput Ticinum, venenum, ut tradunt, accepto, moritur, postquam sex regnaverat annos.

Langobardi ex comuni consilio suae regine Teudelindę licentiam tribuerunt, quali[f] ipsa suo sociare voluisset coniugio, tali[g] et illi regem constituisset.

Quid multa? Accepit Agilulf[h] ducem Taurinensium et regnavit annis XXV[i] et mortuus est.

Et regnavit pro eo filio suo Adalovald annos X; de regno eiectus est.

Eius regnum suscepit[j] Arioald et regnavit annos XII et mortuus est.

Regnavit pro eo Rothari, qui edictum Langubardorum conposuit. Reliqua eius dignitatem et fortia et bella quas gessit, nonne hec scripta sunt in cronica[k] Langubardorum, ut supra?

---

[a] reliquis *Waitz.* [b] Venetiarum *Waitz.* [c] Cleb *B Waitz.* [d] urbe *Waitz.* [e] su *V.* sub *Waitz.* [f] *V corrects* qualis *to* quali. [g] *V corrects* talis *to* tali. [h] *V adds* l *to* Agiluf. [i] *V corrects* XXVII *to* XXV. [j] *V corrects* successit *to* succepit. suscepit *Waitz.* [k] coronica *V Waitz.*

[26] Cividale is the modern name of *Forum Iulii*.
[27] Paul the Deacon, *Historia Langobardorum*, II, 9.
[28] Paul the Deacon writes *Venetia* which was the name of the *VIII provincia Venetia et Histria*, created by the Roman Emperor Diocletian at the end of the third century: Azzara, *Venetiae*, pp. 9-69. Paul the Deacon adds that Alboin did not conquer Padua, Monselice, and Mantua. Paul the Deacon, *Historia Langobardorum*, II, 14.
[29] Pavia is the modern name of *Ticinum*. Andreas of Bergamo utilized both this term and *Papia*.
[30] Tuscia corresponds roughly to modern Tuscany and northern Latium.
[31] Paul the Deacon, *Historia Langobardorum*, II, 26.
[32] Paul the Deacon, *Historia Langobardorum*, II, 27.

Alboin gave Cividale[26] and some Lombard nobles to his nephew Gisulf.[27] In those days, the Lombards invaded Italy, took Vicenza, Verona, and other cities of the Venetias,[28] and besieged Ticinum[29] for three years. Meanwhile Alboin conquered everything as far as Tuscia,[30] except Rome and Ravenna.[31]

The Ticinians held out for three years thanks to the hostages they had given. Seeing that their troops had already surrendered, they surrendered to the Lombards.[32]

I will say a few things out of many.

After reigning for three years and six months, King Alboin was killed because of a plot organized by his wife.[33]

By common decision the Lombards elected the most noble Cleph as king in the city of the Ticinians; he reigned for a year and six months.[34] His throat was cut with a sword by a man of his retinue.[35] After his death, the Lombards had no king for ten years, but remained under the rule of the dukes.[36]

After ten years, they elected Authari, Cleph's son.[37] Authari married a woman named Theodelinda, the saintly and most noble daughter of the Bavarians' King Garibald.[38] She built the church of Saint John, located in Monza.[39]

King Authari, as they narrate, died in Ticinum from taking poison after reigning for six years.[40]

By common decision the Lombards gave their queen Theodelinda the permission to marry whomever she wanted and to make him king.

Why should I say more? She took the Duke of the Turinese, Agilulf.[41] He reigned for twenty-five years, then died.[42]

And his son Adaloald reigned in his place for ten years. He was driven out from the kingdom.[43]

Arioald took his kingdom, reigned for twelve years, and died.[44]

In his place reigned Rothari who wrote the Edict of the Lombards.[45] Are not the other things concerning his rule, his strength, and the wars he had made written in the chronicle of the Lombards, like the things mentioned above?[46]

---

[33] Paul the Deacon, *Historia Langobardorum*, II, 28. Alboin died in 572.

[34] Cleph (572-574).

[35] Paul the Deacon, *Historia Langobardorum*, II, 31.

[36] Paul the Deacon, *Historia Langobardorum*, II, 32.

[37] Paul the Deacon, *Historia Langobardorum*, III, 16.

[38] Paul the Deacon, *Historia Langobardorum*, III, 30.

[39] Paul the Deacon, *Historia Langobardorum*, IV, 21.

[40] Paul the Deacon, *Historia Langobardorum*, III, 35. Authari (584-590).

[41] Paul the Deacon, *Historia Langobardorum*, III, 35.

[42] Paul the Deacon, *Historia Langobardorum*, IV, 41. Agilulf (590-616).

[43] Paul the Deacon, *Historia Langobardorum*, IV, 41. Paul the Deacon narrates that Adaloald was a young boy when he succeeded his father and that he was overthrown because he went mad. Adaloald ruled with his mother Theodolinda from 616 to 626.

[44] Paul the Deacon, *Historia Langobardorum*, IV, 41-42, who says that Arioald ruled for ten years (626-636).

[45] Rothari had the Lombard laws written down. Paul the Deacon, *Historia Langobardorum*, IV, 42.

[46] Paul the Deacon, *Historia Langobardorum*, IV, 45.

Regnavit Rotari annos XVI et mortuus est. Rodoaldi filio suo regnum reliquid. Rodoald vero dum uxore cuiusdam stuprasset, ab eodem interfectus est, postquam V regnaverat annis septemque diebus.

Huic successit in regno Aripert; regnavit annis novem et mortuus est. Reliquid regnum duobus filii sui, Pertarit et Gudiperti. Inter ipsis fratres malis hominibus discordia facientes in tantum, ut alterium regnum invaderent.

Grimoald Beneventanorum suorum ducem per fraudulenter missum eorum mandatum veniens, Gudiperto gladio interemit, expleto anno post mortem patris et sex menses. Pertarit fuga aripuit, Grimoald regnum accepit.

Multa quidem eius storiole continet, sed pauca in hac adbreviationem conscribam. Hic in aedicto Langubardorum novem conposuit capitula; regnavit annos nove[a] et mortuus est. Reliquid regnum Garibaldi, filio suo.

Pertarit vero, unde iam diximus, qui fuga lapsus erat, egressus de Galia navem ascendit, ad Britaniam insolam ad regnum Saxonum transmeare; et dum pelago navigasset, divinus nuntius eidem ad ripam clamans et dixit: «Revertere, Pertarit, in terra tua, quia tertia die est hodie, quod Grimoald defunctus est.»

Quid plura?

Reversus est, et gratanter ab[b] Langubardis susceptus et ad regna gubernacula eum constituerunt mense tertio post mortem Grimoaldi.

Regnavit Pertarit annos decem et septem et mortuus est. Cuniperti, suum filium, regnum reliquid. Multa quidem eius storiole scripta invenimus.

Contra Halahis tirrannum fatigatione sustentus; sed Cunipert triumphum victoriae <obtinuit> cum exultatione Dei. Italia regnavit post mortem patris annos XII. In campo Coronate, ubi bellum contra Alahis gessit, in honore beati Georghi[c] martiris monasterium[d] construxit.

Reliquid regnum Liutperti, filio suo. Surrexit contra eum Aripert et vivum comprehendit; non post multos dies in balneo vita privavit.

Regnavit Aripert annis XII. In flumen Ticinum ab aquis negatus est.

Ansprand eius regnum aripuit; regnavit menses tres.

Reliquid regnum Liutprandi, filio suo.

---

[a] novem *Waitz.* [b] ad *V Waitz.* [c] Georgii *Waitz.* [d] *V adds* u *above the second* o *of* monasteriom.

[47] Rothari (636-652).
[48] Paul the Deacon, *Historia Langobardorum*, IV, 48. Rodoald actually ruled for only five months (652-653). The confusion between years and days is present in Paul the Deacon's work as well.
[49] Paul the Deacon, *Historia Langobardorum*, IV, 48.
[50] Aripert (653-661).
[51] Paul the Deacon, *Historia Langobardorum*, IV, 51.
[52] Paul the Deacon, *Historia Langobardorum*, IV, 51. Godepert (661-662).
[53] Paul the Deacon, *Historia Langobardorum*, V, 1-3.
[54] Paul the Deacon, *Historia Langobardorum*, V, 5, 7, 9, 10, 16, 19-22, 25-29, 32, 33.
[55] Paul the Deacon reports only that Grimoald added a few chapters to the Edict. Paul the Deacon, *Historia Langobardorum*, V, 33. The information provided by Andreas of Bergamo is correct. See *Grimualdi Leges*, pp. 129-135.

Rothari reigned for sixteen years and died.[47] He left the kingdom to his son Rodoald. As Rodoald had raped the wife of a certain man, he was killed by this man after reigning for five years and seven days.[48]

Aripert succeeded him in the kingdom.[49] He reigned for nine years and died.[50] He left the kingdom to his two sons, Perctarit and Godepert.[51] Some evil men created discord between the two brothers to a such degree that each invaded the kingdom of the other.

Deceptively invited by a messenger of theirs, the Duke of the Beneventans, Grimoald, came to them and killed Godepert with a sword, one year and six months after the death of their father.[52] Perctarit fled and Grimoald took the kingdom.[53]

There are many stories about him,[54] but I will write a few of them in this summary. He composed nine chapters in the Edict of the Lombards.[55] He reigned for nine years and died.[56] He left the kingdom to his son Garibald.[57]

Perctarit, who, as we have already said, had fled, departed from Gaul, and embarked on a ship to pass over to the island of Britain, to the kingdom of the Saxons. And while he was sailing through the sea, a divine messenger called him from the shore and told him: «Perctarit, return to your land, because today is the third day since Grimoald died.»[58]

Why should I say more?

Perctarit went back and was received by the Lombards with joy; they put him at the head of the kingdom three months after Grimoald's death.[59]

Perctarit reigned for seventeen years and died.[60] He left the kingdom to his son Cunipert.[61] We have found many written accounts about him.

He underwent many troubles from the tyrant Alahis, but, by God's will, Cunipert obtained the triumph of the victory.[62] After the death of his father, he reigned in Italy for twelve years.[63] He constructed a monastery in honor of the blessed martyr George in the plain of Coronate[64] where he had fought against Alahis.[65]

He left his kingdom to his son Liutpert. Aripert rebelled against Liutpert, captured him alive[66] and, after not many days, deprived him of his life in a bath.[67]

Aripert reigned for twelve years.[68] He drowned in the river Ticinum.[69]

Ansprand took his kingdom; he reigned for three months.

He left his kingdom to his son Liutprand.[70]

[56] Grimoald (662-671).
[57] Paul the Deacon, *Historia Langobardorum*, V, 33.
[58] Paul the Deacon, *Historia Langobardorum*, V, 33.
[59] Paul the Deacon, *Historia Langobardorum*, V, 33.
[60] Perctarit (672-688).
[61] Paul the Deacon, *Historia Langobardorum*, V, 37.
[62] Paul the Deacon, *Historia Langobardorum*, V, 38-41.
[63] Cunipert (688-700).
[64] Coronate d'Adda is near Como (North Italy).
[65] Paul the Deacon, *Historia Langobardorum*, VI, 17.
[66] Paul the Deacon, *Historia Langobardorum*, VI, 19.
[67] Paul the Deacon, *Historia Langobardorum*, VI, 20. Liutpert (700-701).
[68] Paul the Deacon, *Historia Langobardorum*, VI, 35. Aripert II (701-712).
[69] Paul the Deacon, *Historia Langobardorum*, VI, 35.
[70] Paul the Deacon, *Historia Langobardorum*, VI, 35.

Fuit autem Liutprand multae sapientiae, clemens, pudicus, orator, pervigil, elemosinis largus. Legem quidem Langubardorum ampliavit et in edicti corpore conscribere iussit. Regnavit annis treginta et uno septemque mensibus et mortuus est.

[2.] Haec autem superscripta summationem cui incredibile aparet, relegat[a] tota historia Langubardorum; omnia hec ibi veraciter invenit, in quantum hic scripta sunt et plures multa illuc invenitur nobilitatem eorum vel victorie et bella quas gesserunt.

Haec autem adbreviationem superscripta, in quantum potui, exerpsi[b] ego[c] Andreas, licet indignus, presbyter de historiae Langubardorum; et quorum hic super continet eorum historiae minime ad nostram pervenit notitiam, sed in quantum per seriem litterarum seu per antiquos homines potui veraciter[d] scire, hic scrivere delectatus sum.

[3.] Defuncto itaque Liutprand, Ratchis electus a Langubardis rex elevatus est; regnavit annos V et posuit in edicto capituli octo[e].

Hoc quoque defuncto, Aistolfi, germano suo, regnum reliquid.

Eorumque factis retinere non possumus; sed quantum audivimus, audaces uterque fuerunt et suorum tempore Langubardi a nulla gens terruerunt. Regnavit annos octo et posuit in edicto capitula XIII[f] et mortuus est.

Desiderii regnum reliquid. Qui cum regnasset annos tres, suus filius, Adelchis nomine, ex consensu Langubardorum sub se regem constituit; sub quorum tempore in aliquantum pax fuit.

Quidam et etiam filiam suam, Berterad[g] nomine, Karoli, Pipini filius, Francorum rex, coniugio sotiavit; alia vero filia, Liuperga nomine, sotiavit Taxiloni Baioariorum rex. Et pax firmissima ex utraque partis firmaverunt, sed minime conservaverunt.

Causa autem discordiae ista fuit. Habebat Carolus suus germanus maior se Karlemannus nomine, ferebundus et pessimus; contra Carolum iracundus surrexit, eum iurare fecit, ut ipsa Berterad[h] ultra non haberet coniuge.

Quid multa?

---

[a] relega V. relegat *Waitz.* [b] *V adds* p *to* exersi. [c] *V erases* de *before* ego. [d] *V adds* ci *to* verater. [e] *V adds* et posuit in edicto capituli octo *interlineally.* [f] *V adds* et posuit in edicto capitula XIII *interlineally.* [g] *V writes* Berterad *on an erased word.* [h] *V writes* Berterad, *correcting* rte *on erased letters and adding* rad *interlineally.*

[71] Paul the Deacon, *Historia Langobardorum*, VI, 58.

[72] Paul the Deacon does not mention this detail. For the laws issued by Liutprand, see *Livtprandi Leges*, pp. 137-235.

[73] Liutprand (712-744).

[74] Paul the Deacon's *Historia Langobardorum*.

[75] This was a common topos among medieval authors. Curtius, *European Literature and the Latin Middle Ages*, pp. 83-85.

[76] Liutprand was succeeded by his nephew Hildeprand. After eight months of rule, Hildeprand was deposed and the Duke of Friuli, Ratchis, ascended to the throne. Wickham, *Early Medieval Italy*, p. 45.

[77] Ratchis (744-749).

[8] Ratchis added fourteen chapters. See *Ratchis Leges*, pp. 233-247.

[79] Ratchis actually retired to the monastery of Montecassino, probably as a result of a coup. Wickham, *Early Medieval Italy*, p. 45.

[80] For Aistulf's rule, see the introduction, "Carolingian Italy."

Liutprand was very learned, merciful, virtuous, eloquent, tireless worshipper, and generous in alms.[71] He augmented the laws of the Lombards and ordered them to be written in the collection of the Edict.[72] He reigned for thirty-one years and seven months and died.[73]

2. For whom this seems incredible, the above-written summary contains all the *History of the Lombards*.[74] There you can find all these things truthfully written as well as it has been done here; many other things can be found there about their nobility and victories and the wars they waged.

The things written above in this summary, I, the priest Andreas, although unworthy,[75] took from the *History of the Lombards* in so far as I could. The things written below did not come to our knowledge from their histories, but I truthfully learned them from some letters and some old men and I have enjoyed writing them here.

3. Liutprand having then died, Ratchis was elected by the Lombards and made king.[76] He reigned for five years[77] and put eight chapters in the Edict.[78]

He having died too, he left the kingdom to his brother Aistulf.[79]

We cannot report their deeds, but, in so far as we have heard, they were both brave and in their times the Lombards were not afraid of any people.[80]

Aistulf reigned for eight years,[81] put thirteen chapters in the Edict,[82] and died.

He left the kingdom to Desiderius.[83] After reigning for three years, with the agreement of the Lombards, he appointed his son as king under him. Their times were somewhat peaceful.

Desiderius also gave in marriage one of his daughters, named Berterad,[84] to the King of the Franks, Charles,[85] Pippin's son.[86] He gave another daughter, named Liutperga, in marriage to the King of the Bavarians, Tassilo.[87] Both parties signed a very strong peace, but they did not preserve it at all.

This was the cause of the discord. Charles had an elder brother named Carloman,[88] a terrible and evil man. The choleric Carloman rose against Charles and had him swear that he would not have Berterad as his wife anymore.

Why should I say more?

---

[81]   Aistulf (749-756).

[82]   Aistulf added twenty-two chapters to the Edict. See *Ahistulfi Leges*, pp. 279-291.

[83]   Upon Aistulf's death, Ratchis tried to take possession of the Lombard crown, but Desiderius was able to obtain the support of the Franks and the pope, who convinced Ratchis to go back to Montecassino. Wickham, *Early Medieval Italy*, p. 46.

[84]   Contemporary sources do not mention the name of Desiderius's daughter, as if there were a sort of *damnatio memoriae*. The name Ermengard is a modern invention. On this topic, see Barbero, *Charlemagne*, p. 41; Gasparri, *I Longobardi tra oblio e memoria*, pp. 263-269, and the introduction, p. 37.

[85]   Charlemagne.

[86]   Pippin III, son of Charles Martel, was king of the Franks from 751 to 768.

[87]   In reality Tassilo was duke of the Bavarians. Cf. Depreux, *Tassilon III et le roi des Francs*, pp. 23-73. This marriage, celebrated in 763, was arranged to mark the alliance of the Lombards with the Bavarians against the Franks. Tassilo, in fact, wished to get rid of the Frankish tutelage. In general, on Desiderius's marriage policy, see Nelson, *Making a Difference*, and Gasparri, *Il passaggio dai Longobardi ai Carolingi*, p. 29. Rosamond McKitterick has hypothesized that Charlemagne never married the Lombard princess. McKitterick, *Charlemagne*, pp. 86-88.

[88]   According to the *Annales qui dicunt Einhardi*, year 769, Charles was the elder.

Remisit eam Ticino, unde dudum eam duxerat. Mater vero eorum hęc separatio audiens, Carlemanni filii sui blasphemiam intulit, oculorum cecitate perculsus est, cum periculo vita finivit.

[4.] His temporibus aecclesiae Romane Leo papa regebat et oppressiones a Langubardis multa patiebat. Ex sede propria exiens Francia repetavit cum multis sapientissimis ars litterarum, maxime cantores.

Francorum gens haec audiens, magno gavisi sunt gaudio. Karolus cum suis obviam eius adventum pedibus venerunt, ei obtimum consedere locum fecerunt civitatem, quae[a] dicitur Meties. Qui ibidem per annos tres resedentes, tanta quidem dignitatem cantores ibi fecerunt, ut per totam Franciam Italiamque pene multe civitates ornamentum[b] aecclesie usque hodie consonant.

Papa vero probata gens Francorum astuti et nobiles, consilium eorum dedit, ut super Langubardos venirent, Italiam possiderent; ipse vero ad suam sede Romanae eclesie[c] remeavit.

[5.] Karulus siquidem vero, adnitentibus suis, oblitus est tantorum benignitatis, quod ei Desiderius rex tribuit. Congregata multorum Francorum exercitum, ex iussu apostolici sacramenta irrita[d] facta sunt. Italia contro[e] Langobardos veniens, divino iudicio terror in Langubardus inruit, absque grave pugna Italiam invasit, anno Desiderii octavo decimo et Adelchis XV, indictione XII, cum iam CCV anni essent evoluti, postquam Langubardi Italia ingressi sunt.

Desiderio vero eodem tempore mortuus est. Adelchis, eius filius, navium preparans, ultra mare egressus est.

Tantaque tribulatio fuit in Italia, alii gladio interempti, alii fame perculsi, aliis bestiis occisi, ut vix pauci remanerent in vicos vel in civitates.

---

[a] *V writes* q *with an abbreviation mark.* qui *Waitz.* [b] *V writes* ornamentum *twice.* [c] *V adds* eclesie *interlineally.* [d] *V adds* irrita *interlineally.* [e] contra *Waitz.*

[89] Charlemagne's biographer Einhard states that he does not know the motive for the repudiation. Einhard, *Vita Karoli Magni*, ch. 18.

[90] Carloman died at the end of 771. Einhard reports that there was always harmony between the two brothers although some of Carloman's partisans plotted to break the alliance between them. Einhard, *Vita Karoli Magni*, ch. 3. For the relationships between Charles and Carloman, see Barbero, *Charlemagne*, pp. 22-24.

[91] In reality, it was Pope Hadrian who, shortly after Carloman's death, in January 771, asked the Frankish sovereign to intervene in the conflict, but the pontiff never actually crossed the Alps. It was Pope Stephen II who made that trip at the end of 753 when the ruler of the Franks was Pippin III. Leo III traversed the mountains in 799, but with the aim of obtaining Charlemagne's help against the Romans who had made an attempt on the pope's life. Noble, *The Republic of St Peter*, pp. 292-293; Barbero, *Charlemagne*, pp. 19, 27-28, 89-91.

[92] According to the eleventh-century Italian *Cronaca di Novalesa*, III, 6, God indicated Charlemagne should go to Italy.

[93] In Spring 773, Charlemagne gathered an army near Geneva, bypassed Lombard defenses on the Alps and entered the Po valley. The Lombard army, weakened by many defections, disbanded and King Desiderius took refuge in Pavia, the capital of the Lombard kingdom, that fell in June 774. Wickham, *Early Middle Ages*, p. 47;

He sent her back to Ticinum whence he had earlier taken her.[89] When their mother heard this, she cursed her son Carloman. Struck by blindness, he ended his life badly.[90]

4. In those times Pope Leo governed the Roman Church. He suffered great violence from the Lombards. He left his see and went to Francia with many men very learned in letters, mainly cantors.

The people of the Franks rejoiced very much upon hearing that. Charles and his men went to the pope on foot and had him reside in a very good place, the city called Metz. The pope stayed there for three years and the cantors acquired there such great fame that their chanting has resounded as an ornament of the Church to the present day in almost all the cities of Francia and Italy.

Because the pope judged the people of the Franks to be astute and noble, he suggested that they attack the Lombards and take possession of Italy. He then returned to his see in the Church of Rome.[91]

5. With the agreement of his men, Charles forgot the many good things that King Desiderius had given to him. Oaths were invalidated by order of the pope and Charles gathered a large army of Franks and went to Italy against the Lombards.[92] Through divine will, terror seized the Lombards and Charles invaded Italy without a serious battle in the eighteenth year of Desiderius's rule, the fifteenth year of Adelchis, in the twelfth indiction, when two hundred five years had already elapsed since the Lombards had entered Italy.[93]

In that time Desiderius died.[94] His son Adelchis prepared some ships and went beyond the sea.[95]

There was a great distress in Italy — some were killed by the sword, others struck by hunger, others killed by wild animals — to a such degree that few remained in the villages and in the cities.[96]

Barbero, *Charlemagne*, pp. 28-31. Agnellus of Ravenna, *Liber pontificalis ecclesiae Ravennatis*, ch. 160, recounts that the Archbishop of Ravenna, Leo, showed the Franks the way to Italy through one of his deacons. On the other hand, the *Cronaca di Novalesa*, III, 9-14, narrates that Charlemagne managed to avoid the Lombard defenses in the Alps thanks to the help of a Lombard minstrel.

[94] The *Cronaca di Novalesa*, III, 14, relates that Charlemagne was able to enter Pavia because Desiderius's daughter, who was in love with the Frankish king, opened a gate of the city to him, and that Charlemagne had the Lombard king blinded. This latter detail is also reported by the tenth-century *Chronicon Salernitanum*, ch. 9.

[95] According to the *Annales regni Francorum*, year 774, Adelchis escaped to Constantinople. In 787, with the support of the Byzantines, Desiderius's son landed in southern Italy, but was defeated by the Beneventan Lombards. Bertolini, *Adelchi, re dei Longobardi*, pp. 258-259. The *Cronaca di Novalesa*, III, 21-22, recounts that Adelchis secretly went back to Italy and that he ate at Charlemagne's table in disguise giving proof of great strength.

[96] Other sources emphasize that the Frankish invasion provoked serious damage to the Lombard kingdom. For example, in a document composed shortly before the fall of Pavia, it is stated that they were living in a period of «barbarous events.» The new ruler understood that the situation was grave. In 776 Charlemagne ordered that the contracts of the people, who, «forced by hunger,» sold themselves into slavery or sold their possessions at reduced prices, be annulled. Fumagalli, *Il regno italico*, pp. 3-5; Barbero, *Charlemagne*, pp. 33-36; Cammarosano, *Nobili e re*, p. 102.

[6.] Foroiulanorum dux tunc[a] temporis Rotcausus preerat et in Vincentia Gaidus. Qui auditu Francorum devastatione et eius adventum quod in Foroiuli properaret, congregatisque ut poterant, obviam eorum ad ponte qui dicitur Liquentia exierunt et ibidem magna strages de Francis fecerunt.

Karolus vero haec audiens, mandans eorum fidelitatis fidem suscepturos et honoraturos. Rotcausus et Gaidus ducibus cum nobilis Foroiulanorum consilio inito, ut se viriliter contendissent[b]. Erat quidem ex ipsis, cui iam munera Caroli excecaverat cor, tale dedit consilio: «Quid faciemus? Quomodo eorum resistere[c] possumus? Capud non habemus. Regem confortationis nostrae iam devictus est. Eamus eorum fidelitate; bene nobis erit.» Quid dicam? Ut obtabat, fecerunt. Et tamen eorum Carolus servavit honorem.

[7.] Igitur, subiugata et ordinata Italia, ad Romam perrexit; ibidem palatium construxit. Deinde terra[d] pacificata et sacramenta data, Pipinus suus filius regendum Italia concessit. Ipse vero Carolus post aliquantum tempus Francia reversus est, obsides[e] quoque ducentes secum quicquid Italia maiores nati et nobiliores erant. Post non multum tempus ab eodem Carolus meruerunt et honorati sunt ab ipso, ad suam reversi sunt patria.

Pipinus vero, vivente patre, defunctus est. Reliquid filium, Bernardum[f] nomine, cui Karolus Italia concessit.

Qui cum esset penuriae famis Italia[g] preucupata, subito ut Bernardo regnum accepit, dignitatem ubertatemque advenit et sic fuit dum ipse regnavit. Karolus autem, qui cum sex annos in Frantia et postquam in Italia ingressus est XLI annos regnasset, defunctus est in pace senesque aetatis et plenum dierum. Qui per eum nomen Francorum longe lateque percrebuit, sicut est nunc usque ad hodiernum diem.

Reliquid sedem suam in Francia Hludowici, filio suo. Iste incipit vocare imperator ex Francorum genus.

---

[a]   *V adds* u *above the* e *of* tenc. [b] contendsset *V, which writes* dsset *on erased letters.* contenisset *Waitz.*
[c] *V adds* si *to* restere *interlineally.* [d] *V adds* terra *interlineally.* [e] *V corrects* obsedes *to* obsidis. [f] *V writes* um
above o *of* Bernardo. [g] Italiae *Waitz.*

[97]   The *Annales regni Francorum*, year 776, state that Charlemagne appointed Rotcausus duke. On this duke, see Gasparri, *I duchi longobardi*, pp. 71-72.
[98]   Andreas's *Historia* is the only source mentioning Gaidus. Cf. Gasparri, *I duchi longobardi*, p. 56.
[99]   The Livenza is actually a northeastern Italian river.
[100]   At the end of 775, Pope Hadrian sent Charlemagne a letter saying that the dukes of Spoleto, Benevento, Chiusi, and Friuli were plotting with the Byzantines to give the Lombard crown to Desiderius's son Adelchis. *Codex Carolinus*, number 57. Cf. Cammarosano, *Nobili e re*, p. 102, and Gasparri, *Il passaggio dai Longobardi ai Carolingi*, pp. 35-36.
[101]   In the *Annales regni Francorum*, year 776, the name of the duke of Friuli is Hrodgaud. The same source narrates that, when Charlemagne heard that the Lombards were planning a revolt, he immediately went to Italy, killed the duke of Friuli, conquered the rebellious cities, and put them under the command of Franks. For a comparison of the sources, see the introduction, p. 22.

6. In that time Rotcausus was in command as duke of the Friulans[97] and in Vicenza there was Gaidus.[98] When they heard of the devastation caused by the Franks, of the arrival of Charles and that he was going to Cividale, they gathered all the men they could find, went towards them and, at the bridge called Livenza,[99] made great carnage of the Franks.[100]

Having heard these things, Charles sent the Lombards a message saying that he would receive and honor their oath of fidelity. The Dukes Rotcausus and Gaidus summoned a council with the nobles of the Friulans in order to oppose Charles in a manly way. One of those nobles, whose heart had been blinded by Charles's gifts, gave this counsel: «What will we do? How can we resist them? We have no chief. The king, who gave us courage, has already been defeated. Let us swear fidelity to them; it will be well for us.» What can I say? They did as he wished and Charles preserved them in their offices.[101]

7. Having then subjugated Italy and reestablished order, Charles went to Rome where he built a palace.[102] Having pacified that territory and received oaths, he let his son Pippin rule Italy.[103] After some time, Charles went back to Francia, taking also the first-born children and the noblest men of all Italy with him as hostages. After not much time, they were honored by the same Charles and deserved to return to their homeland.[104]

Pippin died while his father was still alive.[105] He left a son, named Bernard, to whom Charles gave Italy.[106]

Italy had been distressed by famine, but, as Bernard took the kingdom, it attained to prestige and abundance, and thus it was for as long as he ruled. Having ruled for six years in Francia and forty-one after he had entered Italy, Charles, who was of old age and full of days, died in peace.[107] Thanks to him, the fame of the Franks grew greatly far and wide, as it has up to the present day.

He left his place in Francia to his son Louis.[108] The latter began to be called emperor of the people of the Franks.

---

[102] The late ninth-century *Libellus de imperatoria potestate* recounts that on that occasion Charlemagne resided in the palace of Saint Peter. *Libellus de imperatoria potestate in urbe Roma*, p. 198.

[103] That is, the part of the Lombard kingdom Charlemagne conquered. Pippin was born in 777/778 and, on Easter 781, was baptized and anointed king of Italy by Pope Hadrian. In general, on Pippin, see Manacorda, *Ricerche sugli inizi*; Wickham, *Early Medieval Italy*, p. 49; Cammarosano, *Nobili e re*, pp. 140-142.

[104] The *Annales regni Francorum*, year 787, report that Charlemagne took thirteen hostages from the Beneventans among whom there was Grimoald, son of the Duke of Benevento, Arechis. The Frankish king later let Grimoald to return to Benevento. Cf. Kosto, *Hostages in the Carolingian World*, pp. 139-141.

[105] Pippin died in 810.

[106] Bernard was about thirteen when he became king of Italy. Because of his young age, Charlemagne gave him some assistants, among whom there was Adalard, who had held the same position under Pippin. Albertoni, *L'Italia carolingia*, p. 33; Wickham, *Early Medieval Italy*, p. 49. Einhard, *Vita Karoli Magni*, ch. 19, emphasizes that, by allowing Bernard to succeed Pippin, Charlemagne gave proof of the affection he bore for his grandson.

[107] Charlemagne died in 814.

[108] It is Louis the Pious (814-840), the only surviving son of Charlemagne.

[8.] Coniux vero eiusdem Hludowici, Hermengarda nomine, inimicitia contra Bernardo, Langubardorum regem, orta est, mandans ei, quasi pacis gratia ad se venire. Ille ab ipsis nobiles legatarii sacramenta fidem suscepit, Francia iturus est. Qui mox ut illa potuit, sicut audivimus, nesciente imperatore, oculi Bernardi evulsit. Ab ipso dolore defunctus est, postquam quinque regnaverat annos, duo sub Carolo, tres sub Hludowicus.

[9.] Erat quidam Hludowicus imperator multae sapientiae, consilio prudens, misericors et pacis amator. Habebat tranquillitas magna ex omniumque parte pacis gratia. Diligebat lectores, cantores et cunctis servientibus Deo ministrantibus aecclesiae.

Habuit filios tres, id est Lothario et[a] Hludowicus de Ermengarda et Carolus de Iuditta[b] que post morte Ermengardi in coniugio suscepit. Quidam praedicto imperator Hludowicus suum filium Lothario sub se sedem imperialis constituit, vivente patre.

[10.] Habuit Lotharius filius, Hludowicus nomine, cui avius suus Hludowicus Italiam concessit, Hludowici filii sui Baioaria, Caroli Aquittania.

Honor autem maior, id est imperialis, crescebat cottidiae Lotharii. Cui inimici homines consilium dederunt, quatenus Iuditta[c], nuvercam suam, genitori suo tollerent et in Italia adducerent; sicuti fecerunt. In civitate Dartonensis in custodia miserunt. Quis potest dicere furore, quam vehementer pater eius iratus fuisset? Sed totam fortia Lotharius ad se retentam habebat.

Igitur non post multos[d] dies dum se recognoscens[e] Lotharius, quod malum aegisset consilium, nubercam suam remittens genitori suo et ira inflamatus contra illos qui ei tam pravum[f] consilium dederunt, alios occidit, alios in exilio misit.

[11.] Tunc temporis ecclesie Mediolanensis Angelbertus archiepiscopus regebat. Volebat imperator dicere, quod ille in ipso consilium fuisset. Qui[g] venientes nobiles eum in gratia miserunt; sed dum ante imperatore ducerent, ille vero tantum caput inclinavit et verba salutatoria dixit. Ad pedes vero noluit venire propter reverentiae honorem aecclesiarum.

---

[a] *V adds* et *interlineally.* [b] *V corrects* Iulitta *to* Iuditta. Iulitta *Waitz.* [c] *V corrects* Iulitta *to* Iuditta. Iulitta *Waitz.* [d] *V adds* non post multos *interlineally.* [e] *V adds* r *to* ecognoscens *interlineally.* [f] *V adds* ra *to* pvum *interlineally.* [g] Et *Waitz.*

[109] The *Annales regni Francorum*, years 817-818, narrate that some evil men suggested Bernard rebel. Louis the Pious immediately prepared an army to go to Italy, but, upon hearing this, Bernard surrendered. The emperor had the leaders of the conspiracy blinded. The biographer of Louis the Pious, Thegan, recounts that the advisors of Louis the Pious ordered the blinding of Bernard who died three days later from the injuries received. Thegan, *Vita Hludowici*, chs. 22-23. According to the other biographer of Louis the Pious, Bernard died because he tried to resist during his blinding. Astronomer, *Vita Hludovici*, ch. 30. For further information and analysis of these events, see the introduction and the works quoted there.

[110] Louis the German.

[111] Louis the Pious actually had three sons from Ermengard. Andreas of Bergamo omitted Pippin. Riché, *The Carolingians*, p. 145.

8. The wife of Louis, named Ermengard, held enmity against the King of the Lombards, Bernard. She sent him a message saying to come to her as if she wanted to make peace. He received oaths about this from some noble ambassadors and went to Francia. We have heard that, as soon as she could, she plucked out the eyes of Bernard. The emperor was unaware of this. Bernard died from the pain. He had reigned for five years, two under Charles and three under Louis.[109]

9. Emperor Louis was very learned, prudent in counsel, merciful, and a lover of peace. Under his rule, there was tranquility and peace everywhere. He loved lectors, cantors, and all those who serve God governing the churches.

He had three sons, that is, Lothar and Louis[110] from Ermengard,[111] and Charles[112] from Judith whom he married after Ermengard's death.[113] While he was still alive, the above-mentioned Louis granted Lothar the imperial title under him.[114]

10. Lothar had a son, named Louis, to whom his grandfather Louis granted Italy.[115] The emperor gave Bavaria to his son Louis and Aquitaine to Charles.

However, day after day, the major office, that is the imperial one, was becoming more and more controlled by Lothar. Evil men suggested that he take his stepmother Judith away from his father and take her to Italy, and they did so. They put her under custody in the city of Tortona.[116] Who could tell of the furor with which his father got vehemently angry? Lothar however had all the forces with him.

Then, after not many days, admitting that he had acted out of bad counsel, Lothar sent his stepmother back to his father and, inflamed with wrath against the men who had given him such evil counsel, he killed some of them and sent others into exile.[117]

11. At that time Archbishop Angilbert was ruling the Church of Milan.[118] The emperor[119] wanted to say that Angilbert had suggested that action. Some nobles went to Angilbert and put him in grace. They took him before the emperor, but he only bowed his head and said words of greeting; indeed, on account of the honor due to the churches, he refused to go to the feet of the emperor.

---

[112] Charles the Bald.

[113] Louis the Pious married Judith in 819, shortly after Ermengard's death. Riché, *The Carolingians*, p. 149.

[114] Louis the Pious made Lothar co-emperor in 817. Riché, *The Carolingians*, pp. 147-148.

[115] This information is not correct, as Louis II became king of Italy in 844, when Louis the Pious was already dead. In reality the latter gave Italy to Lothar. Riché, *The Carolingians*, pp. 147-148.

[116] Louis's biographers too relates this detail. Thegan, *Vita Hludowici*, ch. 42; Astronomer, *Vita Hludovici*, ch. 48.

[117] Andreas's *Historia* greatly simplifies the events. The birth of Charles the Bald led to a new subdivision of the Empire, which displeased the sons Louis the Pious had had from his first marriage. They rebelled against their father on several occasions, but were never able to create a strong alliance because they disagreed on many points. For more information about these struggles, see Riché, *The Carolingians*, pp. 150-157; Nelson, *Charles the Bald*, pp. 76-104.

[118] Angilbert, who was probably Frankish, was archbishop of Milan from about 824 to 859. Bertolini, *Angilberto*, pp. 260-263; Ambrosioni, *Gli arcivescovi nella vita di Milano*, pp. 98-101.

[119] Lothar.

Tunc imperator dixit: «Sic[a] contenis te, quasi sanctus Ambrosius sis!» Archiepiscopus respondit: «Nec ego sanctus Ambrosius, nec tu dominus Deus.» Imperator vero subiunxit ei: «Itae ad genitorem meum, cuius odium me fecistis habere; reducite me ad pristinam gratiam.»

Ille autem haec audiens, perrexit in Frantiam. Hludowicus imperator honorifice eum suscepit. Dum ad mensam uterque reficerent, causa exurgens imperator et dixit: «Bonae archiepiscope, quid debet facere homo de inimicum suum?» Ille respondit: «Dominus dixit in evangelio: "Diligite inimicos vestros et benefacite his qui vos oderunt".» Imperator dixit: «Et si haec non fecero?» Archiepiscopus respondit: «Si non feceris, non habebis vitam aeternam, si in ipso odio mortuus fueris.»[b]

Imperator vero iratus dixit: «Si me vindicabo de adversario meo, non habebo vitam aeternam?» Et statim subiunxit: «Vide Angelbertus, quomodo haec verba defendas.»

Et constituto posito usque in mane. Mane autem facto, coligit imperator sapientes, prout si subito poterant, conflictum habentes de hac verba contra archiepiscopus. Archiepiscopus eorum presentia dixit: «Scitis, quia sumus omnes fratres in Christo?» Illi autem respondentes dixerunt: «Scimus, quia unum patrem vocamus in cęlis.» Ille autem dixit: «Ergo si scitis, quod fratres sumus, sive liber et servus, sive pater et filius, apostolus Iohannes dixit: "Qui odit fratrem suum, omicida est et omnis omicidam non habet vitam eternam in se manentem." Si ergo odiosus[c] omicida reputabitur, quomodo vitam eternam possessurus erit?»

Illi autem convicti, ad haec verba consenserunt. Imperator vero manum in terra ponens, veniam petivit et gratiam filii sui[d] reddidit.

[12.] Imperavit ipse tam solus quam simul cum filio annos XXVII et ipso Lothario sub eodem patre annos XXI.

Indictione tertia sic fuit sol obscuratus in hoc mundo et stellas in celo parebant, III nonas magias, ora nona, in letanias[e] Domini, quasi media ora. Facta est tribulatio magna. Cumque hoc populus intenderent, multi extimabant, quod iam amplius hoc seculum non staret. Sed dum hec angustia contemplarent, refulsit sol et quasi tremidus in antea umbraculum[f] fugire cepit. Ipsa vero nocte sequenti prope matutino facta est lux quasi in die. Haec signa in celo conperta, doctores in suorum monitiones dixerunt: «Estote, fratres, parati, quia adimpletum est quod in evangelio Dominus dixit: "Cum haec signa videritis, scitote, quia prope est die Domini magnus et manifestus?"»

Sequenti autem mense iunio Hludowicus imperator defunctus est, suosque dies finivit in pace.

---

[a] Sic *Waitz*. Si *V*. [b] *V writes* si in ipso odio mortuus fueris *on erased words*. [c] *V corrects* othiosus *to* odiosus. [d] *V adds* sui *interlineally*. [e] latanias *V*. laetanias *Waitz*. [f] umbraculam *Waitz*.

[120] Ambrose (c. 340 - 397) is the patron saint of Milan.
[121] Matt. 5: 44.
[122] 1 John 3: 15.
[123] The *Annales de Saint Bertin*, year 840, too, report that this eclipse occurred in May at the ninth hour. This event is recorded in other sources as well. For example, *Annales Fuldenses*, year 840; Agnellus of Ravenna, *Liber pontificalis*, ch. 172; John the Deacon, *Istoria Veneticorum*, II, 50.

The emperor then said: «So you behave almost as if you were Saint Ambrose!»[120] The archbishop replied: «I am not Saint Ambrose but neither are you the Lord God.» At this the emperor added: «Go to my father whose hatred you made me have; bring me back into his good graces.»

Having heard this, Angilbert went to Francia. Emperor Louis received him with honor. While they were both eating at table, the emperor, raising an issue, said: «Good archbishop, what must a man do with his enemy?» Angilbert answered: «The Lord said in the Gospel: "Love your enemies and benefit those who hate you".»[121] The emperor said: «And if I do not do this?» The archbishop replied: «If you do not do this and if you die with this hatred, you will not have eternal life.»

The angry emperor then said: «If I take revenge on my adversary, shall I not have eternal life?» And immediately he added: «You will see, Angilbert, how you will defend these words.»

Having reached this position they waited until the following day. In the morning the emperor gathered some learned men to see if they could argue immediately with the archbishop about those words. The archbishop said in their presence: «Do you know that we are all brothers in Christ?» They then replied saying: «We know that, as we invoke one Father in Heaven.» Then he said: «So, if you know that we are all brothers, whether free or unfree, father or son, John the Apostle said: "He who hates his brother is a murderer and no murderer will have eternal life dwelling in him." If therefore you are believed to be a hateful murderer, how will you be able to have eternal life?»[122]

They were convinced and agreed to these words. The emperor then placed his hand on the ground, sought forgiveness, and returned his son to favor.

12. Louis reigned both alone and together with his son for twenty-seven years and Lothar for twenty-one years under his father.

In the third indiction, on the third day before the nones of May, at the ninth hour, during the litanies to the Lord, for about half an hour, the sun darkened in this world so much that the stars appeared in the sky.[123] There was great distress. As the people took notice of this, many believed that this world would not last any longer. But while they contemplated these afflictions, a trembling sun shone and began to chase away the shadows. The very night following, around matins,[124] a light appeared as if it were in the day.[125] These signs having appeared in the sky, the learned men said in their warnings: «Brothers, be ready, since what the Lord said in the Gospel has been fulfilled: "When you see these signs, know that it is because the great and manifest day of the Lord is near".»[126]

In the following month of June, Emperor Louis died and ended his days in peace.[127]

---

[124] Early morning prayer.

[125] The author is describing the aurora borealis (also called northern lights). Cf. Fumagalli, *Il regno italico*, p. 40; Id., *Landscapes of Fear*, p. 6.

[126] Luke 21: 31.

[127] Nithard, *Historie des fils de Louis le Pieux*, I, 8, and the *Annales Fuldenses*, year 840, recount that Louis the Pious died in July. On the other hand, *Les Annales de saint Bertin*, year 840, agree with Andreas of Bergamo.

[13.] Post cuius mortem discordia inter ipsis tres germanis surrexit, Hludowicus et Carolus ex una parte, Lotharius ex altera. Cumque nulla parte dantes locum, iungentes se ubi nuncupatur Funtanense, acies hinc et inde ex utraque partis constructe, facta est strages magna, maxime nobiles Aquitanorum. Tantique ibi viri fortes per contentiones malum et improvidentia debellati sunt, quanti potuissent per bonam concordiam et salubrae consilium multa milia sternere contradictorum paganorum. Unde usque hodie[a] sic discipata est nobilitas Aquitanorum, que etiam Nortemanni eorum possedant terrae, nec est[b] eorum fortia qui resistat, sed etiam tributa reddunt[c].

Imperavit Lotharius post mortem patri sui tam solus quam simul cum Hludowicus filio suo annos XV et mortuus est. Reliquid tres filios, id est iam dicto Hludowico, qui sub eo imperavit in Italia annos VI[d], Lothario in Francia, Karolus in Provintia. Sed Carolus non post multos dies defunctus est.

Lotharius ex sede propria exiens, in Italia veniens pacis gratiae videndum germanum suum, ubi cum ipso locutus est finibus Beneventana pago Venosiana. Sed dum iret et reverteret, multa devastantes pauperorum domibus, blasphemia multa incurrit. Reverteni autem, in itinere via egrotare cepit, subito in civitate Placentina defunctus est et ibi corpus eius conditum suisque hominibus a multis simili modo contigerunt.

[14.] Pauca quidem sane dum per gestis filiorum regum seriem apices conponam, animus meus ad reliquis factis percurrit.

Multa fatigatio Langobardi et oppressio a Sclavorum gens sustinuit, usque dum imperator Foroiulanorum finibus[e] Ebherardo principem constituit. Eo defuncto, Unhroch filio suo principatum suscepit.

De Burgundia vero surrexit quidam clericus[f], Hupert nomine, qui aliquanto tempore domno imperatori Hludowici se fidelissimo esse dicebat. Postmodum cum Burgundionibus[g] adiunctus, suorum fines rebellare disponebat; oblitus est tantorum beneficiorum qua[h] ei imperator tribuit et sacramenta quas dederat irrita fecit.

---

    [a] *In V the words* usque hodie *have been erased.* [b] nec qui *V.* nec est *Waitz.* [c] *In V the words* sed etiam tributa reddunt *have been erased.* [d] *V adds* annos VI *interlineally.* sex *Waitz.* [e] fines *Waitz.* [f] clericus *La Placa, p. 71.* dictus *Waitz.* [g] Burgondionibus *Waitz.* [h] quod *Waitz.*

    [128] Lothar's refusal to accept the way Louis the Pious divided the empire caused this dissension. Riché, *The Carolingians*, pp. 160-163.

    [129] Fontenoy is near Auxerre (northeast France).

    [130] The battle of Fontenoy took place in June 841. All primary sources relate that it was a bloody battle, but only Andreas of Bergamo mentions the detail about the Aquitanians. Cf. Nithard, *Histoire des fils de Louis le Pieux*, II, 1-10; Angelbert, *Versus de Bella quae fuit acta Fontaneto*, pp. 138-139.

    [131] Paul the Deacon, *Historia Langobardorum*, VI, 24, uses similar words to criticize a Lombard defeat by the Slavs.

    [132] Lothar died in 855.

13. After his death, dissension arose among these three brothers, with Louis and Charles on one side, and Lothar on the other. As neither side gave way,[128] they met in a place called Fontenoy.[129] After the battle arrays were set up here and there on both sides, there was a great slaughter, mainly of Aquitanian nobles.[130] There, because of evil contentions and improvidence, as many strong men died as, through good harmony and judicious decisions, could have prostrated many thousands of pagan enemies.[131] The nobility of the Aquitanians has been thus wiped out to the present day to the point that the Northmen also own their land and there is no one who can withstand the Northmen's troops, but instead tributes are even given to them.

Lothar ruled after the death of his father both alone and together with his son Louis for 15 years; then he died.[132] He left three children, that is, the above-mentioned Louis, who ruled in Italy under him for six years,[133] Lothar in Francia,[134] and Charles in Provence. Charles however died after not many days.[135]

Lothar left his home and came to Italy to see his brother for the sake of peace. He talked to him in the territory of Benevento, in the village of Venosa.[136] But, on his return, he laid waste many houses of poor people and committed many blasphemous deeds. However, as he was returning, on the way he began to become sick. He suddenly died in the city of Piacenza, where his body was buried; in the same way many diseases struck his men as well.[137]

14. I have written few things about the deeds of the kings' sons; my mind now goes on to other facts.

The Lombards underwent much weariness and harassment by the Slavic people until the emperor set up Everard as leader of the Friulans' territory.[138] After his death, his son Unroch took up the leadership.[139]

In Burgundy, there rose in revolt a certain cleric, named Hupert, who for a while had said that he was very faithful to Emperor Louis. Afterwards he joined some Burgundians and arranged for their lands to rebel, thus forgetting the many benefits that the emperor had bestowed on him and breaking the oaths he had sworn.

[133] Andreas of Bergamo is probably referring to the fact that Louis II was king of Italy from 844 to 850, the year in which Lothar appointed him co-emperor.

[134] Lothar II inherited Lotharingia, i. e. the lands from the Netherlands to the Jura Mountains. Riché, *The Carolingians*, p. 172.

[135] In reality Charles died in 863. *Les Annales de Saint Bertin*, year 863.

[136] Venosa is in Basilicata.

[137] Lothar II went to Italy in 869 to convince Pope Hadrian II to let him divorce his wife, Theutberga, and marry Waldrada. On this case, see Heidecker, *The Divorce of Lothar II*. Lothar II's journey in Italy is described also by the *Annales de Saint Bertin*, year 869, which, however, do not mention the evil deeds the Frankish king committed.

[138] Everard was appointed leader of Friuli around 830, when Lothar, Louis II's father, was still ruling in Italy. Everard was Frankish and his wife was Gisela, daughter of Louis the Pious and his second wife Judith. In general, on Everard, see Fees, *Eberardo, marchese del Friuli*, pp. 252-255, and La Rocca and Provero, *The Dead and their Gifts*, pp. 225-280. Everard's deeds against the Slavs are praised also by Sedulius Scotus, *Carmina*, p. 220.

[139] Everard died around the mid-860s.

Domnus Hludovicus haec audiens, Cunrath cum reliquis fidelibus suis dirixit[a] et eodem Hupert in campo comprehendit et occidit; et multi quidem da eius pars interempti sunt.

Igitur antequam haec rebellatio facta fuisset, tanta quidem nivem Italia cecidit, ut per centum dies in planis locis teneret. Fuit gelus gravissimus, multa semina mortua fuerunt; vitae pene omnibus in planis locis siccaverunt et vinum intra vascula glaciavit, quae etiam per foramen spinarum nihil exibat, donec rumperetur ipsa glatia cum fuste ab ante ipsa spina.

Hoc fuit tempus domni Hludowici imperatoris anno X indictione octava.

His itaque sub brivitate[b] rei veritas transcurris, adventum primi ordinis, sicut cepimus, exsequamur.

[15.] At vero domnus Hludowicus augustus multa quidem oppressionem a Sarracinorum gens in finibus Beneventanis sustinuit et eorum semper resistit[c]. Amelmasser eorum princeps cum multi Sarracini ibi consistentibus occidit.

Reliqui in castro qui dicitur Bari se fortiter munierunt, ubi domnus imperator per V annos eos[d] cum Franci et Langobardi et ceteris nacionum suorum fidelium possidens, simul etiam cum sua coniuge[e] Angelberga nomine et multi eorum[f] similiter.

[16.] Circa haec tempora in Vulgarorum gens divina aspiracio accensa est, quatenus christiani fierent et Christum dominum colerent, quo in[g] tanto[h] amor caritatis in eorum regem pervenit, ut per se ipse ad aecclesia beati Petri Roma veniens et ibi dona obtulit et a[i] domno papa[j] Nicholaus catholica fide monitus, divinitatis scientiae instructus, baptiçatus et fide[k] sancta confirmatus, recepit doctores ab eodem domno apostolico, suam reversus est patriam.

[17.] Igitur dum domnus Hludowicus cum[l] suis[m] Bari custodirent, nuncii venerant de finibus Calabriae dicentes: «Domine imperator, vestri[n] esse volumus et per vestram defensionem salvi fore confidimus. Gens Sarracinorum venerunt, terra nostra dissipaverunt,

[a] direxit *Waitz.* [b] *V adds* vi *to* britate. [c] *V corrects* restitit *to* resistit. [d] eas *V Waitz.* [e] iuge *V.* coniuge *Waitz.* [f] *V adds* eorum *interlineally.* [g] qin in *V with abbreviation marks above* q *and* i. quoniam *Waitz.* [h] *V corrects* tantum *to* tanto. [i] *V adds* a *interlineally.* [j] *V adds* papa *interlineally.* [k] *V adds* e *to* fid *interlineally.* [l] *In V* c *with abbreviation mark.* cus *Waitz.* [m] *V adds* cum suis *interlineally.* [n] *V writes* vestri *on a word beginning with* t.

[140] Hupert, brother of Theutberga, Lothar II's wife, was a cleric who was able to create an autonomous dominion on the border between southwestern Switzerland and France. Riché, *The Carolingians*, p. 184. The *Annales de Saint Bertin*, year 864, recount that Hupert took some of Louis II's possessions in France and that he was killed in 864. According to the *Annales Xantenses*, year 864, the Count of Auxerre, Conrad, and the abbot of Saint Germain of Auxerre killed Hupert.

[141] *Annales Fuldenses*, year 860, report that in that year it was so cold that merchants could go to the Venetian islands using horses and carts instead of boats.

[142] Amalmasser was probably the chief of the Muslim mercenaries whom the Prince of Benevento, Radelchis, hired, and who took control of Benevento in the late 840s. Louis II was asked to put an end to their raids. Musca, *L'emirato di Bari*, pp. 24-25, 33, 38-39. Kreutz, *Before the Normans*, pp. 30-32. The *Cronicae Sancti Benedicti Casinensis*, II, 14, relates that Louis had the Saracen leader beheaded. This source

As the lord Louis heard these things, he sent Cunrath with other of his men against Hupert. Cunrath captured Hupert on the battlefield and killed him. Many of Hupert's faction were killed.[140]

Before this revolt occurred, so much snow had fallen in Italy that it remained on the plains for a hundred days. The cold spell was so severe that many seeds died, vines dried up on almost all the plains and the wine froze in the vessels to a such degree that nothing came out from the taps of the vessels until one broke the ice in front of the taps with a club.

This occurred in the tenth year of the lord Emperor Louis, in the eighth indiction.[141]

Having considered these things briefly and truthfully, we continue to follow the original plan, just as we began it.

15. In the territory of Benevento the Augustus, lord Louis, experienced much harassment from the people of the Saracens, but he always stood up against them. He killed their leader, Amalmasser, along with many Saracens who were there.[142]

Those who remained fortified themselves in the citadel called Bari, which the emperor besieged for five years[143] with Franks, Lombards and allies of other nations.[144] Louis's wife, named Angelberga, and many others were also with him.

16. Around this time a divine inspiration was kindled among the Bulgarian people, inasmuch as they became Christians and began to worship the Lord Christ. So great a love of charity came upon their king, that, by his own decision, he went to the church of the blessed Peter in Rome and brought gifts there. He was advised about the Catholic faith by the lord Pope Nicholas,[145] instructed in the knowledge of divine things, baptized and confirmed in the holy faith. He received some teachers from the same apostolic lord and went back to his homeland.[146]

17. While the lord Louis was keeping watch over Bari with his men, messengers came from the territory of Calabria, saying: «O lord emperor, we wish to be your subjects and we are confident that we will be rescued through your protection. The people of the

and Erchempert, however, call him Massar, while in the works of Ado of Vienne and of John the Deacon he is mentioned under the names of Amalmater and Abomasale. Erchempert, *Ystoriola Longobardorum Beneventum degentium*, ch. 18; Ado of Vienne, *Chronicon*, p. 323; John the Deacon, *Istoria Veneticorum*, II, 52. It is believed that this episode occurred in 848. Gasparri, *Il ducato e il principato di Benevento*, p. 118.

[143] Probably in 847 some Muslim mercenaries, hired by the Prince of Benevento, Radelchis, took possession of Bari and created an autonomous emirate. The Saracens held the city until 871. In his account Andreas of Bergamo synthesizes several of Louis II's campaigns. Cf. Musca, *L'emirato di Bari*.

[144] A letter of Louis II to the Byzantine emperor Basil records the presence of a Slavic fleet. *Chronicon Salernitanum*, p. 117. It is believed that it was led by the Slavic ruler Domagoj, who wanted to drive the Muslims out of the Adriatic sea. Musca, *L'emirato di Bari*, p. 111. The Venetians, too, contributed to the military operations against the Saracens by defeating a Muslim fleet near Taranto. John the Deacon, *Istoria Veneticorum*, III, 5.

[145] Nicholas (858-867).

[146] In reality the Bulgarian sovereign never went to Rome. He did, however, send some emissaries to the pope who gave them a letter for their king describing the precepts for being a good Christian. Riché, *The Carolingians*, p. 176.

civitates desolaverunt, aecclesias suffuderunt; tantum ad vos petimus, ut des nos caput confortacionis, qui nos adiuvent et confortent. Sacramenta vobis damus, tributa solvimus.»

Tunc domnus imperator misericordia motus, non gaudens cupiditatis eorum[a] promissa, sed de illorum dolens malitia, elegit strenuis et nobilissimis viris, Hotone de finibus Bergomensis, Oschis et Gariardus episcopis, et confortavit eos domnus imperator et dixit: «Ite in pace, fideles Christi, angelus Domini bonus commitetur vobiscum, ut et ego videam vos et labores quam[b] vobis inpono merear.»

Tunc simul cum ipsis missis perrexerunt et unde[c] egerunt firmitatis sacramenta receperunt et adunantes secum magis ac magis fideles populus.

Cumque venerunt in quedam valle, ubi ipsis Sarracini fidentes absque ullo timore, annonam[d] metentes, simul cum captivi quas habebant, tunc christiani inruentes super illos et Sarracini quanti ibi invenerunt occiderunt; captivi liberaverunt.

Ut haec audivit eorum principe, Cincimo nomine, de civitate Amantea[e] obviam eorum exiit, preparatus viriliter. Et exinde Franci conperti sunt et iungentes se hii ex una parte[f] et illi ex altera, facta est strages magna Sarracinorum, qui fuga petiens, christiani vero post eos, interficientes usque ad portam civitatis.

Oto vero et praedicti episcopi et suorum secutores triumphatores reversi sunt ad domno imperatore. Imperator vero magnum gavisus est gaudium, honorem dignitatis eorum tribuit.

[18.] Cincimo vero de suis et patrie sue adiutorium colligentes multitudo Sarracini, iter pergentes, Bari secum euntes, multa dispendia adiutorium soldani.

Erat eorum nunciatum, quod christiani celebrarent magnum diem, festum sicut erat, hoc est nativitas domini nostri Iesu Christi, dicentes: «Deum suum colunt die illa; neque pugnaturi neque arma levatori sunt. Eamus super illos, comprahendamus eos omnes in simplicitate sua.»

Hoc consilium domno imperatori nunciatum est. Tunc moniti, ut gallotinnio matutinis et[g] summo diluculo episcopis et sacerdotibus missarum sollemnia celebrarent et populus communionem vel benedictionem acciperent, sicuti et fecerunt. Et exierunt querentes Sarracini et illis querentes Franci iuncti sunt in loco ...[h]

---

[a] *V erases* sed *before* eorum. [b] *V corrects* quas *to* quam. [c] *V adds* unde *interlineally.* [d] *V adds* n *to* anonam *interlineally.* [e] *V adds* Amantea *interlineally.* [f] *V adds* parte *interlineally.* [g] *V adds* et *interlineally.* [h] *Blank space.*

---

[147] Otto was count of Bergamo. Jarnut, *Bergamo*, pp. 21, 22, 68, 256.

[148] The presence of bishops at the head of troops was not unusual in the early Middle Ages. Prinz, *Klerus und Krieg im früheren Mittelalter.*

[149] It is probably the valley of Crati. Musca, *L'emirato di Bari*, p. 113. Noyé, *La Calabre entre Byzantins, Sarrasins et Normands*, p. 91, note 4.

Saracens came, sacked our land, emptied the cities, and destroyed the churches. We ask of you only that you grant us a commander who can help and strengthen us. We will swear oaths to you and will give tributes to you.»

Then, the lord emperor, moved with compassion, not rejoicing in their lucrative promise, but feeling sorrow over their ills, chose strong and very noble men: Otto of the territory of Bergamo,[147] and the bishops Oschis and Gariard.[148] The lord emperor comforted the messengers and said: «Go in peace, faithful of Christ; the good angel of the Lord will come with you so that I might also see you and be worthy of the hardships I lay upon you.»

They then left with the envoys and, wherever they went, they received oaths of fealty and gathered more and more supporters from that people.

As they arrived in a certain valley,[149] where the Saracens, confident and without any fear, were harvesting together with the captives they had, the Christians rushed upon them, killing all of the Saracens they found there, and freed the captives.

When their prince, named Cincimo, heard these things, he departed from the city of Amantea[150] and went towards them fully armed. The Franks found this out and met the Saracens, the former on one side and the latter on the other. There was a great slaughter of Saracens, who fled. The Christians went after them, killing them up to the city gate.

Otto, the bishops, and their followers then went back to the lord emperor in triumph. The emperor rejoiced very much and granted them offices.[151]

18. From his men and with the help of his homeland, Cincimo gathered a multitude of Saracens, who undertook the trip and went to Bari with him to repair the many losses of the *soldanus*.[152]

It was reported to them that the Christians would celebrate a great day, as it was a feast day, that is, the nativity of our Lord Jesus Christ. Therefore they said: «They are worshiping their god on that day. They will neither fight nor take up arms. Let us go upon them and take them all in their guilelessness!»

This suggestion was reported to the emperor. He then ordered that, at dawn, at the cockcrow, the bishops and the priests would celebrate solemn masses, and that the people would receive communion and the benediction, and they did so. And they went out searching for the Saracens, and the Saracens searching for the Franks; they met each other at the place ...

---

[150] Amantea is on the Calabrian Tyrrhenian coast, southwest of Cosenza.

[151] The defeat inflicted on the Muslims in Calabria is also mentioned in *Chronicon Salernitanum*, ch. 108.

[152] In this period, the ruler of Bari was Sawdān. Other Latin sources call him Seodan, Saugdan etc. It has been argued that this word indicated the name of the emir, not the office of sultan which would represent an anachronism for the ninth century. Musca, *L'emirato di Bari*, p. 61; Vasil'ev, *Byzance et les Arabes*, p. 264, note 2. This has been later denied by Lewis, *The Political Language of Islam*, pp. 51-52. As Andreas of Bergamo calls him *soldanus*, which seems to indicate a confusion between the name and the office, I have decided to keep this term. It is worth noting that the Byzantine Emperor, Constantine VII, refers to this ruler as Andreas does. Constantine VII Porphyrogenitus, *De administrando imperio*, p. 128.

Factum est sonitus magnus clangore bucine, innita equorum, strepidus populorum. Cumque prope se coniungerent, fideles Christi oraverunt dicentes: «Domine Iesu Christe, tu dixisti: "Qui manducat carnem meam et bibit sanguinem meum, in me manet et ego in eum." Ergo "si tu nobiscum, quid contra nos?"»

Statim commissum est prelium. Cumque forti intencione pugnantes, arma celestis confortavit christianos; pagani vero terga vertentes fugire ceperunt. Christiani autem post eos cedentes, non cessabant, donec multitudo paganorum interficerent et stipendia quicquid soldani pergebat tullerunt.

[19.] Soldanus hec audiens, metus magnus tristare cepit. Sequenti mense febroario, quinto expleto anno quod Bari possessas habebat, domnus imperator comprehendit soldanus et reliqui Sarracini ibi consistentibus interemit, anno XXI, indictione IIII.

Sarracini vero in suorum terra haec audiens, elegentes se fortissimi viri, sicut audivimus viginti milia hominum, dicentes: «Grandis ignominiam de occisorum nostrorum consonant; eamus illuc.»

Cumque navigio prepararent, ascenderunt et navigaverunt et exierunt in finibus Beneventana. Tunc dixerunt per suorum audatiae elationis: «Quid nobis fiducie habere debemus in navibus nostris? Dissipemus eas, quia Franci adversum nos nihil possunt. Et sic prevaluerint adversum nos, sine ullo metu in regnum nostrum pergere possunt.» Et dictis factis, Franci querere ceperunt.

Nunciatum est[a] domno imperatori, quoniam statim mittens principibus suis, id est Hunroch, Agefrid et Boso, cum electa manus Francorum et Langobardorum vel ceterorum[b] nationes. Iungentes se loco ad sancto Martino, ad strada scilicet[c] prope Capua ad Vulturno, acies hinc et inde, utraque partis forti intenciones pugnantes, Dei adiuvante misericordia, Sarracini devicti et debellati sunt multitudo innumerabiles[d]. Quia quod gladius non interemit, in fluvio Vulturno negati sunt; reliqui fuga vix[e] evaderunt.

Sic Dei iudicio complacuit; "qui venerant exaltati, facti sunt humiliati."

[20.] Ad haec victoria patrata, domnus imperator in Beneventi palatio sedebat. Tunc Adelchis principatum Beneventanorum regebat, cui imperator se et omnia credebat, et dilectione caritatis inter se diliebant.

Anticus hostis, qui semper contra dilectionem inimicitiam querit, exsurgentes per malos homines, inter se occulte dicentes: «Quid grabati sumus sub potestatem Francorum?»

---

[a] Nunciatum id est *Waitz*. [b] *V adds* ce *to* terorum *interlineally*. [c] scilicae *V Waitz*. [d] *V erases a word after* innumerabiles. [e] vis *V Waitz*.

[153] John 6: 56.
[154] Rom. 8: 31.
[155] The Venetian chronicler John the Deacon relates that Bari was conquered on the second of February. On the other hand, a Cassinese calendar and eleventh-century annals, which report the wrong year, state that the city's fall occurred on the third of February. N. Cilento and G. Musca are in favor of the latter date.

They made a loud sound of trumpets, of horses neighing, and of clashing of peoples. As they joined together, the faithful of Christ prayed, saying: «O Lord Jesus Christ, you said: 'He who eats my flesh and drinks my blood will remain in me and I in him.'[153] So, "if you are with us, what is against us?"»[154]

The battle was joined immediately. As they were fighting with forceful exertion, heavenly weapons helped the Christians. The pagans turned their backs and began to flee. The Christians went after them and did not stop until they had killed a multitude of pagans and taken the money intended for the *soldanus*.

19. Hearing this, the *soldanus* began to be sad with great fear. In the following month of February,[155] in the twenty-first year of his rule,[156] in the fourth indiction, having passed the fifth year since the siege of Bari, the lord emperor captured the *soldanus* and killed the Saracens who remained there.[157]

When the Saracens heard of these things in their land, they chose the strongest men among them – twenty thousand, as we have heard – saying: «The dishonor of our men who have been killed is echoing loudly; let us go there!»

Having prepared a fleet, they boarded, sailed, and arrived in the territory of Benevento. Then they said in their arrogant impudence: «Why do we have to rely on our ships? Let us destroy them, for the Franks can do nothing against us. And should they prevail against us, they could go to our kingdom without any fear.» Having done what they had said, they began to look for the Franks.

This was reported to the lord emperor, who immediately sent his commanders, that is, Hunroch, Agefrid, and Boso, with a chosen host of Franks, Lombards, and men of other nations. They met at Saint Martin, on the road near Capua, on the Volturno. The troops fought with great energy on both sides and, thanks to the help of God's mercy, a countless multitude of Saracens was overcome and vanquished, as those whom the sword did not slay drowned in the Volturno river. The others managed to flee, albeit with difficulty.

Thus God's justice was pleased: "those who had come exalted were humbled."[158]

20. Having obtained the victory, the lord emperor resided in the palace of Benevento. At that time Adelchis was governing the principality of the Beneventans.[159] The emperor fully trusted him and they esteemed each other with the love of charity.

The ancient enemy,[160] who always seeks enmity against love, acted through evil men, who were secretly saying to each other: «Why are we oppressed under Frankish dominance?»

John the Deacon, I*storia Veneticorum*, II, 6; Lupus Protospatharius, *Annales*, p. 52; Lowe, *Die ältesten Kalendarien aus Monte Cassino*, p. 15; *Cronaca della dinastia di Capua*, p. 319, note 7; Musca, *L'emirato di Bari*, p. 115, note 50.

[156] 871.

[157] Also the other sources mentioning the conquest of Bari – see Musca, *L'emirato di Bari*, p. 114, note 50 – are as laconic as Andreas of Bergamo. The only exception is John the Deacon, *Istoria Veneticorum*, III, 6.

[158] Cf. Matt. 23: 12, and Luke 14: 11.

[159] Adelchis was prince of Benevento from 853 to 878. Cilento, *Adelchi (Adelgiso)*, p. 259.

[160] The devil.

Taliter Beneventani per fraudem uno consilio ingerunt, ut rederent malum pro bonum[a]; quatenus ubicumque fidelissimi imperatoris[b] invenissent, ibi custodirent, et ad imperatorem non dimisissent redirent. Erant enim Franci separati per castellas vel civitates, fidentes absque ullo terrore, credentes fide Beneventanorum. Fuit autem iste contrarius discessionis dies XXXV, id est idus augusti usque quintodecimo kalendas octobris indictione V.

Sed Deus, qui domno imperatore ad regni gubernacula imperialis ordinaverat, cum ipso erat, sicut legitur: "Cor regis in manum[c] Dei est." Et taliter fideles suos ad eum venire fecit.

Caelestis timor super Beneventanos inruit; vis[d] illorum fuit, ut pacifice potuissent, illos dimiterent. Qui letabundi a domno imperatore reversi sunt[e].

[21.] Eodem anno evoluto, multa signa monstrata sunt. Vinum quomodo vindemiatum et intra vascula[f] misso, statim turbulentus, qui dicitur versio, fuit. In ipsa Pascha Domini per arbores vel reliqua folia et loca parebat quasi terra pluvisset; sequenti autem IIII nonas magi pruina[g] cecidit, multe vites in planis locis seu in vallibus palmites cum uva siccaverunt; similiter et silves tenerrimum cum sua folia aride facte sunt. Sequenti autem mense augusto multarum locustarum[h] advenit de Vicentina partibus in finibus Bresiana, deinde in Cremonensis finibus; inde vero perrexerunt in Laudensis partibus, sive etiam in Mediolanensis. Erant enim unates pergentibus, sicut Salamon dixit: "Locusta regem non habent, set per turmas ascendunt." Devastaverunt enim multas granas minutas, id est milio vel panico.

Completi anno centesimo ex co Francorum gens Italia ingressi sunt, anno domni[i] Hludovici imperatoris XXIII et mensis IIII indictione VI finita.

Ingrediente VII indictione, hoc est anni ab incarnationis domini nostri Ihesu Christi octogenti LXXIII transacti, imperator vero veniens de finibus Beneventana post multa victoria super Sarracini facta.

---

 a   bnum *V.* b imperatori *Waitz.* c manu *Waitz.* d vix *V Waitz.* e *V writes* reversi sunt *on an erasure.* f vescula *V.* vascula *Waitz.* g proina *Waitz.* h locustaram *V.* locustarum *Waitz.* i *V adds* domni *interlineally.*

161 Cf. Prov. 17: 13. Jer. 18: 20. Rom. 12: 17. 1Thess. 5: 15. 1.
162 Prov. 21:1.
163 According to the southern Lombard chronicler Erchempert, the prince of Benevento imprisoned Louis II because the Franks, inspired by the devil, were persecuting his subjects. Erchempert, *Ystoriola Longobardorum Beneventum degentium*, ch. 34. The *Annales de Saint Bertin*, year 871, report that the Beneventans rebelled as Louis II, instigated by his wife, was planning to exile Adelchis. The empress is explicitly blamed for what happened in *Chronicon Salernitanum*, ch. 109. The Neapolitan chronicler John the Deacon narrates that the Duke of Naples, Sergius, fomented the Lombards against the emperor as the latter had intervened against the duke in defense of the bishop of Naples. *Gesta episcoporum Neapolitanorum*, ch. 65. On the other hand, Regino of Prüm, *Chronicon*, year 871, recounts that the Byzantines incited the prince of Benevento to capture Louis II, while the Byzantine emperor, Constantine VII, states that the emir of Bari was responsible for that. Constantine VII Porphyrogenitus, *De administrando imperio*, p. 130.

The Beneventans acted all together fraudulently to return evil for good.[161] Wherever they found the emperor's men, they held them in those places in order not to let them go back to the emperor. The Franks were in fact spread out in castles and cities, free from all fear and trusting in the loyalty of the Beneventans. This hostility lasted for thirty-five days, from the ides of August until the 15th day from the kalends of October, in the fifth indiction.

But God, who had appointed the lord emperor to govern the imperial kingdom, was with him, just as one reads: "The heart of the king is in God's hand."[162] And therefore he had his men go to the emperor.

A heavenly fear rushed upon the Beneventans; the number of the Franks was so great that, in order to have peace, the Beneventans freed them. Full of joy, the Franks returned to the lord emperor.[163]

21. As the year went on, many signs appeared. After being harvested and put into vessels, the wine became immediately agitated, an event which is called turning.[164] On that Easter it seemed as if dirt were raining down among the trees, the leaves and other places. Moreover, on the fourth day of the nones of the following month of May, hoar-frost fell. In the plains and in the valleys many vine-leaves and grapes dried up, and in a similar way the forests and their tender leaves withered. In the following month of August, many locusts came from the region of Vicenza to the territory of Brescia, then to the territory of Cremona. Finally they proceeded to the area around Lodi, and also to Milan. They were proceeding all together, just like Solomon said: "Locusts have no king, but proceed in throngs."[165] They destroyed many small grains, that is, millet and foxtail millet.[166]

This happened on the completion of the hundredth year since the Franks entered Italy, in the twenty-third year of the lord Emperor Louis's rule, in the fourth month, at the end of the sixth indiction.[167]

At the beginning of the seventh indiction, that is, 873 years from the incarnation of our Lord Jesus Christ, the emperor left the territory of Benevento after achieving many victories over the Saracens.[168]

For a detailed analysis of the different versions, see Granier, *La captivité de l'empereur Louis II à Bénévent*, pp. 13-39. The imprisonment of Louis II is attributed to the Beneventans' fear that the sovereign intended to annex Southern Italy. Russo Mailler, *La politica meridionale*, pp. 12-14; Gasparri, *Il ducato e il principato di Benevento*, pp. 125-126; Kreutz, *Before the Normans*, pp. 45-47.

[164] A deterioration of wine.

[165] Prov. 30: 27.

[166] At this time, these types of cereals were chosen for their resistance to bad weather. Montanari, *L'alimentazione contadina*, pp. 114, 133-144.

[167] Many sources mention the damages the locusts caused in 873 in different parts of Europe. *Les Annales de saint Bertin*, year 873; *Annales Fuldenses*, year 873; *Annales Vedastini*, year 873; *Annales Xantenses*, year 873; Regino of Prüm, *Chronicon*, year 873.

[168] The *Chronicon Salernitanum*, chs. 117-118, provides a detailed account of the way Louis II was convinced to help the Lombards against the Muslims and how his troops defeated the Saracens.

[22.] Igitur post annum, hoc est indictione octava, stella commetis in caelo comparuit, similtudo[a] radientibus longinque caude per totum mense iunium, mane et vespere. Deinde in mense iulio Sarracini venerunt et civitate Cummaclo igne cremaverunt.

Sequenti autem mense augusto[b] Hludowicus imperator defunctus est, pridie idus augusti in finibus Bresiana.

Antonius vero, Bresiane episcopus, tulit corpus eius et posuit eum in sepulchro in aecclesia sanctae Mariae, ubi corpus[c] sancti Filastrici requiescit.

Anspertus Mediolanensis archiepiscopus mandans ei per archidiaconum suum, ut reddat corpus illud; ille autem noluit. Tunc mandans Garibaldi Bergomensis episcopus et Benedicti Cremonensis episcopus cum suorum sacerdotes[d] et cunctum clero venire, sicut ipse archiepiscopus faciebat. Episcopis vero ita facerunt et illuc perrexerunt; trahentes eum a terra et mirifice condientes, dies quinto post transitum in pharetro posuerunt, cum omni honore, hymnis Deo psallentibus, in Mediolanum perduxerunt.

Veritatem in Christo loquor. Ibi fui et partem aliquam portavi et cum portantibus ambulavi[e] da[f] flumen qui dicitur Oleo usque ad flumen Adua. Adductus igitur in civitate cum magno honore et lacrimabili fletu, in ęclesia beati Ambrosii confessoris sepelierunt die septimane suae.

Qui imperavit annos XXVI, id est vivente patre annos VI, post mortem patris annos XX[g].

[23.] Post cuius obitum magna tribulatio in Italia advenit. Colligentes se maiores nati in civitate Ticino simul cum Angelberga suorum regina, mense septembri, indictione nona[h] et pravum agentes consilium, quatenus ad duo mandarent reges[i], id est Karoli in Frantia et Hlodovici in Baioaria; sicut et fecerunt.

Tunc Karolus veniens, nesciens de Hludovico. Hludovicus nesciebat quod Karolus venisset; misit filium suum Karolus nomine; propter distantiam ceperunt homines Karoleto nominare. Karolo rex veniens in Papiam, Karlito in finibus Mediolanensis. Cumque de[j] patruum suum compertum fuisset quod esset in Papia, ceperunt homines, qui[k] se ad Carlito coniunxerunt, multa malitia facere; hoc est Beringherio[l] cum reliquas multitudo statim venerunt in finibus Bergomensis, resedente in monasterio Fara per

    [a]   *V adds* l *to* simitudo *interlineally.* similitudo *Waitz.* [b] augustus *V.* augusto *Waitz.* [c] corps *V.* [d] sorcerdotes *V.* sacerdotes *Waitz.* [e] *V adds* vi *to* ambula *interlineally.* [f] a *Waitz.* [g] *V adds* annos – XX *in the margin of the folio.* [h] *V adds* mense septembri indictione nona *interlineally.* [i] regi *Waitz.* [j] *V adds* de *interlineally.* [k] qu *V.* qui *Waitz.* [l] *V adds* h *to* Beringerio *interlineally.*

    [169]   This comet is mentioned by the *Annales Fuldenses*, year 875, as well.
    [170]   The Venetian chronicler John the Deacon narrates that, before attacking Comacchio, the Muslims tried to sack Grado, but lifted the siege when they heard that the Venetian fleet was arriving. John the Deacon, *Istoria Veneticorum*, III, 12.
    [171]   Also the *Annales Fuldenses*, year 875, report that Louis II was buried in St. Ambrose.
    [172]   They are respectively Charles the Bald and Louis the German, who were Louis II's uncles.

22. Then, after a year, that is, in the eighth indiction, a comet star, resembling a tail with long rays, appeared in the sky for the whole month of June, from morning to evening.[169] Then in the month of July the Saracens came and burned the city of Comacchio.[170]

In the following month of August, Emperor Louis died, on the day before the ides of August in the territory of Brescia.

The Bishop of Brescia, Anthony, took his body and placed it in a tomb in the church of St. Mary, where the body of Saint Filastricus rests.

Through his archdeacon, the Archbishop of Milan, Anspertus, ordered the bishop of Brescia to return the body, but the bishop refused. Then the archbishop told the Bishop of Bergamo, Garibald, and the Bishop of Cremona, Benedict, to go there with their priests and all their clerics, just as the archbishop himself did. And the bishops did so and went there. They pulled the emperor out from the ground and wonderfully embalmed him. They placed him in a coffin five days after his death and brought him to Milan with every honor, singing hymns to God.

I speak the truth in Christ. I was there, I carried it for a part of the trip and I walked with the bearers from the river, which is named Oglio, to the river Adda. Having then taken him to the city of Milan, they buried him with great honor and tearful weeping in the church of the blessed confessor Ambrose[171] in a day of the saint's week.

He was emperor for twenty-six years, that is, for six years while his father was still alive, and for twenty years after his father's death.

23. After his death, great distress came upon Italy. The aristocrats gathered in the city of Ticinum with their queen Angelberga in the month of September, in the ninth indiction, and they gave her evil counsel, inasmuch as they wanted to invite two kings, that is, Charles in Francia and Louis in Bavaria;[172] so they did.[173]

Charles then came, not knowing about Louis. Nor did Louis know that Charles was coming. Louis sent his son, named Charles,[174] and, on account of the distance, the men began to call him Little Charles. King Charles went to Pavia; Little Charles went to the territory of Milan. And when he found out that his uncle was in Pavia, the men, who had joined Little Charles, began to do many evil deeds. Berengar[175] immediately went to the territory of Bergamo with another great multitude of men and remained in the monastery of Fara[176] for one week, devastating houses, committing adulteries,

---

[173] Louis II died without a male heir, which led to fights among his relatives for the succession. Wickham, *Early Medieval Italy*, pp. 169-170; Riché, *The Carolingians*, pp. 199-205. According to the *Libellus de imperatoria potestate*, pp. 207-208, Pope John VIII invited Charles the Bald, while Empress Angelberga solicited Carloman, Louis the German's son.

[174] Charles the Fat.

[175] Berengar, who was the son of Everard, became leader of Friuli after the death of his brother Unroch. In 888 Berengar was able to obtain the crown of king of Italy. Wickham, *Early Medieval Italy*, pp. 169-170; Arnaldi, *Berengario I*, pp. 1-26.

[176] The modern Fara Gera d'Adda. Cf. Del Bello, *Indice toponomastico altomedievale del territorio di Bergamo*, p. 77, note 22.

aedomada una, domibus devastantes, adulteria vel incendia fatientes. Tunc multi Bergomensis relinquentes domos suas plena vino et anona, tantum cum uxuribus et paramentum in civitate vel in montibus perrexerunt.

Karolus rex haec audiens, statim prae[a] ipsis malefactores[b] cum multitudo populorum perrexit de finibus Bergomensis in Bresiana, inde in Verona, inde vero in Mantua.

Karlito perrexit in Baioaria. Tunc Karleman, germanus eius, oviam veniens Karoli rex, barbani sui, ad fluvio, qui dicitur Brenta, et pacificis verbis se ad invicem salutaverunt et pactum usque in mensem madio firmaverunt.

Carlemanus ivit in Baioaria. Karolus rex perrexit ad Romam et ad ecclesiam beati Petri dona obtulit; ab apostolico Iohanne unctus et ab honore[c] imperii coronatus, in Papia reversus est, mense ianuario, suprascripta indictione[d] nona.

[24.] Cumque idem Karolus imperator de Roma reversus in Papia sederet, audivit quod Karlomannus, Hludowici filius, contra eum veniret. Cumque exercitum suum adunare vellet et cum eo bellum gerere, quidam de suis, in quorum fidelitatem maxime confidebat, ab eo defecti, ad Carlemannum se coniungebat. Quod ille videns, fugam iniit et Galliam repedavit statimque in ipso itinere mortuus est.

Carlomannus vero regnum Italie disponens, post non multum tempus ad patrem in Baioariam reversus est.

Inter hec Hludovicus rex[e]

   [a]   *V writes* p *with an abbreviation mark.* post *Waitz.* [b] *In V, a word has been erased after* malefactores.
   [c] *V adds* honore *interlineally.* [d] ianuario, indictione suprascripta indictione *V.* [e] *V writes this sentence at the end of f. 86ʳ.*

   [177]   Bergamo.
   [178]   The inhabitants of Bergamo's territory were forced to seek shelter in the city or mountains probably because there were no fortified structures in that area. Cf. Settia, *Castelli e villaggi nell'Italia padana*, pp. 51 and 444; Id., *Potere e sicurezza nella bergamasca del secolo X*, pp. 53-54.
   [179]   It is not clear whether the chronicler meant ecclesiastical ornaments or the clothing of the Bergamasques.
   [180]   The *Annales Fuldenses*, year 875, which report the "German" version of these events, narrate that, when Louis the German heard that Charles the Bald went to Italy, he immediately sent his son Carloman to Italy. Charles the Bald, described as a fearful person, gave Carloman many precious gifts, promising him the Italian crown and that he would go back to France if the son of Louis the German would withdraw. Charles the Bald however did not keep his word and went to Rome where he was crowned emperor. The "French" version is narrated in *Annales de Saint Bertin*, year 875, which recount that Charles the Bald put Charles the Fat to flight and that, when Carloman arrived, he chose to make an agreement with his uncle and to go back to Germany.
   [181]   Andreas of Bergamo is probably referring to the throne, known as *cathedra Petri*, and the Bible of St. Paul. Nees, *Charles the Bald and the «cathedra Petri»*, pp. 343-344.

and setting fires. Many Bergamasques then abandoned their houses full of wine and the harvest and went to the city[177] or the mountains[178] with only their wives and paraments.[179]

When King Charles heard about these things, he immediately proceeded after these evildoers with a multitude of people from the territory of Bergamo, went to Brescia, then to Verona, and then to Mantua.

Little Charles went to Bavaria. His brother Carloman then went to meet his uncle, King Charles, and came to the river which is called Brenta; they greeted each other with peaceful words, and established a truce until the month of May.[180]

Carloman went to Bavaria. King Charles went to Rome, brought gifts to the church of Saint Peter,[181] and was anointed and crowned emperor by Pope John.[182] Charles then returned to Pavia in the month of January, in the above-mentioned ninth indiction.[183]

24. Emperor Charles returned to Pavia from Rome and, while he was residing there, he heard that the son of Louis, Carloman, was coming against him.[184] While he was gathering his army to fight him, some of his men, whose fidelity he trusted greatly, abandoned him and joined Carloman.[185] Having seen that, Charles fled and went to Gaul, but died suddenly during the journey.[186]

Having established order in the kingdom of Italy, Carloman returned to his father in Bavaria shortly thereafter.[187]

Meanwhile, King Louis[188]

[182] Pope John VIII (872-882) crowned Charles the Bald emperor on Christmas 875. On this event, see Nelson, *Charles the Bald*, pp. 239-242, and Arnaldi, *Natale 875: Politica, ecclesiologia e cultura del papato altomedievale*. The *Annales Fuldenses*, year 875, state that Charles the Bald obtained the imperial crown by bribing the Romans in the same way as Jugurtha had done with the ancient Romans.

[183] At Pavia the archbishop of Milan as well as some bishops and counts swore loyalty to Charles the Bald and elected him king of Italy. Cammarosano, *Nobili e re*, p. 169.

[184] Andreas of Bergamo made a mistake as, after being elected king of Italy, Charles the Bald went back to France. He returned to Italy in Summer 877. Nelson, *Charles the Bald*, pp. 243-253.

[185] The *Annales de Saint Bertin*, year 877, recount that, while Charles the Bald was in Tortona (Italy) with Pope John VIII and was waiting for the arrival of the most important aristocrats of his kingdom, he heard that they were organizing a plot, that they would never go to Italy, and that Carloman was coming. The emperor then decided to return to France. Nelson, *Charles the Bald*, pp. 251-252.

[186] According to the *Annales de Saint Bertin*, year 877, Charles the Bald died because his Jewish doctor had poisoned him. On the other hand, the *Annales Fuldenses*, year 877, relate that the emperor died of dysentery.

[187] The *Annales Fuldenses*, year 877, report that Carloman fell ill and was taken to Germany by using a litter.

[188] As the sentence is unfinished, one cannot be sure whether the author was referring to Louis, Charles the Bald's son, or to Louis the German, Carloman's father.

DE PIPPINI REGIS VICTORIA AVARICA

KING PIPPIN'S VICTORY OVER THE AVARS

[DE PIPPINI REGIS VICTORIA AVARICA]

I	Omnes gentes qui[a] fecisti, tu Christe, Dei sobules,
II	terras, fontes, rivos, montes et formasti hominem,
III	Avares, quos[b] converstistis[c] ultimis temporibus.

IV	Multa mala iam fecerunt ab antico tempore,
V	fana Dei dextruxerunt atque monasteria,
VI	vasa aurea sacrata, argentea, fictilia.

VII	Vestem sanctam polluerunt de ara sacratissima,
VIII	linteamina levitę et sanctęmonialium
IX	mulieribus[d] tradatam[e], suadente demone.

X	Misit Deus Petrum sanctum, principem apostulum[f],
XI	in auxilium Pippini, magni regis filium,
XII	ut viam eius comitaret et Francorum aciem.

XIII	Rex accintus Dei virtute Pippinus[g], rex catholicus,
XIV	castra figit super flumen albidum[h] Danubium,
XV	hostibus accingens[i] totum undique presidia.

XVI	Unguimeri satis pavens, Avarina genere,
XVII	regis dicens satis forte: «Tu Cacane perdite!»
XVIII	atque Catunę mulieri, malidictae coniugi:

---

[a] quas *Holder-Egger.* [b] Avaresque *Duemmler.* [c] convertisti *Duemmler Holder-Egger.* [d] muliebribus *D.* mulieribus *Holder-Egger.* [e] tradata *Duemmler Holder-Egger.* [f] apostolum *Duemmler.* [g] Pippin *Duemmler.* [h] albi *D.* albidum *Duemmler Holder-Egger.* [i] *D adds* n *to* accinges *interlineally.*

KING PIPPIN'S VICTORY OVER THE AVARS

1	O Christ, son of God, you, who made all peoples,
2	lands, springs, rivers and mountains, and formed man,
3	have converted the Avars[1] in the recent past.
4	They have done many evil deeds for a very long time;
5	they destroyed shrines of God, monasteries,
6	consecrated vessels of gold, silver items, and pottery.[2]
7	They polluted the holy trappings of the most sacred altars
8	and the linen vestments of the deacons and the nuns,
9	and, on the demon's advice, gave them to their wives.
10	God sent Saint Peter, the prince of the apostles,
11	in aid of Pippin, the great king's son,[3]
12	to accompany him and the army of the Franks.
13	King Pippin, a catholic king, girded with God's power,
14	pitched his camp near the white river Danube,
15	placing lookout posts against the enemy everywhere.
16	Unguimer of the Avar people, greatly frightened by that,
17	said to his king very loudly: «Oh Cacan,[4] you have lost!»,
18	and to the woman Catuna,[5] his accursed wife:

[1] The Avars were a nomadic people, who settled in Pannonia, an area corresponding approximately to present-day Hungary, in the second half of the sixth century after the Lombards left that region to move to Italy. For a general overview of the Avars, see Pohl, *Die Awaren*.

[2] Cf. 2 Tim. 2: 20.

[3] Pippin († 810) was Charlemagne's son.

[4] The rulers of the Avars held the title of khagan. Pohl, *Die Awaren*, pp. 293-300. Like many early medieval authors, the poet used Cacan as if it were a name and for this reason I have preferred to leave the term Cacan in the translation.

[5] The wife of the khagan had the title of katun. Pohl, *Die Awaren*, pp. 305-306. In this case too, the author seems to employ this term as if it were a name.

XIX	«Regna vestra consumata, ultra non regnabitis,
XX	regna vestra diu longa[a] cristianis tradita
XXI	a Pippino demollita, principe catholico.
XXII	Adpropinquat rex Pippinus forti cum[b] exercitu,
XXIII	fines tuos occupare, depopularet[c] populum,
XXIV	montes, silvas[d] atque colles poneret[e] presidia.
XXV	Tolle cito, porta tecum copiosa munera:
XXVI	sceptrum[f] regis adorare, ut paululum[g] possis vivere,
XXVII	aurum, gemmas illi offert, nec[h] te tradat funeri.»
XXVIII	Audiens Cacanus rex, undique perterritus,
XXIX	protinus ascendens mulam cum Tarcanis[i] primatibus
XXX	regem venit adorare[j] et plagaret[k] munere.
XXXI	Regi dicens: «Salve princeps, esto noster dominus,
XXXII	regnum meum tibi trado cum festucis et foliis,
XXXIII	silvas, montes atque colles cum omnibus nascentiis.
XXXIV	Tolle tecum proles nostras, parent tibi obsequia,
XXXV	de primatibus nec parcas, terga verti acie[l],
XXXVI	colla nostra, proles nostras, dicioni tradimus.»
XXXVII	Nos fideles cristiani Deo agamus gratiam,
XXXVIII	qui regnum regis confirmavit super regnum Uniae,
XXXIX	et victoriam donavit illi[m] de paganis gentibus.

[a] longe *Duemmler.* [b] cum forti *Holder-Egger.* [c] occupare, depopulare *Duemmler Holder-Egger.* [d] *B adds* a *to* silvs *interlineally.* [e] ponere Duemmler. [f] exceptrum *D.* sceptrum *Duemmler Holder-Egger.* [g] paullum *Duemmler.* [h] offer, ne *Duemmler.* [i] Tarcan *Duemmler.* [j] *D corrects* adoraret *to* adorare. [k] plagare *Duemmler.* [l] aciem *Holder-Egger.* [m] *D adds* illi *interlineally. Duemmler and Holder-Egger omit* illi.

19	«Your kingdoms are finished; you will reign no more.
20	Your kingdoms will be destroyed by the catholic prince Pippin
21	and will be given to the Christians for a very long time.

22	King Pippin approaches with a strong army
23	in order to take possession of your territories, to sweep away your people
24	and to place his garrisons on your mountains, forests and hills.

25	Rise up quickly and take many gifts with you;
26	pay homage to the scepter of the king so that you might live a little longer.
27	Offer him gold and gems so that he does not deliver you to death.»

28	Hearing this, King Cacan was completely terrified.
29	He immediately mounted on a she-mule and, with the noble Tarcans,[6]
30	went to pay homage to the king and to placate him with gifts.

31	He said to the king: «Greetings, prince! Be our lord!
32	With these branches and leaves,[7] I hand over to you my kingdom,
33	forests, mountains, and hills, with everything that springs forth from them.

34	Take our children with you; let them offer their allegiance to you;
35	do not spare the nobles; turn back with your army;
36	We will hand over to your authority our necks and our children.»

37	We, faithful Christians, give thanks to God,
38	who established the kingdom of our king over the kingdom of the Huns[8]
39	and bestowed upon him the victory over the pagan peoples.

---

[6] Tarcan was a title held by the most important Avars. Pohl, *Die Awaren*, pp. 301-302.

[7] This seems to be a reference to a common medieval practice according to which any transfer of land was symbolized by the gift of a small branch by the old to new owner.

[8] Many medieval authors called Huns the Avars.

XL	Vivat, vivat rex Pippinus in timore domini,
XLI	avus regnat et senescat et procreet filios,
XLII	qui palatia conservent[a] in vita et post obitum.
XLIII	Qui conclusit regnum crande, amplum, potentissimum,
XLIV	quę regna terrę non fecerunt usque ad diem actenus,
XLV	neque cesar et pagani, sed divina gratia.
XLVI	Gloria aeterna patri, gloria sit filio.

---

[a] conservet *Holder-Egger.*

40	May King Pippin live, live in fear of the Lord,
41	may he grow old and reign on in old age and beget sons,
42	who will preserve his palaces in his lifetime and after his death.
43	He created a great, wide, and most powerful kingdom,
44	something that the kingdoms of the earth were not able to do up to this day;
45	neither Caesar nor the pagans did this, but the grace of God did this.
46	Eternal glory be to the father and glory to the son.

RYTHMUS DE CAPTIVITATE LHUDUICI IMPERATORIS
RYTHMUS ON EMPEROR LOUIS'S CAPTIVITY

[RYTHMUS DE CAPTIVITATE LHUDUICI IMPERATORIS]

I	Audite, omnes fines terre,	orrore[a] cum tristitia
II	quale scelus fuid factum	in Benevento civitas:
III	Lhuduicum compreenderunt	sancto pio augusto.
IV	Beneventani se adunarunt	ad unum consilium,
V	Adelferio loquebatur	et dicebant principi:
VI	«Si nos eum vivum dimitemus,	certe nos peribimus;
VII	Celus magnum praeparavit	in istam provintiam,
VIII	regnum nostrum nobis tollit	nos habet pro nihilum,
IX	plures mala nobis fecit	rectum est ut moriad.»
X	Deposuerunt sancto pio	de suo palatio
XI	Adelferio illum ducebat	usque ad pretorium;
XII	ille vero gaudevisum[b]	tamquam ad martirium.
XIII	Exierunt Sado et Saducto	inoviabant imperio;
XIV	et ipse sancte pius	incipiebat dicere:
XV	«Tamquam ad latronem venistis	cum gladibus et fustibus.
XVI	Fuid namque tempus	vos allevavi[c] in omnibus,
XVII	modo vero surrexistis	adversum me consilium;
XVIII	nescio pro quid causam	vultis me occidere.

[a] errore *C.* orrore *Russo Mailler.* [b] gade visum *C Russo Mailler.* [c] allevavit *C.* allevavi *Russo Mailler.*

[1] Louis II, son of emperor Lothar, became king of Italy in 844, co-emperor in 850, and was emperor from 855 to 875.

[2] The *Rythmus* is the only narrative source mentioning Adelferius

[3] In this period, Adelchis (853-878) was the prince of Benevento.

[4] The author wrote *celus* instead of *scelus* because, according to the rules of this kind of poem, a word beginning with c was needed.

[5] A similar detail is reported in the *Chronicon Salernitanum*, ch. 109, which, however, recounts that it was the emperor's wife who harassed the Beneventans and held them in low esteem.

RYTHMUS ON EMPEROR LOUIS'S CAPTIVITY

1   Hear, in every part of the earth, with horror and sadness,

2   what impiety was done in the city of Benevento:

3   they seized the holy, pious augustus, Louis.[1]

4   The Beneventans gathered in one council

5   and Adelferius[2] talked to them. They told their prince:[3]

6   «If we release him alive, we will certainly die.

7   He did a great impiety[4] in this province,

8   he took our kingdom away from us, has no consideration of us,[5]

9   and did many evil things to us;[6] it is just that he dies.»[7]

10   They pulled the pious holy man down from his palace.[8]

11   Adelferius took him to the pretorium,

12   yet Louis was as happy as if he went to martyrdom.

13   Sadus[9] and Saductus[10] came forward, mocking the empire,

14   and the pious holy man began to say:

15   «You came to me with swords and clubs as if I were a thief.[11]

16   There was a time when I helped you in everything[12]

17   and now all of you have risen up against me.

18   I do not know the reason for which you want to kill me.

[6]   For the reasons leading to Louis II's imprisonment, see the introduction and the note in Andreas of Bergamo, *Historia*, ch. 20.

[7]   The gathering of the Beneventans and the discussion are recorded only in this source. For an analysis of the various versions of this episode, see Granier, *La captivité de l'empereur Louis II à Bénévent*.

[8]   According to Andreas of Bergamo, *Historia*, ch. 20, and *Chronicon Salernitanum*, ch. 109, Louis II resided in a palace. The *Annales de Saint Bertin*, year 871, on the other hand, recount that the emperor took refuge in a tower where he faced the Beneventans' attacks for three days.

[9]   He is the Emir of Bari, Sawdān, who was captured after the conquest of Bari by Louis II. Other Latin sources call him *Saudan, Seodan, Saugdan*, etc.

[10]   A Capuan family of this period had this name. Erchempert recounts that the Saducti fled to Capua following a conflict with the gastald of Capua, Landulf. Erchempert, *Ystoriola Longobardorum Beneventum degentium*, ch. 15. A Saductus is mentioned among the signatories of the principality of Benevento's division. *Chronicon Salernitanum*, ch. 84[b].

[11]   Luke 22: 52. For the meaning of this passage, see the introduction.

[12]   The fact that the southern Lombards asked Louis II for his help is also related by *Cronicae Sancti Benedicti Casinensis*, I, 6, II, 14, and Erchempert, *Ystoriola Longobardorum Beneventum degentium*, chs. 19-20.

XIX	Generacio crudelis	veni interficere,
XX	ecclesieque sanctis Dei	venio diligere,
XXI	sanguine veni vindicare	quod super terram
	fusus est.»	

XXII	Kalidus ille temtator	ratum adque nomine
XXIII	coronam imperii sibi in caput	ponet et dicebat populo:
XXIV	«Ecce sumus imperator,	possum vobis regere.»

XXV	Leto animo habebat	de illo que fecerat,
XXVI	a demonio vexatur,	ad terram ceciderat:
XXVII	exierunt multe turme	videre mirabilia.

XXVIII	Magnus dominus Jesus Christus	iudicavit judicium:
XXIX	multa gens paganorum	exit in Calabria,
XXX	super Salerno pervenerunt	possidere civitas.

XXXI	luratum est ad	sante Dei reliquie
XXXII	ipse regnum defendendum	et alium requirere.

---

[13] Sawdān. The sentence is not very clear, but it seems that the author did a play on words with Sadus/Sawdān and Satan.

[14] The *Rythmus* is the only source that mentions these episodes. The fact that the emir of Bari enjoyed a certain amount of freedom during his captivity in Benevento and acted to create conflicts between the Beneventans and Louis II is, however, recorded by the *Chronicon Salernitanum*, ch. 109, and Constantine Porphyrogenitus, *De administrando imperio*, p. 130. Cf. Russo Mailler, *La politica meridionale*, p. 16.

19	I came to kill a cruel people.
20	I came because I love the Church of the holy God,
21	I came to avenge the blood that had been poured out on the earth.»
22	Behaving according to his name, that cunning tempter[13]
23	put the imperial crown on his head and told the people:
24	«Here I am the emperor and I can rule you.»
25	He was happy with what he had done,
26	but he fell to the ground, struck by the demon.
27	A great crowd hastened to see the wondrous event.[14]
28	The great Lord Jesus Christ expressed his judgment.
29	Many pagans left Calabria
30	and went against Salerno to take possession of the city.[15]
31	Oaths were sworn on the holy relics of God
32	that the emperor would defend the kingdom and would seek another one.[16]

[15] According to Erchempert, God had the Muslims come from Africa in order to avenge the offense to Louis II. They raided Campania and besieged Salerno. Erchempert, *Ystoriola Longobardorum Beneventum degentium*, chs. 34-35. The same story is recounted in the *Chronicon Salernitanum*, ch. 111, which adds that the Saracens came from Africa, but landed in Calabria, thus supporting the version reported in the *Rythmus*.

[16] The author is probably referring to the fact that, after liberating Louis II and forcing him to swear he would never go back to their land with an army without their permission, the Beneventans asked for his help against the Muslims who were devastating Campania.

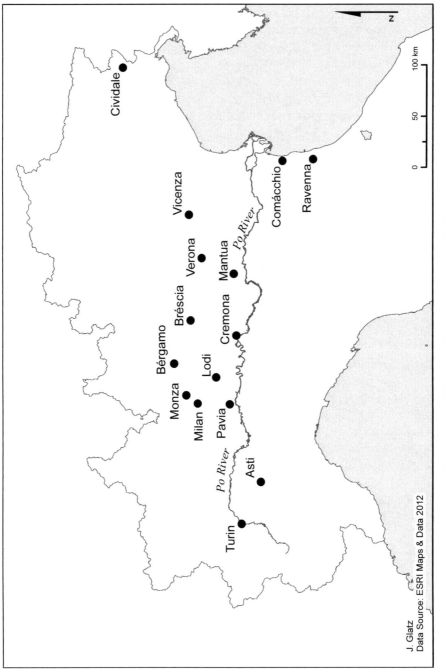

Northern Italy and the main locations mentioned in the texts.

J. Glatz
Data Source: ESRI Maps & Data 2012

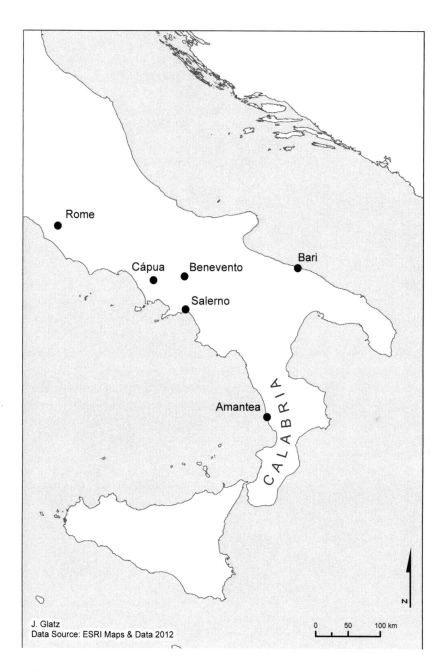

Central and Southern Italy and the main locations mentioned in the texts.

INDEX OF BIBLICAL QUOTATIONS

Historia Langobardorum codicis Gothani

Ps. 112: 7-8	ch. 1
Matt. 9: 13	ch. 1
John 10: 16	ch. 1
Rom. 5: 13	ch. 1

Andreae Bergomensis Historia

Prov. 21: 1	ch. 20
Prov. 30: 27	ch. 21
Matt. 5: 44	ch. 11
Matt. 23: 12	ch. 19
Luke 14: 11	ch. 19
Luke 21: 31	ch. 12
1 John 3: 15	ch. 11
John 6: 56	ch. 18
Rom. 8: 31	ch. 18

Rythmus de captivitate Lhuduici imperatoris

Luke 22: 52	line 15

INDEX VERBORUM*

Accendere: AB, ch. 16: «in Vulgarorum gens divina aspiracio accensa est».

Accidere: G, ch. 6: «ut per fęmeneum primum exordium accidit mala suasio peccati».

Accingere: VA, line 15: «hostibus accingens totum undique presidia».

Accintus: VA, line 13: «Rex accintus Dei virtute Pippinus».

Accipere: G, ch. 10; AB, ch. 1, pp. 70, 72.

Accusare: AB, ch. 1, p. 68.

Acies: G, ch. 2; AB, chs. 13, 20; VA, lines 12, 35.

Adbrevatio/Adbreviatio: AB, ch. 1, pp. 66, 72, ch. 2.

Adducere: G, chs. 5, 11; AB, chs. 10, 22.

Adimplere: AB, ch. 12.

Adipiscere: G, ch. 10; AB, ch. 1, p. 68.

Adiungere: G, ch. 10; AB, ch. 14: «Postmodum cum Burgundionibus adiunctus».

Adiutor: G, ch. 8: «sacerdotum facti sunt adiutores», chs. 10, 11; AB, ch. 1, p. 68.

Adiutorium: AB, ch. 23.

Adiuvare: AB, chs. 17, 19.

Adiuvator: G, ch. 10.

Adniti: AB, ch. 5: «adnitentibus suis».

Adorare: VA, line 26: «sceptum regis adorare», line 30: «regem venit adorare».

Adpropinquare: VA, line 22.

Adtrahere: AB, ch. 1, p. 66.

Adulterium: AB, ch. 23: «adulteria vel incendia fatientes».

Adunare: AB, ch. 17: «adunantes secum magis ac magis fideles populus», ch. 24; R, line 4.

Advenire: AB, chs. 21, 23.

Adventus: AB, chs. 4, 6, 14.

Adversarius: AB, ch. 11: «Si me vindicabo de adversario meo, non habebo vitam aeternam?».

Adversum: R, line 17.

Aecclesia/Ecclesia: G, ch. 1; AB, ch. 1, p. 70, ch. 4: «aecclesiae Romane Leo papa regebat... ornamentum aecclesie», ch. 9, ch. 11: «ecclesie Mediolanensis Angelbertus archiepiscopus regebat... Ad pedes vero noluit venire propter reverentiae honorem aecclesiarum», chs. 16, 17, 23; R, line 20.

Aedomada: AB, ch. 23.

Aetas/etas: AB, ch. 1, p. 66: «iuvenili etate», ch. 7: «senesque aetatis».

Aeternus/Eternus: AB, ch. 11; VA, line 46.

Agere: VA, line 37.

Agnus: G, ch. 1: «postea agni inter dominicum gregem pascentes».

Albidus: VA, line 14.

Allevare: R, line 16.

Altus: G, ch. 1: «ut ex alto salutem consequeretur».

Amabilis: AB, ch. 1, p. 68.

Amator: AB, ch. 9.

---

* Abbreviations: G = Historia Langobardorum Codicis Gothani; AB = Andreae Bergomatis Historia; VA = De Pippini Regis Victoria Avarica; R = Rythmus de Captivitate Lhuduici imperatoris.

Ambulare: AB, ch. 22.

Amen: G, ch. 11.

Amicicia: G, ch. 2: «foedus amicicię», ch. 5: «pactum et foedus amicicię».

Amicus: AB, ch. 1, p. 68.

Amnis: G, ch. 2: «Vindilicus dicitur amnis».

Amor: AB, ch. 16.

Ampliare: AB, ch. 1, p. 74: «Legem quidem Langubardorum ampliavit».

Amplissimus: AB, ch. 1, p. 68.

Amplius: AB, ch. 12.

Amplus: VA, line 43.

Angaria: G, ch. 6.

Angelus: AB, ch. 17.

Angustia: AB, ch. 12.

Animus: G, ch. 2: «ardentissimo animo»; AB, ch. 1, p. 68, ch. 14; R, line 25.

Annona/Anona: AB, ch. 17: «annonam metentes», ch. 23: «relinquentes domos suas plena vino et anona».

Annus: G, chs. 2, 3, 4, 5, 6, 7, 8, 9; AB, ch. 1, pp. 66, 68, 70, 72, 74, chs. 3, 5, 7, 8, 12, 13, 14, 15, 19, 21, 22.

Antiquus/Anticus: G, ch. 1: «antiqui parentes Langobardorum», ch. 2: «sicut nostri antiqui patres», ch. 11: «sicut fecit antiquissimis diebus»; AB, ch. 2: «antiqui homines», ch. 20: «anticus hostis»; VA, line 4: «multa mala iam fecerunt ab antico tempore».

Aparere: AB, ch. 2: «cui incredibile aparet».

Aperilis/Aprilis: G, ch. 5; AB, ch. 1, p. 68.

Apices: AB, ch. 14.

Apostolicus: AB, chs. 5, 16, 23.

Apostolus: G, ch. 10; AB, ch. 11; VA, line 10.

Appellare: AB, ch. 1, p. 66.

Aqua: G, ch. 1: «ad aquam vivam poscendam»; AB, ch. 1, p. 72: «In flumen Ticinum ab aquis negatus est».

Ara: VA, line 7: «Vestem sanctam polluerunt de ara sacratissima».

Arbitrium: G, ch. 8: «nam antea per cadarfada et arbitrio seu ritus fierunt causationes».

Arbor: AB, ch. 21.

Archiepiscopus: AB, chs. 11, 22.

Ardens: G, ch. 2: «ardentissimo animo».

Argenteus: VA, line 6.

Aridus: AB, ch. 21: «silves tenerrimum cum sua folia aride facte sunt».

Aripere: AB, ch. 1, p. 72.

Arma: AB, ch. 18: «arma celestis confortavit christianos».

Ars: AB, ch. 4: «cum multis sapientissimis ars litterarum».

Ascendere: AB, ch. 1, pp. 66, 72, chs. 19, 21; VA, line 29.

Asper: G, ch. 1: «sanguinea et aspera progeines».

Aspiracio: AB, ch. 16.

Astutus: AB, ch. 4: «Papa vero probata gens Francorum astuti et nobiles».

Attingere: G, ch. 2: «deinde certantes Saxonię patria attigerunt».

Audatia: AB, ch. 19.

Audax: AB, ch. 1, p. 66, ch. 3: «audaces uterque fuerunt».

Audire: AB, ch. 1, p. 68, ch. 3: «quantum audivimus», chs. 4, 6, 8: «sicut audivimus», chs. 11, 14, 17, 19, 23, 24; R, line 1: «Audite, omnes fines terre».

Augustus: AB, ch. 1, p. 68, ch. 15: «domnus Hludowicus augustus», chs. 20, 22: «Sequenti autem mense augusto Hludowicus imperator defunctus est, pridie idus augusti»; R, line 3: «Lhuduicum compreenderunt sancto pio augusto».

Aureus: VA, line 6: «vasa aurea».

Aurum: VA, line 27.

Auxiliare: AB, ch. 1, p. 66: «Deo auxiliante».

Auxilium: G, ch. 5; AB, ch. 1; VA, line 11.

Avus: AB, ch. 10; VA, line 41.

Balneum: AB, ch. 1, p. 72.

Bando: G, ch. 4: «tulit bandonem ipsius».

Baptisma: G, ch. 1: «salutem invenerunt baptismatis».

Baptiçare: AB, ch. 16.

Barba: G, ch. 1: «nomen mutati sunt pro eo ad barba prolixa et numquam tonsa»; AB, ch. 1, p. 66.

Barbanus: G, ch. 4; AB, ch. 23.

Beatus: AB, ch. 1, p. 72.

Bellum: G, ch. 2: «bella et vastationes quę fecerunt reges eorum», chs. 5, 6; AB, ch. 1, pp. 68, 70, 72, chs. 2, 24.

Benedictio: AB, ch. 18.

Benefacere: AB, ch. 11.

Beneficium: AB, ch. 14.

Benignitas: AB, ch. 5.

Bestia: AB, ch. 5.

Bibere: G, ch. 6; AB, ch. 18.

Blasphemia: AB, ch. 3: «Mater vero eorum hęc separatio audiens, Carlemanni filii sui blasphemiam intulit».

Blasphemium: AB, ch. 13: «Sed dum iret et reverteret, multa devastantes pauperorum domibus, blasphemia multa incurrit».

Bona: G, ch. 4: «praedavit omnia bona eorum».

Bonum: AB, ch. 20: «malum pro bonum».

Bonus: G, ch. 1: «numerum bonorum effecti sunt», ch. 10; AB, chs. 11, 13: «per bonam concordiam», ch. 17: «angelus Domini bonus».

Breviare: G, ch. 1.

Brevitas: AB, ch. 14.

Bucina: AB, ch. 18.

Cadarfada: G, ch. 8: «nam antea per cadarfada et arbitrio seu ritus fierunt causationes».

Cadere: AB, ch. 1, p. 66, ch. 14: «tanta quidem nivem Italia cecidit», ch. 21: «pruina cecidit»; R, line 26: «ad terram ceciderat».

Caelestis/Celestis: AB, ch. 17: «arma celestis confortavit christianos», ch. 20: «Caelestis timor super Beneventanos inruit».

Caelum: AB, chs. 11, 22.

Campus: G, ch. 4: «in campis Filda»; AB, ch. 1, pp. 66, 72, ch. 14: «Hupert in campo comprehendit».

Canalis: G, ch. 2: «Albiae fluvii canalis».

Cannonicus: G, ch. 8: «Langobardi ad cannonica tenderunt certamina».

Cantor: AB, chs. 4, 9.

Capere: AB, ch. 1, p. 70.

Capitalis: G, ch. 11: «capitalem subierunt sentenciam».

Capitulum/Capitulus: AB, ch. 1, p. 72: «in aedicto Langubardorum novem conposuit capitula», ch. 3: «posuit in edicto capituli octo... posuit in edicto capitula XIII».

Captivus: G, chs. 3, 11; AB, ch. 17.

Capud/caput: AB, chs. 6, 11, 17; R, line 23.

Caritas: AB, chs. 16, 20.

Carnis: AB, ch. 18.

Carta: G, ch. 5: «cartam conscriptionis».

Castellum: AB, ch. 20: «Erant enim Franci separati per castellas vel civitates».

Castrum: AB, ch. 15: «in castro, qui dicitur Bari»; VA, line 14: «castra figit».

Catholicus: AB, ch. 16; VA, line 13: «rex catholicus», line 21: «principe catholico».

Cauda: AB, ch. 22: «stella commetis in caelo comparuit, similtudo radientibus longinque caude».

Causa: AB, chs. 3, 11; R, line 18.

Causatio: G, ch. 8: «arbitrio seu ritus fierunt causationes».

Cecitas: AB, ch. 3: «oculorum cecitate perculsus est».

Cedere: AB, ch. 18: «Christiani autem post eos cedentes, non cessabant».

Celebrare: AB, ch. 18.

Celus (= scelus): R, line 7: «Celus magnum praeparavit in istam provintiam».

Certamen: G, chs. 5, 8.

Certare: G, ch. 2.

Certe: R, line 5: «Si nos eum vivum dimitemus, certe nos peribimus».

Cesar: VA, line 45.

Cessare: AB, ch. 18.

Christianus/Cristianus: AB, chs. 16, 17, 18; VA, lines 20, 37.

Cito: VA, line 25.

Civis: G, chs. 6, 11.

Civitas: G, chs. 6, 7; AB, ch, 1, p. 70, chs. 4, 5, 10, 13, 17, 20, 22, 23; R, lines 2, 30.

Clamare: AB, ch. 1, p. 72.

Clangere: G, ch. 2: «in Beovinidis aciem et clauses seu tuba clangencium».

Clangor: AB, ch. 18: «Factum est sonitus magnus clangore bucine».

Clericus: AB, ch. 14.

Clerus: AB, ch. 22.

Cognomen: G, ch. 1.

Colere: AB, chs. 16, 18.

Coligere/Colligere: AB, chs. 11, 18, 23.

Collis: VA, lines 24, 33.

Collum: G, ch. 6; VA, line 36.

Comendare: AB, ch. 1, p. 68.

Comitare: VA, line 12.

Commetis: AB, ch. 22.

Commitere: G, ch. 4; AB, chs. 17, 18.

Commorari: AB, ch. 1, p. 66.

Communio: AB, ch. 18.

Comperire/Conperire: AB, chs. 12, 17, 23.

Complacere: AB, ch. 19.

Componere: AB, ch. 1, p. 66.

Comprehendere/Compreendere: AB, chs. 4, 18; R, line 3.

Comunis: AB, ch. 1, p. 70.

Concedere: G, chs. 10, 11; AB, ch. 1, p. 70, chs. 7, 10.

Concidere: AB, ch. 1, p. 66.

Concludere: VA, line 43.

Concordia: AB, ch. 13.

Condere: AB, ch. 13.

Condire: AB, ch. 22: «trahentes eum a terra et mirifice condientes».

Confessor: AB, ch. 22.

Confidare: AB, chs. 17, 24.

Confirmare: AB, ch. 16; VA, line 38.

Conflictum: AB, ch. 11.

Confortare: AB, ch. 17, ch. 18: «arma celestis confortavit christianos».

Confortacio/Confortatio: AB, ch. 6: «Regem confortationis nostrae iam devictus est», ch. 17: «tantum ad vos petimus, ut des nos caput confortacionis».

Congregare: AB, ch. 1, p. 66, chs. 5, 6.

Coniugium: AB, ch. 1, pp. 68, 70, chs. 3, 9.

Coniungere: AB, chs. 18, 23, 24.

Coniux: AB, ch. 1, p. 70, chs. 3, 8, 15; VA, line 18.

Conponere: AB, ch. 1, pp. 70, 72, ch. 14: «Pauca quidem sane dum per gestis filiorum regum seriem apices conponam».

Conscribere: AB, ch. 1, pp. 72, 74.

Conscriptio: G, ch. 5: «cartam conscriptionis», ch. 8.

Consedere: AB, ch. 1, p. 66, ch. 4.

Consensum: AB, ch. 3.

Consentire: AB, ch. 11.

Conservare: AB, ch. 3: «et pax firmissima ex utraque partis firmaverunt, sed minime conservaverunt»; VA, line 42.

Consilium: G, ch. 6; AB, ch. 1, p. 70, chs. 4, 6, 9, 10, 11, 13, 18, 20, 23; R, line 4: «Beneventani se adunarunt ad unum consilium», line 17.

Consistere: AB, chs. 15, 19.

Consonare: AB, ch. 4, ch. 19: «Grandis ignominiam de occisorum nostrorum consonant».

Constituere: AB, ch. 1, pp. 66, 70, 72, chs. 3, 9, 11, 14.

Construere: AB, ch. 1, p. 72, ch. 7, ch. 13: «acies hinc et inde ex utraque partis constructe».

Consuetudo: G, ch. 6: «feminalis tenet consuetudo peccandi».

Consumare: VA, line 19: «Regna vestra consumata».

Consumere: G, ch. 11: «cives eorum igne sunt exanimati et consumpti».

Contemplare: AB, ch. 12.

Contendere: AB, ch. 6.

Contentio: AB, ch. 13.

Contexere: AB, ch. 1, p. 66: «Longobardorum gesta... a Paulo viro philosopho contesta... pauca de multis in hac adbrevatione contexere nisi sumus».

Continere: AB, ch. 1, pp. 70, 72, ch. 2: «hic supter continet eorum historiae».

Contingere: AB, ch. 13: «suisque hominibus a multis simili modo contigerunt».

Contradictor: AB, ch. 13: «multa milia sternere contradictorum paganorum».

Contrarius: AB, ch. 20: «Fuit autem iste contrarius discessionis dies XXXV».

Conversatio: G, ch. 2: «Hic incipiens originem et nationem seu parentelam Langobardorum, exitus et conversationem eorum».

Convincere: AB, ch. 11: «Illi autem convicti, ad haec verba consenserunt».

Copiosus: VA, line 25.

Cor: G, ch. 1: «duricia cordis»; AB, ch. 6: «cui iam munera Caroli excecaverat cor», ch. 20.

Corona: G, ch. 10; R, line 23: «coronam imperii sibi in caput ponet».

Coronare: AB, ch. 23: «ab apostolico Iohanne unctus et ab honore imperii coronatus».

Corpus: AB, ch. 1, p. 74: «in edicti corpore conscribere iussit», chs. 13, 22.

Cotidiae: AB, ch. 10.

Crinis: AB, ch. 1, p. 66.

Credere: AB, ch. 20.

Cremare: AB, ch. 22: «civitate Cummaclo igne cremaverunt».

Crescere: AB, ch. 10: «Honor autem maior, id est imperialis, crescebat cottidiae Lotharii».

Cronica: AB, ch. 1, p. 70.

Crudelis: G, ch. 11; R, line 19.

Cubicularius: G, ch. 6.

Culpa/Culpare: G, ch. 10: «innumerabilibus viris, qui eidem culparunt incessanter, culpas dimisit».

Cupere: AB, ch. 1, p. 66.

Cupiditas: G, ch. 10: «nulli lucri cupiditas peragrare»; AB, ch. 17.

Custodia: AB, ch. 10: «in custodia miserunt».

Custodire: AB, chs. 17, 20.

Debellare: G, ch. 5; AB, chs. 13, 19.

Defendere: AB, ch. 1, p. 68, ch. 11; R, line 32.

Defensare: G, chs. 10, 11.

Defensator: G, ch. 10: «defensator domni Petri principis apostolorum», ch. 11.

Defensio: AB, ch. 17.

Deficere: AB, ch. 24: «quidam de suis, in quorum fidelitatem maxime confidebat, ab eo defecti, ad Carlemannum se coniungebat».

Defungere: AB, ch. 1, pp. 66, 72, chs. 3, 7, 8, 12, 13, 14, 22.

Delectare: AB, ch. 2: «hic scrivere delectatus sum».

Delere: AB, ch. 1, p. 68.

Demollire: G, ch. 10: «poterat omnia demollire»; VA, line 21.

Demon: VA, line 9: «suadente demone».

Demonium: R, line 26: «a demonio vexatur, ad terram ceciderat».

Deponere: AB, ch. 1, p. 68; R, line 10.

Depopulare: VA, line 23.

Desolare: AB, ch. 17.

Devastare: AB, chs. 13, 21, 23.

Devastatio: AB, ch. 6.

Devincere: AB, chs. 6, 19.

Dextruere: VA, line 5.

Dicere: G, chs. 1, 2, 11; AB, ch. 1, pp. 66, 70, 72, chs. 4, 6, 10, 11, 12, 13, 14, 15, 17, 18, 19: «Tunc dixerunt per suorum audatiae elationis... Et dictis factis, Franci querere ceperunt», chs. 20, 21, 22; VA, lines 17, 31; R, lines 5, 14, 23.

Dicio: VA, line 36: «colla nostra, proles nostra, dicioni tradimus».

Dies: G, chs. 2, 6, 11: «Praesentem diem per eius adiutorium splenduit Italia, sicut fecit antiquissimis diebus»; AB, ch. 1, pp. 68, 70, 72, ch. 7: «senesque aetatis et plenum dierum», ch. 12: «facta est lux quasi in die... prope est die Domini magnus et manifestus... suosque dies finivit in pace», chs. 13, 14, 18, 20, 22; VA, line 44.

Dignitas: G, ch. 10; AB, ch. 1, p. 68: «pommorum genera vel reliqua dignitate transmittens», p. 70, ch. 4: «tanta quidem dignitatem cantores ibi fecerunt», ch. 7: «dignitatem ubertatemque advenit», ch. 17: «honorem dignitatis eorum tribuit».

Dignus: G, chs. 10, 11.

Dilectio: AB, ch. 20.

Diligere: AB, chs. 9, 11, 20: «dilectione caritatis inter se diliebant».

Diluculum: AB, ch. 18: «summo diluculo».

Dimitere: AB, ch. 20.

Dirigere: AB, ch. 1, p. 68, ch. 14.

Discessio: AB, ch. 20.

Discordia: AB, ch. 1, p. 72, chs. 3, 13.

Dispendium: AB, ch. 18: «multa dispendia adiutorium soldani».

Disponere: AB, ch. 14: «suorum fines rebellare disponebat», ch. 24: «Carlomannus vero regnum Italie disponens».

Dissipare/Discipare: AB, ch. 13: «discipata est nobilitas Aquitanorum», ch. 17: «terra nostra dissipaverunt», ch. 19: «Quid nobis fiducie habere debemus in navibus nostris? Dissipemus eas».

Distantia: AB, ch. 23.

Dividere: AB, ch. 1, pp. 66, 68.

Divinare: G, 1: «nisi divinandum perspicerit».

Divinitas: AB, ch 16: «divinitatis scientiae instructus».

Divinus: AB, ch. 1, p. 72, ch. 5: «divina aspiracio», ch. 16; VA, line 45.

Divitiae: AB, ch. 1, p. 68.

Doctor: AB, ch. 12: «doctores in suorum monitiones dixerunt», ch. 16: «recepit doctores ab eodem domno apostolico».

Dogma: G, ch. 3.

Dolere: AB, ch. 17.

Dolor: AB, ch. 8.

Dominator: G, ch. 10: «Baivariam dominator existet».

Dominicus: G, ch. 1: «agni inter dominicum gregem pascentes».

Dominium: AB, ch. 1, p. 66.

Dominus/Domnus: G, ch. 5: «factus est dominus Italię», ch. 11: «magno et glorioso filio suo domno Pippino magno regi... domno Pippino... per domni nostri merita»; AB, ch. 1, p. 68, chs. 11, 12, 13, 14, 15, 16, 17, 18, 19, 20, 21; VA, lines 31, 40; R, line 28.

Domus: G, ch. 2; AB, chs. 13, 23.

Donare: VA, line 39.

Donum: AB, chs. 16, 23.

Ducere: AB, ch. 1, p. 70: «duxit uxorem, Teudolinda nomine», chs. 3, 7, 11.

Duricia: G, ch. 1: «duricia cordis».

Dux: G, ch. 7; AB, ch. 1, pp. 66, 70, 72, ch. 6.

Edictum/Aedictum: AB, ch. 1, p. 70: «edictum Langubardorum conposuit», p. 72, p. 74: «in edicti corpore conscribere iussit», ch. 3.

Edificare: AB, ch. 1, p. 70.

Egredi: AB, ch. 1, pp. 66, 72, ch. 5.

Egrotare: AB, ch. 13.

Elatio: AB, ch. 19.

Electus: AB, ch. 1, p. 68, ch. 19.

Elegere: AB, ch. 1, p. 70, chs. 3, 17, 19.

Elemosina: AB, ch. 1, p. 74.

Elevare: AB, ch. 2.

Emittere: G, ch. 2: «foedus amicicię emiserunt».

Episcopus: AB, chs. 17, 18, 22.

Equus: AB, ch. 18.

Estimare: AB, ch. 1, p. 66.

Eunuchus: AB, ch. 1, p. 68.

Europa: AB, ch. 1: «In septentrionali plaga Europae».

Evacuare: G, ch. 11: «Abari sunt evacuati et superati».

Evadere: AB, ch. 19: «reliqui fuga vix evaderunt».

Evangelium: AB, chs. 11, 12.

Evellere: AB, ch. 8: «oculi Bernardi evulsit».

Evolvere: AB, ch. 1, p. 68, chs. 5, 21.

Exaltare: AB, ch. 19: «qui venerant exaltati».

Exanimare: G, ch. 11.

Excecare: AB, ch. 6: «cui iam munera Caroli excecaverat cor».

Exercitus: G, chs. 3, 11; AB, ch. 24; VA, line 22.

Exilium: AB, ch. 10.

Exire: G, ch. 6; AB, ch. 1, p. 68, chs. 4, 6, 13, 14, 17, 18, 19; R, lines 13, 27, 29.

Exitus: G, chs. 1, 2.

Exordium: G, ch. 1: «per femeneum primum exordium accidit mala suasio peccati».

Explere: AB, ch. 1, p. 72.

Expugnare: G, chs. 2, 4.

Exsequi: AB, ch. 14: «adventum primi ordinis, sicut cepimus, exsequamur».

Extimare: AB, ch. 12.

Extremum: G, ch. 2: «ab extremis Gallie finibus».

Exultatio: AB, ch. 1, p. 72.

Exurgere: AB, ch. 11: «causa exurgens».

Facere: G, chs. 2, 4, 5, 7, 8, 10, 11; AB, ch. 1, pp. 66, 68, 72, chs. 3, 4, 5, 6, 10, 11, 12, 13, 14, 17, 18, 19, 20, 21, 23; VA, lines 1, 4, 44; R, lines 2, 25.

Facies: AB, ch. 1, p. 66.

Factum: AB, ch. 3: «Eorumque factis retinere non possumus», ch. 14: «animus meus ad reliquis factis percurrit».

Facultas: G, ch. 10.

Famis: AB, ch. 1, p. 66, chs. 5, 7.

Fanum: VA, line 5.

Fatigatio: AB, ch. 1, p. 72: «Contra Halahis tirrannum fatigatione sustentus», ch. 14: «Multa fatigatio Langobardi et oppressio a Sclavorum gens sustinuit».

Febroarius: AB, ch. 19.

Femeneus: G, ch. 6: «per femeneum primum exordium accidit mala suasio peccati».

Femina: AB, ch. 1, p. 66.

Feminalis: G, ch. 6: «usque ad presentem diem feminalis tenet consuetudo peccandi».

Ferebundus: AB, ch. 3.

Ferre: AB, ch. 18: «stipendia quicquid soldani pergebat tullerunt», ch. 22: «tulit corpus eius».

Fertilis: AB, ch. 1, p. 66.

Festuca: VA, line 32: «regnum meum tibi trado cum festucis et foliis».

Festum: AB, ch. 18: «celebrarent magnum diem, festum sicut erat, hoc est nativitas domini nostri Iesu Christi».

Fictilia: VA, line 6.

Fidelis: AB, ch. 14: «se fidelissimo esse dicebat... cum reliquis fidelibus suis dirixit», chs. 15, 17, 18, 20: «quatenus ubicumque fidelissimi imperatoris invenissent»; VA, line 37.

Fidelitas: AB, ch. 6: «mandans eorum fidelitatis fidem suscepturos et honoraturos... Eamus eorum fidelitate», ch. 24.

Fidere: AB, ch. 1, p. 66, chs. 17, 20.

Fides: AB, chs. 6, 8, 16, 20.

Fiducia: AB, ch. 19.

Filia: G, chs. 4, 5, 6; AB, ch. 1, pp. 68, 70, ch. 3.

Filius: G, ch. 1: «misericors filius Dei», chs. 4, 5; AB, ch. 1, pp. 66, 68, 70, 72, chs. 3, 5, 7, 9, 10, 11, 12, 13, 14, 23, 24; VA, lines 11, 41, 46.

Finire: G, ch. 2: «Ligurius fluvius Albię fluvii canalis inundans et nomen finitur», ch. 10: «Hic finitum est regnum Langobardorum»; AB, ch. 3: «vita finivit», ch. 21.

Finis: G, ch. 2; AB, ch. 1, p. 66, chs. 13, 14, 15, 17, 19, 21, 22, 23; VA, line 23; R, line 1.

Firmare: AB, chs. 3, 23.

Firmitas: AB, ch. 17.

Firmus: AB, ch. 3: «et pax firmissima ex utraque partis firmaverunt».

Fletus: AB, ch. 22.

Floridus: AB, ch. 1, p. 66: «barba florida».

Fluere: G, ch. 1: «fluentem lac et mel».

Flumen: AB, ch. 1, pp. 66, 72, ch. 22; VA, line 14.

Fluvius: G, ch. 2; AB, chs. 19, 23.

Foedus: G, chs. 2, 5.

Folia: AB, ch. 21; VA, line 32.

Foramen: AB, ch. 14.

Forte: VA, line 17: «dicens satis forte».

Fortia: AB, ch. 1, p. 70, ch. 10: «Sed totam fortia Lotharius ad se retentam habebat», ch. 13: «nec est eorum fortia qui resistat».

Fortis: AB, ch. 13: «viri fortes», ch. 18: «Cumque forti intencione pugnantes», ch. 19: «elegentes se fortissimi viri... utraque partis forti intenciones pugnantes»; VA, line 22.

Fortiter: AB, ch. 15: «se fortiter munierunt».

Fortitudo: G, ch. 11: «Deus patri concessit fortitudinis gratiam».

Frater: AB, ch. 1, p. 72, chs. 11, 12.

Fraudulenter: AB, ch. 1, p. 72.

Fraus: AB, ch. 20: «Beneventani per fraudem uno consilio ingerunt».

Fuga: G, ch. 6; AB, ch. 1, p. 72, chs. 17, 19, 24.

Fugire: AB, chs. 12, 18.

Fundere: R, line 21: «sanguine veni vindicare, quod super terram fusus est».

Funus: VA, line 27.

Furor: AB, ch. 10: «Quis potest dicere furore, quam vehementer pater eius iratus fuisset?».

Fustis: AB, ch. 14; R, line 15.

Gallotinnium: AB, ch. 18: «gallotinnio matutinis et summo diluculo episcopis et sacerdotibus missarum sollemnia celebrarent».

Gaudere: AB, ch. 1, p. 68, ch. 4: «magno gavisi sunt gaudio», ch. 17: «non gaudens cupiditatis eorum promissa... vero magnum gavisus est gaudium».

Gaudevisus: R, line 12.

Gaudium: AB, ch. 1, p. 68, chs. 4, 17.

Gelus: AB, ch. 14: «fuit gelus gravissimus».

Gemma: VA, line 27.

Generacio: R, line 19: «Generacio crudelis veni interficere».

Generare: G, ch. 2: «in multis partibus bella et pericula generarunt».

Genitium (= Gyneceum): AB, ch. 1, p. 68.

Genitor: AB, chs. 10, 11.

Gens: G, ch. 10: «super innumerabiles gentes eius timor irruit»; AB, ch. 1, p. 68, chs. 3, 4, 14, 15, 16, 17, 21; VA, line 1: «omnes gentes qui fecisti, tu Christe», line 39; R, line 29.

Genus: G, ch. 5: «Audoin ex genere fuit Gausus», ch. 7: «Clephs de genere Peleos»; AB, ch. 1, p. 68, ch. 7; VA, line 16.

Gerere: AB, ch. 1, pp. 70, 72 ch. 24.

Germanus: AB, ch. 1, p. 66, chs. 3, 13, 23.

Gesta: AB, ch. 1, p. 66, ch. 14.

Gignere: G, ch. 7: «genuit Aioald rex de Teodelinda filia nomine Gudebergam».

Glaciare: AB, ch. 14: «vinum intra vascula glaciavit».

Gladius: AB, ch. 1, pp. 70, 72; R, line 15.

Glatia: AB, ch. 14: «rumperetur ipsa glatia cum fuste ab ante ipsa spina».

Gloria: VA, line 46.

Gloriosus: G, ch. 10: «gloriosissimum Carolum regem», ch. 11.

Grabare: AB, ch. 20: «Quid grabati sumus sub potestatem Francorum».

Granum: AB, ch. 21: «granas minutas».

Grandis/Crandis: AB, ch. 19; VA, line 43: «regnum crande».

Gratanter: AB, ch. 1, p. 72.

Gratia: G, chs. 1, 11; AB, chs. 8, 9, 11, 13; VA, lines 37, 45.

Gravis: AB, ch. 5: «grave pugna», ch. 14: «Fuit gelus gravissimus».

Grex: G, ch. 1: «postea agni inter dominicum gregem pascentes».

Gubernacula: AB, ch. 1, p. 72: «ad regna gubernacula eum constituerunt», ch. 20: «ad regni gubernacula imperialis ordinaverat».

Gustare: G, ch. 6: «cumque gustasset, intellexit, quod malignum biberat».

Habitare: G, chs. 2, 3; AB, ch. 1, pp. 66, 68.

Habitatio: G, ch. 2.

Habundare: G, ch. 11: «sicut omnipotens Deus patri concessit fortitudinis gratiam, ita et in filio habundavit.»

Hereditas: G, ch. 2: «in Pannonię urbis patriam suam hereditatem afflixerunt».

Historia: AB, ch. 2.

Hodie: AB, ch. 1, p. 72, ch. 4, ch. 13: «usque hodie sic discipata est nobilitas Aquitanorum».

Hodiernus: AB, ch. 7: «usque ad hodiernum diem».

Homo: AB, ch. 1, p. 72, ch. 2: «antiqui homines», chs. 10, 11, 13, 19, 20, 23; VA, line 2.

Honor: G, ch. 10: «imperii honor adeptus est»; AB, ch. 1, p. 72, chs. 6, 17, 23.

Honorare: AB, ch. 1, p. 68, chs. 6, 7.

Honorifice: AB, ch. 11.

Hostis: AB, ch. 20: «Anticus hostis»; VA, line 15.

Humiliare: AB, ch. 19: «qui venerant exaltati, facti sunt humiliati».

Hymnus: AB, ch. 22.

Hystoriola: AB, ch. 1, p. 66.

Ianuarius: AB, ch. 23.

Ignis: G, ch. 11: «cives eorum igne sunt exanimati et consumpti»; AB, ch. 22.

Ignominia: AB, ch. 19: «Grandis ignominiam de occisorum nostrorum consonant».

Imperare: AB, chs. 13, 22.

Imperator: G, ch. 6; AB, ch. 1, p. 68, chs. 7, 8, 9, 11, 12, 14, 15, 17, 18, 19, 20, 21, 22, 24; R, line 24.

Imperialis: AB, ch. 9: «sedem imperialis constituit», ch. 10: «Honor autem maior, id est imperialis», ch. 20: «ad regni gubernacula imperialis ordinaverat».

Imperium: G, ch. 10; R, lines 13, 23.

Impius: G, ch. 11.

Inauditus: G, ch. 1: «mirumque est omnibus et inauditum videre».

Incarnatio: AB, ch. 1, p. 68, ch. 21.

Incendium: AB, ch. 23.

Incessanter: G, ch. 10.

Inchoare: G, chs. 8, 10.

Inclinare: G, ch. 4: «inclinavit Wacho Suavus sub regno Langobardorum»; AB, ch. 11: «ille vero tantum caput inclinavit».

Incredibilis: AB, ch. 2: «haec autem superscripta summationem cui incredibile aparet, relegat tota historia Langubardorum».

Indictio: G, ch. 5; AB, ch. 1, p. 68, chs. 5, 12, 14, 19, 20, 21, 22, 23.

Indignus: AB, ch. 2: «exerpsi ego Andreas, licet indignus».

Inferre: AB, ch. 3: «Mater vero eorum hęc separatio audiens, Carlemanni filii sui blasphemiam intulit».

Inflamare: AB, ch. 10: «ira inflamatus».

Ingerere: AB, ch. 20: «uno consilio ingerunt».

Ingredi: AB, ch. 1, p. 66, chs. 5, 7, 21.

Inimicitia: AB, chs. 8, 20.

Inimicus: G, chs. 10, 11; AB, chs. 10, 11.

Inire: AB, ch. 1, p. 68.

Iniuria: G, ch. 4.

Innitum: AB, ch. 18: «innita equorum».

Innumerabilis: G, ch. 10; AB, ch. 19: «Sarracini devicti et debellati sunt multitudo innumerabiles».

Inoviare: R, line 13.

Inponere: AB, ch. 17.

Inruere: G, ch. 10; AB, chs. 5, 17, 20.

Insidia: AB, ch. 1, p. 70.

Instruere: AB, ch. 16: «divinitatis scientiae instructus».

Insula/insola: G, chs. 7, 11; AB, ch. 1, pp. 66, 72.

Intelligere: G, ch. 6.

Intencio: AB, chs. 18, 19.

Intendere: AB, ch. 12.

Interficere: AB, ch. 1, p. 72, chs. 17, 18; R, line 19.

Interimere: AB, ch. 1, pp. 66, 70, 72, chs. 14, 19.

Internitio: AB, ch. 1, p. 68.

Introire: AB, ch. 1, p. 68.

Inundare: G, ch. 2: «Ligurius fluvius Albię fluvii canalis inundans et nomen finitur».

Invadere: AB, ch. 1, pp. 70, 72, ch. 5.

Invenire: AB, ch. 1, pp. 66, 72, chs. 17, 20.

Invidia: AB, ch. 1, p. 68.

Invitare: G, ch. 5.

Ira: AB, ch. 10.

Iracundus: AB, ch. 3.

Iratus: AB, chs. 10, 11.

Irritus: AB, ch. 5: «ex iussu apostolici sacramenta irrita facta sunt», ch. 14: «sacramenta quas dederat irrita fecit».

Irruere: AB, ch. 1, pp. 66, 68.

Iter: AB, chs. 13, 24.

Iubere: AB, ch. 1, p. 74.

Iudex: G, ch. 7.

Iudicare: R, line 28.

Iudicium: AB, ch. 5: «divino iudicio», ch. 19: «Dei iudicio»; R, line 28.

Iugulare: AB, ch. 1, p. 70.

Iulius: AB, ch. 22: «in mense Iulio».

Iungere: G, ch. 7: «iunxit Teodelindę reginę»; AB, chs. 13, 17, 19.

Iunius: AB, chs. 12, 22.

Iurare: AB, ch. 3; R, line 31: «iuratum est ad sante Dei reliquie».

Iussus: G, ch. 11; AB, ch. 5.

Iustitia: G, chs. 8, 10.

Iustus: G, ch. 1.

Iuvenilis: AB, ch. 1: «iuvenili etate».

Kalendae: AB, ch. 1, p. 68, ch. 20.

Kalidus: R, line 22: «Kalidus ille temtator».

Labor: AB, ch. 1, p. 66: «pro famis labore», ch. 17: «labores quam vobis inpono».

Lac: G, ch. 1: «In terra Italiae adventantes, fluentem lac et mel».

Lacrimabilis: AB, ch. 22: «lacrimabili fletu».

Laetabundus: AB, ch. 20.

Lana: AB, ch. 1, p. 68.

Lapsare: AB, ch. 1, p. 72: «fuga lapsus erat».

Largus: AB, ch. 1, p. 74: «elemosinis largus».

Late: AB, ch. 1, p. 68, ch. 7: «longe lateque».

Latro: R, line 15.

Laus: G, ch. 1.

Lector: AB, ch. 9.

Legatarius: AB, ch. 8.

Legatus: AB, ch. 1, p. 68.

Legere: AB, ch. 1, p. 66: «propter multitudinem populorum legimus populum illum in tres partes esse sorte divisum», ch. 20: «sicut legitur».

Letania: AB, ch. 12.

Letus: R, line 25.

Levare: G, ch. 2: «Ibique primum regem levaverunt», ch. 7; AB, ch. 18: «neque pugnaturi neque arma levatori sunt».

Levita: VA, line 8.

Lex: G, ch. 1: «sanguinea et aspera progeines, et sine lege... Non inputatur peccatum, cum lex non esset», ch. 8: «Per quem leges et iusticiam Langobardis est inchoate», ch. 10: «paternę patrię leges Langobardis misertus concessit», ch. 11: «Leges et ubertas et quietudinem habuit per domni nostri merita»; AB, ch. 1, p. 74: «Legem quidem Langubardorum ampliavit».

Liber: AB, ch. 1, p. 66: «Longobardorum gesta, unum volumen, sex tamen libros», ch. 11: «fratres sumus, sive liber et servus».

Liberare: G, ch. 11; AB, ch. 17.

Licentia: AB, ch. 1, p. 70.

Linteamen: VA, line 8: «linteamina levitae».

Littera: AB, ch. 2: «sed in quantum per seriem litterarum seu per antiquos homines potui veraciter scire».

Litterae: AB, ch. 4: «cum multis sapientissimis ars litterarum».

Locus: G, ch. 2; AB, chs. 4, 13, 14, 18, 19, 21.

Locusta: AB, ch. 21.

Longa: VA, line 20: «regna vestra diu longa cristianis tradita».

Longe: AB, ch. 1, p. 68, ch. 7: «longe lateque».

Loqui: AB, chs. 13, 22: «Veritatem in Christo loquor».

Lucrum: G, ch. 10: «nulli lucri cupiditas peragrare».

Lumen: G, ch. 8: «ortum est lumen in tenebris».

Lupus: G, ch. 1: «Primis lupi rapaces».

Lux: AB, ch. 12.

Madius: AB, ch. 23: «in mensem madio».

Magius: AB, ch. 12: «III nonas magias».

Magnus: G, ch. 11; AB, ch. 1, p. 68, ch. 3: «Habebat Carolus suus germanus maior», chs. 4, 6, 9, 10: «Honor autem maior, id est imperialis», ch. 12, 13, 17, 18: «christiani celebrarent magnum diem», chs. 19, 22, 23; VA, line 11; R, lines 7, 28.

Maiores: AB, ch. 7: «ducentes secum quicquid Italia maiores nati et nobiliores erant», ch. 23: «Colligentes se maiores nati in civitate Ticino».

Maledictus: VA, line 18: «Catunae mulieri, maledictae coniugi».

Malefactor: AB, ch. 23.

Malignus: G, ch. 6: «Cumque gustasset, intellexit, quod malignum biberat».

Malitia: AB, ch. 17: «de illorum dolens malitia», ch. 23: «multa malitia facere».

Malum: AB, ch. 20: «rederent malum pro bonum».

Malus: G, chs. 6, 11; AB, ch. 1, p. 72, chs. 10, 20; VA, line 4; R, line 9.

Mandare: G, ch. 6; AB, ch. 1, p. 72, chs. 6, 8, 23.

Manducare: AB, ch. 18.

Mane: AB, ch. 11: «constituto posito usque in mane. Mane autem facto», ch. 22: «mane et vespere».

Manere: AB, ch. 11: «non habet vitam eternam in se manentem», ch. 18: «Qui manducat carnem meam et bibit sanguinem meum, in me manet».

Manifestus: AB, ch. 12: «prope est die Domini magnus et manifestus».

Manus: AB, ch. 1, p. 68: «Alboin electam manum per mare Adriaticum dirigit», ch. 19: «cum electa manus Francorum», ch. 20: «Cor regis in manum Dei est».

Mare: AB, ch. 1, p. 68, ch. 5: «ultra mare egressus est»,

Martir: AB, ch. 1, p. 72.

Martirium: R, line 12: «ille vero gaudevisum tamquam ad martirium».

Mater: AB, ch. 1, p. 66, ch. 3.

Matrimonium: G, ch. 4.

Matutinum: AB, chs. 12, 18.

Medius: AB, ch. 12: «quasi media ora».

Mel: G, ch. 1: «In terra Italiae adventantes, fluentem lac et mel».

Melior: G, ch. 2: «meliorem ubertatis patrię requirentes».

Mensa: AB, ch. 11: «Dum ad mensam uterque reficerent».

Mensis: G, chs. 5, 6, 7, 9; AB, ch. 1, pp. 68, 70, 72, chs. 12, 19, 21, 22, 23.

Merere: AB, ch. 7: «ab eodem Carolus meruerunt».

Mereri: AB, ch. 17: «ut et ego videam vos et labores quam vobis inpono merear».

Meritum: G, ch. 1: «ubi non fuit meritum parentum», ch. 11: «per domni nostri merita».

Metere: AB, ch. 17: «annonam metentes».

Metropolis: G, ch. 6.

Metus: G, ch. 6; AB, ch. 19: «metus magnus tristare cepit... sine ullo metu».

Miles: G, ch. 6: «Longino prefecto militi Ravenensi... Longino militi».

Milium: AB, ch. 21: «multas granas minutas, id est milio vel panico».

Minae: G, ch. 5: «qui minas Suffię reginę erat perterritus».

Minime: AB, chs. 2, 3.

Ministrare: AB, ch. 1, p. 68, ch. 9: «cunctis servientibus Deo ministrantibus aecclesiae».

Minutus: AB, ch. 21: «Devastaverunt enim multas granas minutas, id est milio vel panico».

Mirabilia: R, line 27.

Mirifice: AB, ch. 22.

Mirus: G, ch. 1: «mirumque est omnibus et inauditum videre».

Misericordia: AB, chs. 17, 19.

Misericors: G, ch. 1; AB, ch. 9.

Misertus: G, ch. 10: «paternę patrię leges Langobardis misertus concessit».

Missa: AB, ch. 18: «missarum sollemnia celebrarent».

Missus: AB, ch. 1, p. 72, ch. 17.

Mittere: G, chs. 4, 6; AB, ch. 1, p. 68, chs. 10, 19, 21, 23; VA, line 10.

Monasterium: AB, ch. 1, p. 72, ch. 23; VA, line 5.

Monere: AB, ch. 16: «a domno papa Nicholaus catholica fide monitus», ch. 18.

Monitio: AB, ch. 12.

Mons: AB, ch. 23; VA, lines 2, 24, 33.

Monstrare: AB, ch. 21: «multa signa monstrata sunt».

Morire: G, chs. 4, 5, 6, 7; AB, ch. 1, pp. 66, 68, 70, 72, chs. 3, 5, 11, 13, 14, 24; R, line 9.

Mors: AB, ch. 1, pp. 70, 72, chs. 9, 13, 22.

Movere: G, ch. 5; AB, ch. 17: «misericordia motus».

Movicio: G, ch. 1.

Mucro: G, ch. 1: «mucrones spinarum».

Mula: VA, line 29.

Mulier: VA, lines 9, 18.

Multitudo: AB, ch. 1, p. 66, chs. 18, 19, 23.

Mundus: AB, ch. 12: «fuit sol obscuratus in hoc mundo».

Munire: AB, ch. 15.

Munus: AB, ch. 1, p. 68, ch. 6; VA, line 25: «porta tecum copiosa munera», line 30.

Mutare: G, ch. 2: «nomen mutati sunt».

Narrare: AB, ch. 1, p. 66.

Natio/Nacio: G, ch. 2: «Hic incipiens originem et nationem seu parentelam Langobardorum, exitus et conversationem eorum»; AB, ch. 15: «cum Franci et Langobardi et ceteris nacionum suorum fidelium», ch. 19: «cum electa manus Francorum et Langobardorum vel ceterorum nationes».

Nativitas: AB, ch. 18: «nativitas domini nostri Iesu Christi».

Natus: AB, ch. 1, p. 68, chs. 7, 23.

Navigare: AB, ch. 1, p. 72, ch. 19.

Navigium: AB, ch. 19.

Navis: G, ch. 6; AB, ch. 1, p. 72, chs. 5, 19.

Necessarius: G, ch. 10: «paternę patrię leges Langobardis misertus concessit et suas, ut voluit, quę necessariae erant Langobardis, adiunxit».

Necessitas: G, ch. 1.

Negare: AB, ch. 1, p. 72: «In flumen Ticinum ab aquis negatus est», ch. 19: «in fluvio Vulturno negati sunt».

Negligentia: AB, ch. 1, p. 66.

Nepos: AB, ch. 1, p. 70.

Nescire: AB, ch. 8: «nesciente imperatore».

Nex: G, ch. 6: «necem Albuini».

Niti: AB, ch. 1, p. 66: «Exinde pauca de multis in hac adbrevatione contexere nisi sumus».

Nix: AB, ch. 14: «tanta quidem nivem Italia cecidit».

Nobilis: AB, ch. 1, p. 70: «Alboin nepoti sui Gisolfi Foroiuli concessit et reliquos nobiles Langobardi», ch. 1, p. 70: «Clef nobilissimum... Teudelinda nomine... sancta et nobilissima», ch. 4: «Papa vero probata gens Francorum astuti et nobiles», ch. 6: «cum nobilis Foroiulanorum», ch. 7: «ducentes secum quicquid Italia maiores nati et nobiliores erant», ch. 8: «nobiles legatarii», ch. 11: «venientes nobiles eum in gratia miserunt», ch. 13: «nobiles Aquitanorum», ch. 17: «elegit strenuis et nobilissimis viris».

Nobilitas: AB, ch. 2: «multa illuc invenitur nobilitatem eorum», ch. 13: «discipata est nobilitas Aquitanorum».

Noctu: AB, ch. 1, p. 66.

Nomen: G, chs. 2, 4, 5, 7; AB, ch. 1, pp. 66, 68, 70, chs. 3, 7: «per eum nomen Francorum longe lateque percrebuit», chs. 8, 10, 14, 15, 17, 23.

Nominare: AB, ch. 23: «ceperunt homines Karoleto nominare».

Nonae: AB, chs. 12, 21.

Nonne: AB, ch. 1, p. 70.

Notitia: AB, ch. 2: «minime ad nostram pervenit notitiam».

Novus: G, ch. 2: «novam habitationem posuerunt».

Nuberca: AB, ch. 10.

Numerus: G, ch. 1: «inter iustorum numerum collocavit».

Nunciare: AB, chs. 18, 19.

Nuntius/Nuncius: AB, ch. 1, p. 72, ch. 17.

Obferre: AB, chs. 16, 23: «ad ecclesiam beati Petri dona obtulit».

Obitus: AB, ch. 23; VA, line 42.

Oblisci: AB, ch. 5: «Karolus... oblitus est tantorum benignitatis, quod ei Desiderius rex tribuit», ch. 14.

Obscurare: AB, ch. 12: «fuit sol obscuratus in hoc mundo».

Obsequium: AB, ch. 1, p. 70: «a puero de suo obsequio gladio iugulatus est»; VA, line 34: «parent tibi obsequia».

Obses: AB, ch. 1, p. 70, ch. 7.

Obtare: AB, ch. 6: «Ut obtabat, fecerunt».

Obtimus: AB, ch. 4.

Obtinere: AB, ch. 1, p. 72.

Occidere: G, chs. 3, 4, 5, 6, 7; AB, chs. 1, 5: «aliis bestiis occisi», chs. 10, 14, 15, 17, ch. 19: «Grandis ignominiam de occisorum nostrorum consonant»; R, line 18.

Occulte: AB, ch. 20: «exsurgentes per malos homines, inter se occulte dicentes».

Occupare: VA, line 23.

October: AB, ch. 20.

Oculus: AB, chs. 3, 8.

Odiare: AB, ch. 11.

Odiosus: AB, ch. 11.

Odium: AB, ch. 11.

Odoramentum: G, ch. 1: «odoramenta aecclesiarum».

Offerre: VA, line 26: «gemmas illi offert».

Omicida: AB, ch. 11.

Omnipotens: G, ch. 10, ch. 11.

Oppressio: G, ch. 1: «parentum oppressione»; AB, chs. 4, 14, 15.

Opprimere: G, ch. 11.

Ora: AB, ch. 12.

Orare: AB, ch. 18.

Orator: AB, ch. 1, p. 74.

Ordinare: G, ch. 7: «ordinavit eum Authari rex ducem in civitatem Austinse»; AB, ch. 7: «subiugata et ordinata Italia», ch. 20: «Deus, qui domno imperatore ad regni gubernacula imperialis ordinaverat».

Ordiri: AB, ch. 1, p. 68.

Ordo: AB, ch. 1, p. 66: «Longobardorum gesta... contesta et per ordinem narrata invenimus», ch. 14: «adventum primi ordinis, sicut cepimus, exsequamur».

Origo: G, ch. 2: «Hic incipiens originem et nationem seu parentelam Langobardorum, exitus et conversationem eorum».

Oriri: G, ch. 8; AB, ch. 8: «inimicitia contra Bernardo, Langubardorum regem, orta est».

Ornamentum: AB, chs. 4, 14.

Orror: R, line 1: «Audite, omnes fines terre, orrore cum tristitia».

Ovis: G, ch. 1: «Habeo alias oves, quę non sunt ex hoc ovili».

Pacificare: AB, ch. 7: «terra pacificata».

Pacifice: AB, ch. 20: «vis illorum fuit, ut pacifice potuissent, illos dimiterent».

Pacificus: AB, ch. 23: «pacificis verbis se ad invicem salutaverunt».

Pactus: G, ch. 5; AB, ch. 23: «pactum usque in mensem madio firmaverunt».

Paganus: AB, chs. 13, 18; VA, lines 39, 45; R, line 29: «multa gens paganorum exit in Calabria».

Pagus: AB, ch. 13.

Palatium: AB, chs. 7, 20; VA, line 42; R, line 10.

Palmes: AB, ch. 21: «palmites cum uva siccaverunt».

Panicum: AB, ch. 21: «multas granas minutas, id est milio vel panico».

Papa: AB, chs. 4, 16.

Paramentum: AB, ch. 23: «tantum cum uxuribus et paramentum in civitate vel in montibus perrexerunt».

Parare: G, ch. 5: «in eorum auxilium essent parati».

Parcere: VA, line 35.

Parens: G, ch. 1.

Parentela: G, ch. 2.

Parere: AB, ch. 12: «stellas in celo parebant», ch. 21: «parebat quasi terra pluvisset»; VA, line 34: «parent tibi obsequia».

Pars: G, ch. 2: «et in multis partibus bella et pericula generarunt... patrias ad suam partem expugnare coeperunt», ch. 5; AB, ch. 1, p. 66, chs. 3, 9, 13: «Hludowicus et Carolus ex una parte, Lotharius ex altera. Cumque nulla parte dantes locum, iungentes se ubi nuncupatur Funtanense, acies hinc et inde ex utraque partis constructe», chs. 14, 17, 19, 21, 22: «partem aliquam portavi».

Pascha: G, ch. 5; AB, ch. 1, p. 68.

Patens: AB, ch. 1, p. 66.

Pater: G, ch. 2: «antiqui patres», ch. 11; AB, ch. 1, p. 72, chs. 7, 9, 10, 11, 12, 13, 22, 24; VA, line 46.

Paternus: G, ch. 11.

Patrare: AB, ch. 1, p. 66, ch. 20.

Patria: G, ch. 2: «et patrias quas vastarunt... Saxonię patria attigerunt... patrias ad suam partem expugnare coeperunt... meliorem ubertatis patrię requirentes... in Pannonię urbis patriam suam hereditatem afflixerunt», ch. 10: «paternę patrię leges»; AB, chs. 7, 16, 18.

Patritius: AB, ch. 1, p. 68.

Patruus: AB, ch. 23.

Pauca: AB, ch. 1, pp. 66, 70, 72, ch. 14.

Pauci: AB, ch. 5: «ut vix pauci remanerent in vicos vel in civitates».

Pauper: G, ch. 1: «de stercore erigens pauperem»; AB, ch. 13: «multa devastantes pauperorum domibus».

Pavere: VA, line 16.

Pax: AB, ch. 1, p. 68, chs. 3, 7, 8, 9, 12, 13, 17.

Peccare: G, ch. 6.

Peccator: G, ch. 1: «Non veni vocare iustos, sed peccatores».

Peccatum: G, ch. 1: «Non inputatur peccatum, cum lex non esset», ch. 6: «suasio peccati».

Pelagus: AB, ch. 1, p. 72.

Pensio: AB, ch. 1, p. 68: «lanas in genitio per pensione dividere».

Penuria: AB, ch. 7: «cum esset penuriae famis Italia preucupata».

Peragrare: G, ch. 10.

Percellere: AB, ch. 3: «oculorum cecitate perculsus est», ch. 5: «fame perculsi».

Percipire: AB, ch. 1, p. 68: «absque pugna perciperent».

Percrebescere: AB, ch. 1, p. 68: «Lombardi vero in Pannonia habitaverunt et longe lateque nomen eorum percrebuit», ch. 7: «Qui per eum nomen Francorum longe lateque percrebuit».

Percurrere: G, ch. 8: «per conscriptionem primis iudices percurrerunt».

Perdire: VA, line 17.

Perdomare: G, ch. 10.

Perducere: G, ch. 3: «ad suam dogmam perduxerunt»; AB, ch. 22.

Perferre: AB, ch. 1, p. 68.

Pergere: G, ch. 5: «in Italiam, in quam ipsi perrexerant», chs. 10, 11; AB, chs. 7, 11, 17, 18, 19, 21, 22, 23.

Periculum: G, ch. 2: «in multis partibus bella et pericula generarunt»; AB, ch. 3: «cum periculo vita finivit».

Perire: R, line 6.

Perpetuus: AB, ch. 1, p. 68: «cum Avaris perpetuam pacem fecit».

Persecutor: G, ch. 11.

Perterrere: G, ch. 5: «minas Suffię reginę erat perterritus»; VA, line 28.

Pervenire: AB, ch. 1, pp. 66, 68; R, line 30.

Pervigil: AB, ch. 1, p. 74.

Pes: AB, ch. 4: «Karolus cum suis obviam eius adventum pedibus venerunt», ch. 11: «Ad pedes vero noluit venire».

Petire: AB, ch. 11, ch. 17: «tantum ad vos petimus... fuga petiens».

Pharetrum: AB, ch. 22: «post transitum in pharetro posuerunt».

Philosophus: AB, ch. 1, p. 66: «Paulo viro philosopho».

Phitonissa: G, ch. 1: «phitonissa inter sibillę cognomina».

Pius: G, ch. 10; R, lines 3, 10, 14.

Plaga: AB, ch. 1, p. 66: «In septentrionali plaga Europae».

Plagare: VA, line 30.

Planus: AB, ch. 14: «in planis locis», ch. 21.

Plenus: AB, ch. 1, p. 68, ch. 7: «plenum dierum», ch. 23.

Plovere: AB, ch. 21: «parebat quasi terra pluvisset».

Plura: AB, ch. 1, p. 72: «Quid plura?».

Plures: AB, ch. 1, p. 66, ch. 2.

Polluere: VA, line 7: «vestem sanctam polluerunt».

Pommum: AB, ch. 1, p. 68.

Ponere: G, ch. 6; AB, ch. 1: «Positis super se ducibus Hibor et Agio», ch. 11: «constituto posito usque in mane»; VA, line 24; R, line 23.

Pons: AB, ch. 6.

Populus: G, chs. 1, 4, 11; AB, ch. 1, p. 66, chs. 12, 17, 18, 23; VA, line 23; R, line 23.

Porta: AB, ch. 17.

Portare: AB, ch. 22: «partem aliquam portavi et cum portantibus ambulavi»; VA, line 25.

Posse: G, ch. 10; AB, ch. 1, p. 68, chs. 3, 6, 10, 11, 19; VA, line 26; R, line 24.

Possedere/Possidere: AB, ch, 1, pp. 68, 70, ch. 4: «Italiam possiderent», ch. 15: «castro, qui dicitur Bari... possidens», ch. 19: «quinto expleto anno quod Bari possessas habebat»; R, line 30: «super Salerno pervenerunt possidere civitas».

Potentissimus: VA, line 43.

Potestas: G, ch. 10: «dignitates Romanę potestatis accepit»; AB, ch. 1, p. 70, ch. 20.

Praedare/Predare: G, chs. 4, 5, 11.

Praeparare: AB, ch. 1, p. 68, chs. 5, 17, 19; R, line 7.

Pravus: AB, chs. 10, 23.

Preda: AB, ch. 1, p. 68.

Predestinare: G, ch. 6.

Preesse: AB, ch. 1, p. 68, ch. 6: «Foroiulanorum dux tunc temporis Rotcausus preerat».

Prefectus: G, ch. 6.

Prelium: AB, ch. 18.

Presentia: AB, ch. 11.

Preses: G, ch. 5: «Narside proconsule et preside Italię».

Presidium: VA, lines 15, 24.

Prestare: G, ch. 11: «prestante domino nostro Ihesu Christo».

Pretorium: R, line 11.

Preucupare: AB, ch. 7: «cum esset penuriae famis Italia preucupata».

Prevalere: AB, ch. 19.

Prevaricatio: G, ch. 11: «suę prevaricationis sacramenti».

Primas: VA, lines 29, 35.

Primis: G, ch. 1, ch. 2: «Primis Winili proprio nomine seu et parentela... postea ad vulgorum vocem Langobardi nomen mutati sunt», ch. 8.

Primus: G, chs. 2, 5, 6; AB, ch. 1, p. 66.

Princeps: G, chs. 1, 10: «domni Petri principis apostolorum»; AB, chs. 14, 15, 17, 19; VA, lines 10, 20, 31; R, line 5.

Principatus: G, ch. 4: «Post Peronem tenuit principatum Langobardorum Claffo»; AB, chs. 14, 20.

Pristinus: AB, ch. 11: «reducite me ad pristinam gratiam».

Privare: AB, ch. 1, p. 72.

Probare: AB, ch. 4: «Papa vero probata gens Francorum astuti et nobiles».

Proconsul: G, ch. 5.

Procreare: VA, line 41.

Progeines: G, ch. 1: «sanguinea et aspera progeines».

Proles: VA, lines 34, 36.

Prolixus: G, ch. 2: «barba prolixa».

Promittere: G, ch. 5.

Properare: AB, ch. 6.

Prophetare: G, ch. 1: «non ut prophetaret quę nesciebat».

Prophetia: G, ch. 1: «davitica impleta prophetia».

Proprietas: G, ch. 2: «primis habitatio et proprietas eorum fuit... ad suam proprietatem perduxerunt».

Protinus: VA, line 29.

Proverbium: G, ch. 1: «ad Iudęos in proverbiis dicens».

Provincia/Provintia: G, chs. 2, 5, 11; R, line 7.

Prudens: AB, ch. 9: «consilio prudens».

Pruina: AB, ch. 21: «sequenti autem IIII nonas magi pruina cecidit, multe vites in planis locis seu in vallibus palmites cum uva siccaverunt».

Psallere: AB, ch. 22: «hymnis Deo psallentibus».

Pudicus: AB, ch. 1, p. 74.

Puer: AB, ch. 1, p. 70: «a puero de suo obsequio gladio iugulatus est».

Pugna: G, ch. 5; AB, ch. 1, p. 68, ch. 5: «absque grave pugna Italiam invasit».

Pugnare: G, chs. 3, 4, 5; AB, ch. 1, p. 66, chs. 18, 19.

Quasi: AB, ch. 1, p. 66, chs. 8, 11, 12, 21.

Querere: AB, ch. 18: «exierunt querentes Sarracini et illis querentes Franci», ch. 19.

Quiescere: AB, ch. 1, p. 66.

Quietudo: G, ch. 11.

Radiens (= Radians): AB, ch. 22.

Rapax: G, ch. 1: «Primis lupi rapaces».

Rapere: G, ch. 11: «multa vasa sanctorum, quae illi crudeles et impii rapuerunt».

Rebellare: AB, ch. 14.

Rebellatio: AB, ch. 14.

Rebellis: G, ch. 7: «occidit tres duces rebellos suos, Zangrulf de Verona,

Mimolfo de insula sancti Iuli et Gaidulfo de Bergamo et alios plures rebellos suos.»

Recipere: AB, ch. 16: «recepit doctores ab eodem domno apostolico», ch. 17: «firmitatis sacramenta receperunt».

Recognoscere: AB, ch. 10: «se recognoscens Lotharius, quod malum aegisset consilium».

Rectum: R, line 9: «rectum est ut moriad».

Reddere: AB, ch. 11: «gratiam filii sui reddidit», chs. 13, 20: «sed etiam tributa reddunt», ch. 22.

Redigere: G, ch. 11: «ad Francorum servitutem est redacta».

Redire: G, ch. 4; AB, ch. 20.

Reducere: AB, ch. 11: «reducite me ad pristinam gratiam».

Reficere: AB, ch. 11: «mensam uterque reficerent».

Refulgere: G, ch. 1: «talis salus refulgere»; AB, ch. 12: «refulsit sol».

Regere: AB, ch. 1, p. 66, chs. 4, 7, 11, 20; R, line 24.

Regina: G, chs. 5, 7; AB, ch. 1, p. 70, ch. 23.

Regio: AB, ch. 1, p. 66.

Regnare: G, chs. 4, 5, 6, 7, 8, 9; AB, ch. 1, pp. 66, 70, 72, chs. 3, 7, 8; VA, lines 19, 41.

Regnum: G, chs. 4, 10: «Hic finitum est regnum Langobardorum et incoavit regnum Italię», ch. 11; AB, ch. 1, pp. 66, 70, 72, chs. 3, 7, 19, 20; VA, lines 20, 32, 38, 43, 44; R, line 8.

Relaxare: G, ch. 5: «ipsam terram relaxarent».

Relinquere: G, ch. 5: «relinquens Italiam»; AB, ch. 1, pp. 66, 72, chs. 3, 7, 13, 23.

Reliquia: R, line 31: «Iuratum est ad sante Dei reliquie».

Reliquus: AB, ch. 1, pp. 68, 70, chs. 14, 15, 19, 21, 23.

Reluctare: G, ch. 2: «cum Abaris reluctantes seu bella plurima».

Remanere: AB, ch. 1, p. 66, ch. 5: «pauci remanerent in vicos vel in civitates».

Remeare: AB, ch. 1, p. 68, ch. 4.

Remittere: AB, ch. 10: «nubercam suam remittens genitori suo»

Repedare/Repetare: AB, chs. 4, 24.

Reputare: AB, ch. 13: «Si ergo odiosus omicida reputabitur».

Requirere: G, ch. 2: «meliorem ubertatis patrię requirentes», chs. 5, 10: «ab Italia perrexerat eius iusticiam requirendam»; R, line 32.

Resedere/Residere: AB, ch. 1, p. 68, chs. 4, 23.

Resistere: AB, chs. 6, 13, 14, 15.

Resolutus: AB, ch. 1, p. 66.

Respondere: AB, ch. 11.

Retinere: AB, ch. 10: «Sed totam fortia Lotharius ad se retentam habebat».

Reverentia: AB, ch. 11: «Ad pedes vero noluit venire propter reverentiae honorem aecclesiarum».

Revertere: G, chs. 5, 11; AB, ch. 1, p. 72, chs. 13, 16, 17, 20, 23, 24.

Rex: G, ch. 2: «bella et vastationes quę fecerunt reges eorum... Ibique primum regem levaverunt nomine Agelmund», chs. 3, 4, 5, 6, 7, 8, 11: «domno Pippino magno regi»; AB, ch. 1, pp. 66, 68, 70, chs. 3, 5, 6: «Regem confortationis nostrae iam devictus est», chs. 8, 16, 20: «Cor regis in manum Dei est», ch. 21: «Locusta regem non habent», ch. 23; VA, lines 11, 13, 17, 22, 25, 26, 28, 30, 31, 38, 40.

Ripa: G, ch. 2; AB, ch. 1, p. 72.

Ritus: G, ch. 8.

Rivus: VA, line 2.

Rosa: G, ch. 1: «ut de spina rosa efficeretur».

Rumpere: AB, ch. 14: «rumperetur ipsa glatia cum fuste».

Sacerdos: G, ch. 8; AB, chs. 18, 22.

Sacramentum: G, ch. 11; AB, ch. 5: «ex iussu apostolici sacramenta irrita facta sunt», chs. 7, 8: «sacramenta fidem suscepit», ch. 14: «sacramenta quas dederat irrita fecit», ch. 17.

Sacratissimus: VA, line 7.

Sacratus: VA, line 6.

Saluber: AB, ch. 18: «salubrae consilium».

Salutare: AB, ch. 23.

Salutatorius: AB, ch. 11: «verba salutatoria dixit».

Salvator: G, ch. 1: «salvator ad Iudęos in proverbiis dicens».

Salve: VA, line 31.

Salvus: AB, ch. 17: «per vestram defensionem salvi fore confidimus».

Sanctimonialis: VA, line 8.

Sanctus/Santus: AB, ch. 1, p. 70, chs. 11, 16: «fide sancta confirmatus», chs. 19, 22; VA, lines 7, 10; R, line 3: «Lhuduicum compreenderunt sancto pio augusto», lines 14, 20, 31: «Iuratum est ad sante Dei reliquie».

Sanguineus: G, ch. 1: «sanguinea et aspera progeines».

Sanguis: AB, ch. 18; R, line 21: «sanguine veni vindicare quod super terram fusus est».

Sapiens: AB, ch. 11.

Sapientia: AB, ch. 1, p. 74, ch. 9.

Sapientissimus: AB, ch. 4.

Scandalum: G, ch. 4: «Iniuriam vindican-dum, Gibites scandalum commiserunt cum Langobardis».

Scelus: R, line 2: «quale scelus fuid factum».

Sceptrum: VA, line 26.

Scientia: AB, ch. 16: «divinitatis scientiae instructus».

Scire: AB, ch. 2: «in quantum per seriem litterarum seu per antiquos homines potui veraciter scire», chs. 11, 12.

Scisma: G, ch. 6: «Unde plures annos scisma et bella inter Langobardos et Romanos fuerunt».

Scribere: AB, ch. 1, pp. 66, 70.

Seculum: AB, ch. 12: «multi extimabant, quod iam amplius hoc seculum non staret».

Secutor: AB, ch. 17.

Sedere: AB, ch. 20: «domnus imperator in Beneventi palatio sedebat», ch. 24: «Karolus imperator de Roma reversus in Papia sederet».

Sedis: AB, chs. 4, 7, 9: «imperator Hludowicus suum filium Lothario sub se sedem imperialis constituit, vivente patre», ch. 13.

Semen: AB, ch. 14: «Fuit gelus gravissimus, multa semina mortua fuerunt».

Senes: AB, ch. 7: «senesque aetatis».

Senescere: VA, line 41.

Sentencia: G, ch. 11: «capitalem subierunt sentenciam».

Separatio: AB, ch. 3.

Separatus: AB, ch. 20: «Erant enim Franci separati per castellas vel civitates».

Sepelire: AB, ch. 22.

September: AB, ch. 23.

Septentrionalis: AB, ch. 1, p. 66: «In septentrionali plaga Europae».

Sepulchrum: AB, ch. 22: «posuit eum in sepulchro in aecclesia sanctae Mariae».

Series: AB, ch. 2: «per seriem litterarum», ch. 14: «gestis filiorum regum seriem apices conponam».

Sermo: AB, ch. 1, p. 66.

Serpens: G, ch. 1.

Servare: AB, ch. 6: «eorum Carolus servavit honorem».

Serviens: AB, ch. 9: «cunctis servientibus Deo ministrantibus aecclesiae».

Servitus: G, ch. 11: «Per quem Tratia provincia una cum Abaris ad Francorum servitutem est redacta».

Servus: AB, ch. 11: «fratres sumus, sive liber et servus».

Sibilla: G, ch. 1.

Siccare: AB, ch. 14: «vitae pene omnibus in planis locis siccaverunt», ch. 21: «palmites cum uva siccaverunt».

Signum: G, ch. 2: «usque hodie pręsentem diem Wachoni regi eorum domus et habitatio apparet signa»; AB, ch. 12: «Haec signa in celo conperta, doctores in suorum monitiones dixerunt: "Estote, fratres, parati, quia adimpletum est quod in evangelio Dominus dixit: 'Cum haec signa videritis, scitote, quia prope est die Domini magnus et manifestus?'"», ch. 21: «multa signa monstrata sunt».

Silva: VA, lines 24, 33.

Silves: AB, ch. 21: «silves tenerrimum cum sua folia aride facte sunt».

Similis: AB, ch. 13.

Similiter: AB, chs. 15, 21.

Similitudo: AB, ch. 1, p. 66: «eorum feminae crine solutae erga faciem ad similitudinem barbae composuerunt».

Simplicitas: AB, ch. 18: «comprahendamus eos omnes in simplicitate sua».

Situs: AB, ch. 1, p. 70.

Sobules: VA, line 1.

Sociare/Sotiare: AB, ch. 1, pp. 68, 70, ch. 3.

Sol: AB, ch. 12.

Solatium: G, ch. 11.

Sollemne: AB, ch. 18: «missarum sollemnia celebrarent».

Solus: AB, ch. 12: «Imperavit ipse tam solus quam simul cum filio annos XXVII», ch. 13.

Solutus: AB, ch. 1, p. 66.

Solvere: AB, ch. 17: «tributa solvimus».

Sonitus: AB, ch. 18: «Factum est sonitus magnus clangore bucine».

Sors: AB, ch. 1, p. 66.

Spina: G, ch. 1: «ut de spina rosa efficeretur»; AB, ch. 14: «vinum intra vascula glaciavit, quae etiam per foramen spinarum nihil exibat, donec rumperetur ipsa glatia cum fuste ab ante ipsa spina».

Splendere: G, ch. 11.

Stare: AB, ch. 12.

Stella: AB, chs. 12, 22.

Stercus: G, ch. 1: «de stercore inter iustorum numerum collocavit... Et de stercore erigens pauperem».

Sternere: AB, ch. 1, p. 68, ch. 13: «quanti potuissent per bonam concordiam et salubrae consilium multa milia sternere contradictorum paganorum».

Stipendium: AB, ch. 18: «stipendia quicquid soldani pergebat tullerunt».

Stirps: G, ch. 11.

Storiola: AB, ch. 1, p. 72: «Multa quidem eius storiole continet, sed pauca in hac adbreviationem conscribam... Multa quidem eius storiole scripta invenimus.»

Strada: AB, ch. 19: «ad strada scilicet prope Capua ad Vulturno».

Strages: AB, ch. 1, p. 68, chs. 6, 13, 17.

Strenuus: AB, ch. 17: «elegit strenuis et nobilissimis viris».

Strepidus: AB, ch. 19: «strepidus populorum».

Stuprare: AB, ch. 1, p. 72.

Suadere: G, ch. 6: «suasit ipsa Rosemonia Longino militi»; VA, line 9: «suadente demone».

Suasio: G, ch. 6: «ut per fęmeneum primum exordium accidit mala suasio peccati».

Subditus: G, ch. 10: «factus est domni Petri apostoli subditissimus filius».

Subicere: G, ch. 6: «colla sua ipsi Albuin regi subicierunt»; AB, ch. 1, p. 68.

Subire: G, ch. 11: «populus eorum capitalem subierunt sentenciam».

Subito: AB, chs. 7, 11, 13.

Subiugare: AB, ch. 1, pp. 66, 70, ch. 7.

Subiungere: AB, ch. 11.

Succedere: AB, ch. 1, pp. 66, 68, 72.

Suffudere (= suffodere): AB, ch. 17: «Gens Sarracinorum venerunt, terra nostra dissipaverunt, civitates desolaverunt, aecclesias suffuderunt».

Summatim: AB, ch. 1, p. 66.

Summatio: AB, ch. 2: «Haec autem superscripta summationem cui incredibile aparet, relegat tota historia Langubardorum».

135

Summus: AB, ch. 18: «summo diluculo».

Superare: G, ch. 11; AB, ch. 1, p. 68.

Supernus: G, ch. 1: «superna visitatione».

Superscriptus: AB, ch. 2.

Surgere: AB, ch. 1, p. 72, chs. 3, 13, 14; R, line 17.

Suscipere: G, ch. 6; AB, ch. 1, pp. 66, 70, 72, chs. 6, 8, 11, 14.

Sustinere: AB, ch. 1, p. 68, p. 72: «Contra Halahis tirrannum fatigatione susten-tus», ch. 14: «oppressio a Sclavorum gens sustinuit», ch. 15: «Hludowicus augustus multa quidem oppressionem a Sarracinorum gens in finibus Bene-ventanis sustinuit».

Tela: AB, ch. 1, p. 68.

Temperare: G, ch. 6: «temperavit venenum».

Tempus: G, chs. 2, 3, 4, 5, 7, 8; AB, ch. 1, pp. 66, 68, chs. 3, 4, 5, 6, 7, 11, 14, 16, 24; VA, lines 3, 4; R, line 16.

Temtator: R, line 22.

Tendere: G, ch. 8: «Langobardi ad cannonica tenderunt certamina».

Tenebrae: G, ch. 8: «ortum est lumen in tenebris».

Tener: AB, ch. 21: «silves tenerrimum cum sua folia aride facte sunt».

Tenere: G, ch. 4: «tenuit principatum».

Tergum: AB, ch. 18: «pagani vero terga vertentes fugire ceperunt»; VA, line 35.

Terminus: G, ch. 10; AB, ch. 1, p. 68.

Terra: G, chs. 1, 5, 11; AB, ch. 1, pp. 66, 72, chs. 7, 11: «manum in terra ponens», chs. 13, 17: «terra nostra dissipaverunt», chs. 19, 21: «parebat quasi terra pluvisset», ch. 22: «trahentes eum a terra et mirifice condientes»; VA, lines 2, 44; R, line 1: «Audite, omnes fines terre», lines 21, 26.

Terrere: AB, ch. 3: «suorum tempore Langubardi a nulla gens terruerunt».

Terror: AB, ch. 5: «divino iudicio terror in Langubardus inruit», ch. 20: «fidentes absque ullo terrore».

Thesaurus: G, ch. 6.

Timor: G, ch. 10: «super innumerabiles gentes eius timor irruit»; AB, ch. 17: «ipsis Sarracini fidentes absque ullo timore, annonam metentes», ch. 20: «Caelestis timor super Beneventanos inruit»; VA, line 40.

Tirrannus: AB, ch. 1, p. 72.

Tollere: AB, ch. 10; VA, lines 25, 34; R, line 8.

Totum: VA, line 15.

Totus: AB, chs. 2, 4: «per totam Franciam Italiamque», chs. 10, 22.

Tradere: G, chs. 4, 11; AB, ch. 1, p. 70; VA, lines 9, 20, 27, 32, 36.

Trahere: AB, ch. 22: «trahentes eum a terra et mirifice condientes».

Tranquillitas: AB, ch. 9: «Habebat tranquillitas magna».

Transcurrere: AB, ch. 14: «His itaque sub brivitate rei veritas transcurris».

Transigere: AB, ch. 21: «anni ab incarnationis domini nostri Ihesu Christi octogenti LXXIII transacti».

Transire: AB, ch. 1, p. 66.

Transitum: AB, ch. 22: «dies quinto post transitum in pharetro posuerunt».

Transmeare: AB, ch. 1, p. 72: «ad Britaniam insolam ad regnum Saxonum transmeare».

Transmittere: G, ch. 6: «transmisit eam Constantinopolim»; AB, ch. 1, p. 68.

Transvehere: AB, ch. 1, p. 68: «in Italiam transvecti».

Tribuere: AB, ch. 1, p. 70, chs. 5, 14, 17.

Tribulatio: AB, ch. 5: «Tantaque tribulatio fuit in Italia», ch. 12: «Facta est tribulatio magna», ch. 23: «Post cuius obitum magna tribulatio in Italia advenit».

Tributum: AB, chs. 13, 17.

Trinitas: G, ch. 1: «vestigia sanctae trinitatis recipientes».

Tristare: AB, ch. 19: «Soldanus hec audiens, metus magnus tristare cepit».

Tristitia: R, line 1: «Audite, omnes fines terre, orrore cum tristitia».

Triumphare: AB, ch. 17: «triumphatores reversi sunt ad domno imperatore».

Triumphus: AB, ch. 1, p. 72: «triumphum victoriae».

Tuba: G, ch. 2.

Turbulentus: AB, ch. 21: «Vinum quomodo vindemiatum et intra vascula misso, statim turbulentus, qui dicitur versio, fuit».

Turma: AB, ch. 21; R, line 27: «exierunt multe turme videre mirabilia».

Ubertas: G, ch. 2: «meliorem ubertatis patrię requirentes», ch. 10: «Deus centies multiplicavit ubertates», ch. 11: «Leges et ubertas et quietudinem habuit»; AB, ch. 7: «subito ut Bernardo regnum accepit, dignitatem ubertatemque advenit».

Ulcisci: AB, ch. 1, p. 66.

Ultimus: VA, line 3.

Umbraculum: AB, ch. 12: «refulsit sol et quasi tremidus in antea umbraculum fugire cepit».

Unare: AB, ch. 21: «Erant enim unates pergentibus, sicut Salamon dixit: "Locusta regem non habent, set per turmas ascendunt."».

Ungere: AB, ch. 23: «ab apostolico Iohanne unctus et ab honore imperii coronatus».

Unia: VA, line 38: «regnum Uniae».

Urbs: G, ch. 2; AB, ch. 1, p. 70.

Uva: AB, ch. 21.

Uxor: G, chs. 4, 5, 6, 7; AB, ch. 1, pp. 68, 70, 72.

Vacuus: G, ch. 6.

Vallis: AB, chs. 17, 21.

Vasculum: AB, chs. 14, 21.

Vastare: G, chs. 2, 11.

Vastatio: G, ch. 1: «bella et vastationes quę fecerunt reges eorum».

Vasum: VA, line 6: «vasa aurea sacrata».

Vehementer: AB, ch. 10: «Quis potest dicere furore, quam vehementer pater eius iratus fuisset?».

Venenum: AB, ch. 1, p. 70.

Venia: AB, ch. 11: «Imperator vero manum in terra ponens, veniam petivit».

Venire: AB, ch. 1, p. 66.

Veraciter: AB, ch. 2: «in quantum per seriem litterarum seu per antiquos homines potui veraciter scire».

Verbum: AB, chs. 11, 23.

Veritas: AB, ch. 14: «His itaque sub brivitate rei veritas transcurris», ch. 22: «Veritatem in Christo loquor».

Versio: AB, ch. 21: «Vinum quomodo vindemiatum et intra vascula misso, statim turbulentus, qui dicitur versio, fuit».

Vertere: AB, ch. 18; VA, line 35.

Vesper: AB, ch. 22: «mane et vespere».

Vestigium: G, ch. 1: «vestigia sanctae trinitatis recipientes».

Vestis: VA, line 7: «Vestem sanctam polluerunt de ara sacratissima».

Vexare: R, line 26.

Via: VA, line 11.

Victor: AB, ch. 1, p. 68.

Victoria: AB, ch. 1, pp. 66, 72, chs. 2, 20, 21; VA, line 39.

Vicus: AB, ch. 5.

Videre: AB, ch. 1, pp. 66, 70.

Vincere: AB, ch. 1, p. 66.

Vindemiare: AB, ch. 21.

Vindicare: G, ch. 4; AB, ch. 11; R, line 21.

Vindicta: AB, ch. 1, p. 66: «super Bulgares vindicta ulcisci cupiebant».

Vinum: AB, chs. 14, 21.

Vir: G, ch. 10; AB, ch. 1, p. 66, ch. 13: «Tantique ibi viri fortes per contentiones malum et improvidentia debellati sunt», chs. 17, 19.

Viriliter: AB, ch. 6: «Rotcausus et Gaidus ducibus cum nobilis Foroiulanorum consilio inito, ut se viriliter contendissent», ch. 17: «obviam eorum exiit, preparatus viriliter».

Virtus: AB, ch. 1, p. 66: «sic omnis Herulorum virtus concidit»; VA, line 13: «Rex accintus Dei virtute Pippinus».

Vis: AB, ch. 20: «vis illorum fuit».

Visitatio: G, ch. 1: «superna visitatione».

Vita: AB, ch. 1, p. 72, chs. 3, 11; VA, line 42.

Vitae (= Vites): AB, ch. 14: «vitae pene omnibus in planis locis siccaverunt».

Vitis: AB, ch. 21: «multe vites in planis locis seu in vallibus palmites cum uva siccaverunt».

Vivere: AB, ch. 1, p. 68, chs. 7, 9, 22; VA, lines 26, 40.

Vivus: G, ch. 1: «ad aquam vivam poscendam»; AB, ch. 1, p. 72: «vivum comprehendit»; R, line 5: «Si nos eum vivum dimitemus, certe nos peribimus».

Vix: AB, ch. 5: «ut vix pauci remanerent in vicos vel in civitates», ch. 19: «reliqui fuga vix evaderunt».

Vocare: G, ch. 1; AB, ch. 1, p. 66: «pars tercia, cui sors cecidit, Winoli vocati sunt», ch. 7: «Iste incipit vocare imperator ex Francorum genus», ch. 11: «unum patrem vocamus in cęlis».

Volumen: AB, ch. 1, p. 66.

INDEX OF PEOPLES, PERSONS AND PLACES

Bergamo, G, ch. 7, AB, chs. 17, 22, 23.

Bernard, grandson of Charlemagne, king of Italy, AB, chs. 7, 8.

Berterad, daughter of the Lombard king Desiderius, AB, ch. 3.

Berthari, see Perctarit.

Boso, commander of Emperor Louis II's army, AB, ch. 19.

Brenta, river, AB, ch. 23.

Brescia, AB, chs. 21, 22, 23.

Britain, AB, ch. 1, p. 73.

Bulgarians, AB, ch. 1, p. 67, ch. 16.

Burgundians, AB, ch. 14.

Burgundy, AB, ch. 14.

Cacan, Avar ruler, VA, lines 16, 28.

Caesar, VA, line 45.

Calabria, AB, ch. 17, R, line 29.

Capua, AB, ch. 19.

Carloman, brother of Charlemagne, AB, ch. 3.

Carloman, son of Louis the German, AB, chs. 23, 24.

Catuna, wife of the Avar ruler, VA, line 18.

Charles (= Charlemagne), king of the Franks, emperor, G, ch. 10, AB, chs. 3, 4, 5, 6, 7, 8, VA, lines 11, 46.

Charles (the Bald), son of Louis the Pious, king of the Western Franks, emperor, AB, chs. 9, 10, 13, 23.

Charles, king of Provence, son of Lothar, AB, ch. 13.

Charles, Little Charles, son of Louis the German, AB, ch. 23.

Chlotar, king of the Franks, G, ch. 5.

Christ/Jesus, G, ch. 11, AB, chs. 16, 17, 18, 21, 22, VA, line 1, R, line 28.

Chusubald, king of the Franks, G, ch. 4.

Cincimo, Muslim leader, AB, chs. 17, 18.

Cividale, AB, ch. 1, p. 71, ch. 6.

Claffo, king of the Lombards, G, ch. 4, AB, ch. 1, p. 67.

Cleph, king of the Lombards G, ch. 7, AB, ch. 1, p. 71.

Clothsuinda, wife of the Lombard King Alboin, AB, ch. 1, p. 69.

Comacchio, AB, ch. 22.

Constantinople, G, ch. 6.

Coronate, plain of, AB, ch. 1, p. 73.

Corsica, G, ch. 11.

Cremona, AB, chs. 21, 22.

Cunibert/Cunipert, king of the Lombards, G, ch. 9, AB, ch. 1, p. 73.

Cunimund, king of the Gepids, G, ch. 5, AB, ch. 1, p. 69.

Cunrath, count of Auxerre, AB, ch. 14.

Danube, VA, line 14.

David, king of Israel, G, ch. 1.

Desiderius, king of the Lombards, G, ch. 9, AB, chs. 3, 5.

Elbe, G, ch. 2.

Ermengard, wife of Louis the Pious, AB, chs. 8, 9.

Europe, AB, ch. 1, p. 67.

Everard, ruler of Friuli, AB, ch. 14.

Fara, monastery of, AB, ch. 23.

Felf, G, ch. 4.

Fewan, king of the Rugians, G, ch. 3.

Filastricus, Saint, AB, ch. 22.

Filda, G, ch. 4.

Fontenoy, AB, ch. 13.

Francia, AB, chs. 4, 7, 8, 11, 13, 23.

Franks, G, chs. 4, 5, 10, AB, chs. 3, 4, 5, 6, 7, 15, 17, 18, 19, 20, 21, VA, line 12.

Friulans, AB, ch. 1, p. 69, ch. 6, ch. 14.

Gaidulf, duke of Bergamo, G, ch. 7.

Gaidus, duke of Vicenza, AB, ch. 6.

Gambara, mother of Ibor and Aio, G, ch. 1, AB, ch. 1, p. 67.

Gariard, bishop, AB, ch. 17.

Garibald, Bavarian ruler, father of Theodelinda, G, ch. 7, AB, ch. 1, p. 71.

Garibald, son of the Lombard king Grimoald, AB, ch. 1, p. 73.

Louis (II), son of emperor Lothar, emperor, AB, chs. 10, 13, 14, 15, 16, 21, 22, R, lines 3, 6, 7, 8, 9, 10, 11, 12, 14, 16, 17, 18, 19, 20, 21, 32.

Ludusenda, first wife of the Lombard king Alboin, G, ch. 5.

Mantua, AB, ch. 23.

Mary, church of Saint, (Brescia), AB, ch. 22.

Mauringa, AB, ch. 1, p. 67.

Menia, mother of the Lombard king Audoin, wife of the Thuringian king Pisen, G, ch. 5.

Metz, AB, ch. 4.

Milan, G, ch. 6, AB, chs. 11, 21, 22, 23.

Mimulf, duke of the island of Saint Iulius, G, ch. 7.

Monza, AB, ch. 1, p. 71.

Moors, G, ch. 11.

Narses, Byzantine general, G, ch. 5, AB, ch. 1, p. 69.

Nicholas, pope, AB, ch. 16.

Normans, AB, ch. 13.

Odovacer, G, ch. 3.

Oglio, river, AB, ch. 23.

Oschis, bishop, AB, ch. 17.

Otto, count of Bergamo, AB, ch. 17.

Pannonia G, chs. 2, 3, 5, AB, ch. 1, p. 69.

Patespruna, G, ch. 2.

Paul, chronicler, AB, ch. 1, p. 67.

Pavia, G, ch. 6, AB, chs. 23, 24.

Pelei, Lombard family, G, ch. 7.

Perctarit/Berthari, king of the Lombards, G, ch. 9, AB, ch. 1, p. 73.

Peredeus, chamberlain of King Alboin, G, ch. 6.

Pero, king of the Lombards, G, ch. 4.

Peter, Saint, G, ch. 10, VA, line 10.

Peter, church of Saint, (Rome), AB, ch. 23.

Piacenza, AB, ch. 13.

Pippin (III), king of the Franks, father of Charlemagne, AB, ch. 3.

Pippin, son of Charlemagne, king of Italy, G, ch. 11, AB, ch. 7, VA, lines 11, 12, 13, 21, 22, 26, 30, 31, 38, 40, 43, 46.

Pisen, king of the Thuringians, G, chs. 4, 5.

Provence, AB, ch. 13.

Ranigunda, wife of the Lombard king Wacho, G, ch. 4.

Ratchis, king of the Lombards, G, ch. 9, AB, ch. 3.

Ravenna, G, chs. 3, 6, AB, ch. 1, p. 71.

Rodelenda, mother of the Lombard king Alboin, G, ch. 5.

Rodoald, king of the Lombards, G, ch. 9, AB, ch. 1, p. 73.

Rodulf, king of the Heruls, G, ch. 4.

Romans, G, ch. 6, AB, ch. 1, p. 69.

Rome, AB, ch. 1, pp. 69, 71, ch. 4, ch. 7, ch. 16, ch. 23, ch. 24.

Rosemund, daughter of the King of the Gepids Cunimund, wife of the Lombard king Alboin, G, chs. 5, 6.

Rotcausus, duke of the Friulans, AB, ch. 6.

Rothari, king of the Lombards, G, ch. 8, AB, ch. 1, pp. 71, 73.

Rugians, G, ch. 3.

Rugiland, AB, ch. 1, p. 67.

Saductus, Beneventan noble, R, line 13.

Sadus (= emir of Bari Sawdān), R, lines 13, 22, 23, 24, 25, 26.

Saint Martin, Campanian location, AB, ch. 19.

Salerno, R, line 30.

Saracens, AB, chs. 15, 17, 18, 19, 22.

Saxons, AB, ch. 1, p. 73.

Saxony, G, chs. 2, 10.

Sawdān, emir of Bari, see Sado, Soldanus.

Scandinavia, AB, ch. 1, p. 67.

Scatenauge, G, ch. 2.

Scoringa, AB, ch. 1, p. 67.

Silenga, third wife of the Lombard king Wacho, G, ch. 4.

Slavs, AB, ch. 14.

Soldanus (= emir of Bari Sawdān), AB, chs. 18, 19.

Solomon, king of Israel, AB, ch. 21.

Sophia, Byzantine empress, G, ch. 5, AB, ch. 1, p. 69.

Spain, G, ch. 10.

Spains, G, ch. 5.

Sueves, G, ch. 4, AB, ch. 1, p. 69.

Tassilo, Bavarian ruler, AB, ch. 3.

Tato/Tatto, king of the Lombards, G, ch. 4, AB, ch. 1, p. 69.

Theodelinda, queen of the Lombards, G, ch. 7, AB, ch. 1, p. 71.

Theudebert, king of the Franks, G, ch. 4.

Thrace, G, chs. 2, 11.

Thuringians, G, chs. 4, 7.

Ticinians, AB, ch. 1, p. 71.

Ticinum, city, AB, ch. 1, p. 71, ch. 3, ch. 23.

Ticinum, river, AB, ch. 1, p. 73.

Tortona, AB, ch. 10.

Totila, king of the Goths, AB, ch. 1, p. 69.

Turin, G, ch. 7.

Turinese, AB, ch. 1, p. 71.

Tuscia, AB, ch. 1, p. 71.

Unguimeri, VA, line 16.

Unichis, father of the Lombard king Wacho, G, ch. 4.

Unroch, see Hunroch.

Vandals, AB, ch. 1, p. 67.

Venetias, AB, ch. 1, p. 71.

Venosa, AB, ch. 13.

Verona, G, chs. 6, 7, AB, ch. 1, p. 71, ch. 23.

Vicenza, AB, ch. 1, p. 71, ch. 6, ch. 21.

Vindilicus, river, G, ch. 2.

Vinsilane, G, ch. 4.

Volturno, river, AB, ch. 19.

Wacho, king of the Lombards, G, chs. 2, 4, AB, ch. 1, p. 69.

Walderada, daughter of the Lombard king, Wacho, G, ch. 4.

Walderada, mother of Theodelinda, G, ch. 7.

Walthari, king of the Lombards, G, chs. 4, 5, AB, ch. 1, p. 69.

Winili, G, ch. 2, AB, ch. 1, p. 67.

Wisicharda, daughter of the Lombard king Wacho, G, ch. 4.

Zangrulf, duke of Verona, G, ch. 7.

Finito di stampare nel mese di novembre 2018
da Tipografia Impressum srl Marina di Carrara (MS)
per conto di Pisa University Press